Narrative Mourning

TRANSITS:
LITERATURE, THOUGHT & CULTURE, 1650–1850

Series Editors
Kathryn Parker, University of Wisconsin—La Crosse
Miriam Wallace, New College of Florida

A long running and landmark series in long eighteenth-century studies, *Transits* includes monographs and edited volumes that are timely, transformative in their approach, and global in their engagement with arts, literature, culture, and history. Books in the series have engaged with visual arts, environment, politics, material culture, travel, theater and performance, embodiment, writing and book history, sexuality, gender, disability, race, and colonialism from Britain and Europe to the Americas, the Far East, and the Middle East. Proposals should offer critical examination of artifacts and events, modes of being and forms of knowledge, material culture, or cultural practices. Works that make provocative connections across time, space, geography, or intellectual history, or that develop new modes of critical imagining are particularly welcome.

Recent titles in the *Transits* series:

Narrative Mourning: Death and Its Relics in the Eighteenth-Century British Novel
Kathleen M. Oliver

Lothario's Corpse: Libertine Drama and the Long-Running Restoration, 1700–1832
Daniel Gustafson

Romantic Automata: Exhibitions, Figures, Organisms
Michael Demson and Christopher R. Clason, eds.

Beside the Bard: Scottish Lowland Poetry in the Age of Burns
George S. Christian

The Novel Stage: Narrative Form from the Restoration to Jane Austen
Marcie Frank

The Imprisoned Traveler: Joseph Forsyth and Napoleon's Italy
Keith Crook

Fire on the Water: Sailors, Slaves, and Insurrection in Early American Literature, 1789–1886
Lenora Warren

Community and Solitude: New Essays on Johnson's Circle
Anthony W. Lee, ed.

The Global Wordsworth: Romanticism Out of Place
Katherine Bergren

For a full list of *Transits* titles, please visit our website: www.bucknelluniversitypress.org.

Narrative Mourning

DEATH AND ITS RELICS IN THE
EIGHTEENTH-CENTURY BRITISH NOVEL

KATHLEEN M. OLIVER

LEWISBURG, PENNSYLVANIA

Library of Congress Cataloging-in-Publication Data

Names: Oliver, Kathleen M., author.
Title: Narrative mourning : death and its relics in the eighteenth-century British novel / Kathleen M. Oliver.
Description: Lewisburg, Pennsylvania : Bucknell University Press, 2020. |
Series: Transits: literature, thought & culture 1650-1850 | Includes bibliographical references and index.
Identifiers: LCCN 2019040874 | ISBN 9781684481910 (paperback) | ISBN 9781684481927 (hardback) | ISBN 9781684481934 (epub) | ISBN 9781684481941 (mobi) | ISBN 9781684481958 (pdf)
Subjects: LCSH: English fiction—18th century—History and criticism. | Death in literature. | Relics in literature. | Mourning customs in literature. | Manners and customs—England—History—18th century.
Classification: LCC PR858.D37 O45 2020 | DDC 823/.5093548—dc23
LC record available at https://lccn.loc.gov/2019040874

A British Cataloging-in-Publication record for this book is available from the British Library.

Copyright © 2020 by Kathleen M. Oliver

All rights reserved

No part of this book may be reproduced or utilized in any form or by any means, electronic or mechanical, or by any information storage and retrieval system, without written permission from the publisher. Please contact Bucknell University Press, Hildreth-Mirza Hall, Bucknell University, Lewisburg, PA 17837–2005. The only exception to this prohibition is "fair use" as defined by U.S. copyright law.

♾ The paper used in this publication meets the requirements of the American National Standard for Information Sciences—Permanence of Paper for Printed Library Materials, ANSI Z39.48-1992.

www.bucknelluniversitypress.org

Distributed worldwide by Rutgers University Press

Manufactured in the United States of America

For those who mourn.
For those whom I mourn.
For things that mourn with us.

CONTENTS

List of Illustrations ix

Introduction: The Relic 1

OBJECTS 21

1 "With My Hair in Crystal": Commemorative Hair Jewelry and the Entombed Saint in Samuel Richardson's *Clarissa* (1748) 25

2 "You Know Me Then": The Relic versus the Real in Ann Radcliffe's *The Mysteries of Udolpho* (1794) 39
  PART I. The Secret Life of Portraits 40
  PART II. Death as the Lost Beloved 57

PERSONS 75

3 "All the Horrors of Friendship": Counting the Bodies in Sarah Fielding's *The Adventures of David Simple* (1744) and *Volume the Last* (1753) 81
  PART I. The Sorrows of Young David: Melancholia 82
  PART II. Double Vision: Allegory 102

4 "It Is All for You!": Dying for Love in Samuel Richardson's *The History of Sir Charles Grandison* (1753) 113

GHOSTS 137

5 "'Tis at Least a Memorial for Those Who
  Survive": The It-Narrator, Death Writing,
  and the Ghostwriter in Henry Mackenzie's
  The Man of Feeling (1771) 139

Conclusion: Death and the Novel 158

Acknowledgments 163

Notes 165

Bibliography 189

Index 199

ILLUSTRATIONS

Figure 1.1 An eighteenth-century Georgian mourning ring, with the decedent's hair "in crystal." Inscription reads "C. P. Galabin, ob 16 April 1812, at 38." — 28

Figure 2.1 Ozias Humphry, 1742–1812. *Portrait of a Lady*. Undated. — 42

Figure 2.2 Wax model of a decomposing body in a walnut coffin, lid off. Italy, 1774–1800. — 63

Figure 2.3 Reclining figure of a man showing muscles, tendons, and inner organs, 1785. — 64

Figure 3.1 *David Simple*. Etching by William Blake, based on an illustration by Thomas Stothard. — 100

Figure 4.1 *Sir Charles Grandison* (London: Heinemann, 1902). Engraving by Anthony Walker from a drawing by Thomas Stothard (1783). — 116

Figure 5.1 *The Man of Feeling* (Paris: Theophilus Barrois, 1807). Engraving by C. L'Epine from a drawing by Louis Lafitte. — 154

Narrative Mourning

INTRODUCTION

The Relic

> When my grave is broke up againe. . . .
> And he that digs it, spies
> A bracelet of bright haire about the bone,
> Will he not let'us alone,
> And thinke that there a loving couple lies,
> Who thought that this device might be some way
> To make their soules, at the last busie day,
> Meet at this grave, and make a little stay?
> —John Donne, "The Relique" (early 1600s)

> I cannot love my friend, without loving his person. It is in this way that every thing which practically has been associated with my friend, acquires a value from that consideration; his ring, his watch, his books, and his habitation. The value of these as having been his, is not merely fictitious; they have an empire over my mind; they can make me happy or unhappy; they can torture, and they can tranquillise; they can purify my sentiments, and make me similar to the man I love; they possess the virtue which the Indian is said to attribute to the spoils of him he kills, and inspire me with the powers, the feelings and the heart of their preceding master.
> —William Godwin, *Essay on Sepulchres* (1809)

IN THE FIRST DECADES OF THE 1600S, the period during which John Donne's elegies are believed to have been composed, the poet and his readers could assume certain things: that on Resurrection Day, the dead would rise again, immortal yet physically recognizable, bodies and souls reunited; and that the wearing of a relic from a loved one—in this instance, a bracelet fashioned from his or her hair—would assure reunion on that "last busie day."[1] However, by century end, following the 1694 publication of the second edition of Locke's *Essay Concerning*

Human Understanding, both assumptions were under contestation. And by the early 1800s, 200 years after the composition of Donne's elegies, the dead body itself was considered an anathema, no longer the final repository of the soul, no longer necessary to salvation, and almost certainly not expected to appear—in any form—at the resurrection. Consciousness—not the body, not the soul, not body and soul together—was now believed to be the sole source of personal identity, and it either died with the physical body, or it became unmoored from that body, able to exist on its own, unfettered by any physical container—the new soul of humanity, one might say. Nonetheless, despite the radical alteration in beliefs regarding the body, the soul, and even resurrection, relics gifted by the living or dying and/or relics taken from the dead remained prized possessions well into the late nineteenth century, functioning as vital and material connections between friends and lovers, whether dead or merely absent. But why did veneration of the relic remain, when the dead and dying body from which it was taken or with which it was associated was reviled? Did the relic mean the same thing in the eighteenth or nineteenth centuries as it did in the sixteenth century, or as it did in the fourteenth century? Or had the relic transformed itself in order to adapt to the new cultural attitudes evinced toward the dead and dying, toward the body and the soul?

This book explores death and its relics as they appear within the confines of the eighteenth-century British novel. It argues that the cultural disappearance of the dead/dying body and the introduction of consciousness as humanity's newfound soul found expression in fictional representations of the relic (object) or relict (person); that the eighteenth-century relic had little to do with reunion in the afterlife (the future), but rather with reunion *in* the present and/or *with* the past; and, last, that the relic/relict functioned as surrogate for the absent (living, dead, or dying) and as reliquary for their "psychic" essence, both historically and within the fictive realms of the novel. The six novels examined in this monograph utilize the concept of the relic/relict as metaphor, trope, symbol, and/or narrative strategy; the appearance of the relic/relict signals narrative mourning. These texts also engage (often obliquely) with changing cultural attitudes toward the dead as regards both the material body and immaterial consciousness. The term "relic" as used within this book refers to a material object that is a physical or psychical remnant of a once-living or otherwise absent person; the term "relict" refers to a fictional personage who exists as the remains of something or someone no longer in existence.

* * *

Prior to 1694, when the second edition of John Locke's *An Essay Concerning Human Understanding* was published with a new chapter entitled "Of Identity and Diversity," the soul was believed by the adherents of Christianity to be immortal and possessed of weight and substance, the latter albeit of an immaterial nature. Within this belief system, as Christopher Fox has admirably demonstrated, the "immaterial substance or soul is by no means the whole person . . . but it *is* that indivisible and immortal part of him which assures his personal continuity and ontological permanence."[2] The soul unified human experience—and it transcended it. However, the body remained an equal component as regards personal identity and final judgment. A single soul existed per single body, and on Resurrection Day, the soul would reanimate the body, breathing it into some semblance of its previous form. On that day, the soul would be weighed and judged based on the person's actions, thoughts, and beliefs during his or her lifetime, and the newly reunited, reanimated, and refurbished physical body would bear the consequences of that judgment, following the soul to its final resting place, whether in heaven or hell. The reanimation and reconstitution of the corporeal body proved an essential part of the notion of resurrection, as not only was the body considered an integral part of personal identity, but the resurrected body—now "immortal and incorruptible"[3]—confirmed Jesus's own resurrection and the idea that he died for humankind's sins.[4] As Lucia Dacome notes, "views of resurrection critically affected the way in which the body was perceived as an integral part of the self"; and, consequently, as Fox argues, the "material body and the immaterial soul must both go into our concept of human identity"—at least up until the time that Locke published his own views of personal identity.[5]

Locke believed that consciousness alone—not the substantial soul, not the corporeal body, not body and soul together—was the source of personal identity, but in arguing thus, he laid open the question of whether such a thing as a substantial soul even existed, which further raised the question of whether the resurrection would or even could occur or, at least, whether it involved the actual raising of the physical body. Consciousness located personal identity in the mind, with consciousness constantly shifting and potentially able to move from one person to another. Because consciousness was inherently unstable—"floating ideas of an ever-changing" nature[6]—with past actions or thoughts, deeds or misdeeds, potentially erased or eradicated from memory, it rendered the madman, the amnesiac, the sleepwalker, the imbecile, or the sufferer of dementia or senility from being held morally accountable for any misbehavior. However, if moral accountability could not be ascribed to those individuals who lacked consciousness of their deeds, then how could they be judged, either in a court of law or on Resurrection Day? As Locke posits, "in the Great Day, wherein the secrets of all hearts shall be laid open, it may be reasonable to think, no one shall be made to answer for what he knows nothing of; but shall receive his doom, his conscience accusing or excusing him."[7] Dacome notes that "Locke's ordinary self, based on consciousness, reserved for itself a right to some kind of omnipotence: it survived death; it could transmigrate through different bodies; and it remained unaffected by physical decay."[8] In other words, consciousness had taken the place of the substantial soul and improved upon it, as it was immortal, it functioned as a moral compass (if memory permitted), it was tethered to no corporeal substance or body, it was judged only by what it was conscious of doing, not by what it had done, and it could move about freely, at will.

Further, Locke dismissed the body as relevant to personhood and to personal identity, as "person" in Locke's lexicon is described as "a thinking intelligent being, that has reason and reflection, and can consider itself as itself, the same thinking thing, in different times and places; which it does only by that consciousness which is inseparable from thinking, and, as it seems to me, essential to it."[9] The body merely identified one as human: "the *idea of a man*" is "of a body, so and so shaped."[10] In life, the body became a mere shell, harboring consciousness and comparable to a suit of clothes, which one may change at will without changing one's self. Through the agency of consciousness, personal identity could be preserved, "whether in the same or different substances"[11]—that is, in the same body or in a different one. By implication, in death, with the soul and/or consciousness departed, the body was nothing but refuse, and one of the concerns (among many) voiced by Locke's critics was that his theories might lead to the dead or dying body being treated without dignity or respect, perhaps even being denied a proper burial.[12]

From the time of publication in 1694 up through the late 1730s, Locke's theories of consciousness and personal identity were hotly debated, and nowhere more heatedly than in the pulpit and in the press. However, beginning in the 1740s, general acceptance of Locke's theory of personal identity as rooted solely in consciousness began to take wider hold, and, combined with other cultural shifts and developments, attitudes toward both the act of dying and the dying/dead body changed slowly yet radically and irrevocably, with the end result being that the dying/dead body became a putrid abomination rather than a mortal (if corrupt) housing essential for the sacred work of resurrection. An unwillingness of the Anglican clergy to bury religious Dissenters or skeptics in the local churchyard; a more mobile population; increased reliance on medical treatment in caring for the sick; scientific arguments advancing the (erroneous) idea that the dead were harmful to the living; nascent consumerism and more abundant consumer goods; and the fact that the body was no longer the source of personal identity or the intimate partner of the substantial soul—these all played their parts in rendering the dying and dead body an unwelcome presence in the home and the community.[13]

INTRODUCTION

Traditionally, the terminally ill were cared for within the confines of the home, their principal—and perhaps only—attendants being members of the immediate family, most often their female relations. Once dead, the body was washed and dressed by female family members, assisted perhaps by some older women from within the community, and, after it was suitably mourned, waked, and prayed for, first in the front parlor (or best room in the house) and later in the church, it made its way to the local churchyard for a final blessing before being committed to the earth, where there the soul of the decedent waited, along with other parish decedents, for "the resurrection of the body and life everlasting."[14] The living remembered the dead, as the churchyard home of the dead was passed regularly on the way into church or in the course of daily life. Most of the bodies in the churchyard were promiscuously jumbled together, mingling in their communal unmarked graves; the churchyard itself was "a lumpy, untidy place,"[15] the earth bulging here and there with the generations of bodies buried beneath. As Thomas W. Laqueur writes, "The churchyard was not primarily a space of individual commemoration or for mourning at a family grave; indeed, there was . . . technically no such thing, even if custom allowed it. Passerby would have seen a few temporary wooden markers; there were wreaths or in some cases plaques inside the church, but outside there was little that was intended to be permanent."[16] As a burial site, the churchyard was "ancient, crowded, hierarchical, exclusively for the use of a small community, grounded in faith, and seething with new burials that all faced east to await the resurrection and displaced older ones in constantly reused land in the heart of the living community."[17] Significantly, the dying and the dead remained members of the community, always close by, always waiting for the living to join them.

However, during the latter half of the eighteenth century, this began to change. Although the vast majority of the sick and dying were still nursed at home, frequent visits from the chirurgeon, the physician, and the apothecary were sought; specific illnesses and diseases were blamed for death, rather than old age or natural causes; and the physician's failure in diagnosis or treatment or the patient's own failure to respond were increasingly identified as culpable and contributing causes. In other words, death was no longer the natural outcome of life, but rather a failure of some sort, whether bodily, diagnostic, and so on. In addition, although the vast majority of the dead were still laid out at home, members of the nascent funerary professions (undertakers) increasingly took over different aspects of burial preparation formerly performed by family members and friends, or by the local carpenter, milliner, and wax chandler; undertakers provided hearses for rent, mourning clothes, palls, coffins, and shrouds,[18] though embalming technically remained under the auspices of the Company of Barber-Surgeons and, later, the

College of Surgeons. Also, during this time, the first cemeteries opened, situated away from the living, outside the city walls or on the outskirts of the town. Unlike the churchyard, the cemetery was a place where anyone could be buried regardless of religious faith (or lack thereof), as long as sufficient funds were available to pay for a burial plot; residence within a community was also not a requirement for burial. The park-like grounds of this new abode for the dead were flat and even, with manicured lawns and marble statuary, resisting the notion that bodies were buried underneath the ground. As Laqueur writes, "Cemeteries need bodies, discretely hidden bodies: there are no mounds and no jumbles of bones; there is no smell."[19]

By century end, the corpse had become an abomination, the repository of disease, dangerous and threatening, its malodorous fumes alone liable to infect the living, and the cemetery dealt with this abomination by sequestering the dead from the living and by removing the more obvious traces—the smells, the lumpy grounds—of their existence.[20] More than ever, the dead body became the abject body, unwanted and unloved. The best way, then, to remember the dead was distantly, through remembrance, memorial, and history: a gravestone marked with the decedent's name; an annual visit to the cemetery, flowers in hand; and memories evoked through objects and places. In sum, several highly significant changes in attitudes toward death initiated in Western European cultures during the eighteenth century: the dying were increasingly placed under medical care;[21] death itself was considered avoidable or, at least, deferrable; the dead body was increasingly considered putrid and vile, dangerous to the health and well-being of the living and thus removed from the immediate environs of the living;[22] and the dead individual became a spectral other, existing not in the dead body but anywhere and everywhere else, as free-floating as consciousness.[23]

As the concealment and disappearance of dead and dying bodies became increasingly accepted practice, mourning rites, ritual, and practices increased in importance across all levels of society, culminating in the Victorian love of elaborate funerals, objects and relics associated with the dead beloved, and numerous prescriptions and proscriptions regarding the actual practices of mourning.[24] The elaborate funeral, followed by stately procession to the cemetery; the black bombazine mourning dress; the commemorative mourning ring—things that had formerly been the sole province of the wealthy now became increasingly available and affordable to all, except for the most impoverished—and they were desired by all, even the poorest.[25] It should also be noted that the majority of mourning objects common in the eighteenth century—several of which are examined in this book—were relatively new in the eighteenth century, at least as objects available to the many: mourning jewelry incorporating the decedent's hair originated in the fourteenth century,[26] though it only became highly fashionable in the eighteenth and nineteenth centuries; miniature portraits had been painted since Elizabethan times, yet their popularity peaked during the eighteenth century;[27] and mourning attire, originally expensive due to the dyestuffs and fabrics used (silk and fine broadcloth), first became available to the middle classes only in the late seventeenth century and only widely available well into the eighteenth century,[28] with the importation of inexpensive dyes, mordants, and fabrics. Thus, what we now consider "traditional" elements of mourning were relatively new in the eighteenth century—at least to the largest numbers of the population.

Why did our eighteenth- and nineteenth-century ancestors respond to the disappearance of death with an increase in mourning? I would suggest that the eighteenth- and nineteenth-century avid interest in mourning—indeed, cultish in the case of the Victorians—was based on two primary factors. First, the attention of late Georgians and Victorians to the accoutrements, rituals, and displays of mourning resulted from the increased availability of relatively inexpensive consumer products and services relative to mourning. Nascent consumerism, fueled by the increasing availability of less expensive products (due to industrialization, expansionism, and colonialism); the entrepreneurial spirit of the emerging mortuary trade; and the increase in the size and wealth of the middle station[29]—these all led our eighteenth- and nineteenth-century ancestors to respond to death's vicissitudes with an increased attention to mourning. Second, the intensive mourning undergone with the death of a loved one may have also included occluded mourning for death itself and for the disappearance of the dying/dead subject. Specifically, with death no longer deemed a companion, as it had been in the past, the culture lost something, whether it be a sense of self (as how a culture views the dead relates directly to its views of the living), a sense of shared community (among our ancestors, ourselves, and our descendents), or a sense of communion with something greater than ourselves (such as with God or Nature). In addition, cultural mourning may not have been just for the loss of death as an intimate companion or for the increasingly absent dying/dead body, but because the body (living/dying/dead) was no longer considered the intimate partner of the soul, a loss in terms of cultural sense of self and of personal identity.

Mourning acknowledges loss and trauma, on both a personal and a cultural level, and the relic—re-imagined to meet new realities—offered itself as a form of recompense, metaphorically becoming the new body for the dead, one more lovely and more lasting than the corpse.

* * *

The Latin noun *reliquiae* refers to the remains of the dead, whether in the form of bodies (newly dead, decomposing, or skeletal), bones or bone shards, fingernails and toenails, teeth, hair, or ashes. Its corresponding verb is *relinquere*, to relinquish, to remain, to leave behind, to bequeath, to abandon, to forsake. Relics, then, as physical objects (and as words), possess an inherent ambiguity: they are evidence of abandonment by the dead, and they are bequests from the dead to the living.

The oldest form of relic, the sacred relic, works through two interrelated means: beneficent contagion and intercession. "Beneficent contagion" refers to the idea that the saint's remains continue to possess sanctity and some measure of sentience; viewing/touching the tomb, the reliquary, or the relic of a saint allows the individual access to the saint's holiness, which, in turn, might positively affect (rub off on, so to speak) the individual, curing illness or disability, increasing fertility, alleviating sin, mending personal difficulties, or positively influencing future behavior. Through his or her bodily remains—an integral part of personal identity that would be rejoined with the soul on Resurrection Day—the saint also acted as intercessor or mediator on behalf of the individual; God presumably would listen to the saint, even if unwilling to listen directly to the lowly petitioner. According to Catholic doctrine, primary relics include bones, teeth, nails, and hair, as well as blood, sweat, and tears; secondary relics include items that have touched the body, such as clothing and jewelry or even instruments of torture (such as the Holy Rood); and tertiary relics are those that have touched primary or secondary relics, accruing sacredness through beneficent contagion.

In England, during the 1530s, in conjunction with the dissolution of the monasteries, Henry VIII authorized the destruction of sacred relics, instituted a prohibition against pilgrimages, and ordered the de-sanctification of many English saints, including Thomas Becket at Canterbury.[30] Some sacred relics remained, secretly prized by Catholic recusants or displayed in the cabinets of antiquarians; new sacred relics were made, as Catholics (and, during the reign of Mary I, Protestants) suffered for their religious beliefs, creating new martyrs to be emulated and venerated, their bits of bone and drops of blood to be treasured;[31] and secular relics, such as Donne's hair bracelet, continued to be worn, assuring reunion with the beloved on Resurrection Day and thus acting in a quasi-religious fashion.[32] However, for most English Protestants, the relic became "associated with a religion that at best was seen as foreign and old-fashioned, and, at worst, suspicious and dangerous."[33] For Protestants, the only true sacred relic was the Bible, or, occasionally, prayer books and other religious texts, which were treated with the veneration previously accorded to relics of saints and martyrs: together, the binding and covers of the Bible functioned as reliquary, containing within the sacred word the "embodiment of spirit in matter" and expressive of "divine power";[34] bibles and other religious books were believed to possess talismanic powers, able to elicit truth from those resting their hands upon their covers.[35] Largely because of this association of the Bible and other religious texts with sacred relics, the relic remained "a powerful literary metaphor in post-Reformation English writing."[36]

Nonetheless, even if "the England of the post-Reformation years did not witness a straightforward replacement of the sacred with the secular,"[37] the post-Reformation relic differed from its medieval counterpart in significant ways. First, the post-Reformation relic tended to be private rather than public and, paradoxically, because of this, more accessible. Most medieval pilgrims had little or no direct contact with the saint's relics; as Robyn Malo notes, "it would have been a rare pilgrim who was permitted to see or touch even the most ordinary relic."[38] However, during the English Reformation, as previously noted, some sacred relics found their way into the homes of recusants, and many recusants themselves became martyrs for their faith. Hidden within the home, these relics could be touched, kissed, or viewed, and, as Malo demonstrates in the case of post-Reformation English martyrs, "Catholic families knew these martyrs in life, and they also, whenever possible, collected their body parts or personal effects after they were dead."[39] The personal—and often literally hidden nature—of the Post-Reformation sacred relic made it more prone to fetishization; it was necessarily secret due to its legal prohibition and because the possession of such relics marked the possessor as potentially treasonous. Second, because of the intimacy between relic and venerator, the relic became more evocative of the decedent. Seeing or touching a medieval relic may have summoned a vague notion of the former corporeal being of the long-dead saint along with a sense of her or his numinous powers, but the post-Reformation relic—specifically, the sacred relic of a newly made martyr or a secular relic from a deceased or absent loved one—evoked a detailed mental portrait of the decedent. Third, the post-Reformation relic was closely aligned with the act of remembrance and thus with the past, in contrast to the medieval relic, which focused on future benefits to the venerator. Fourth, by the eighteenth century, the secular relic increasingly had become an object owned by or associated with the decedent, rather than his or her actual bodily remains. (Although commemorative hair jewelry remained popular up through the end of the nineteenth century, it lacks the deathly association of bones and blood; indeed, a lock of hair defies both aging and death). Finally, the secular relic often functioned simultaneously as a relic of the dead and as a reliquary for the dead. Whereas the sacred relic—a bone, for instance—might be encased in a golden, bejeweled box with glass panes through which to view it, the secular relic—a ring, a book, a portrait—was both relic, being something closely identified with the decedent and left behind by him or her, and reliquary, being an object that encased or encapsulated the spirit or essence of the decedent.

If we compare the relic of Donne's poem with the myriad "relics" listed by Godwin, we can also identify differences between the sixteenth-century relic and one from the late eighteenth or early nineteenth century. Even though Donne is writing post Reformation, his relic—the bracelet fashioned from his lover's hair—retains some of the features of the medieval relic: it possesses a quasi-religious function, and it focuses on the future (the reunion of souls on Judgment Day), the latter admittedly in a teasing and playful fashion. In contrast, Godwin's relics include the ring, watch, and books left behind by his beloved "friend," Mary Wollstonecraft; these objects are the repositories of memory (the past) and conduits for psychic reunion with the beloved (the present). Further, they are objects associated with the deceased, not her bodily remains. Interestingly, the eighteenth-century relic aligns itself with the medieval relic in one specific way: it still offers beneficent contagion. Writing about the "relics" left behind by Wollstonecraft, Godwin asserts that they are able to "make me similar to the man I love; they possess the virtue which the Indian is said to attribute to the spoils of him he kills, and inspire me with the powers, the feelings and the heart of their preceding master."[40]

The eighteenth-century relic, then, is both a material sign of loss and the material compensation for that loss, but more than that, it offers psychic reunion in the present and with the past. While most often relics are material objects—usually small, durable, resistant to decay, easily transportable[41]—a relic may also be a person, such as a widow ("relict") or other persons "left behind" by the decedent. In particular, children may recall the deceased individual in extraordinarily vivid ways. And while "relic" is most often associated with the remains of the dead, the word also signifies any trace, vestige, remnant, mark, footprint, or shadow of something that has, in the main, disappeared physically, psychically, culturally, or historically—but not without leaving some trace, no matter how small.

* * *

Originating in its close association with dying, death, and/or loss, the relic/relict commemorates, signifies, and articulates trauma, both bodily and psychic, as experienced by that person for whom the relic/relict exists as the material remains and by the person (a relict) who functions as survivor/witness. In *The Art of Death*, Edwidge Danticat speaks to these dualities: "I know now, having watched my mother die, that death is a phenomenon of both the body and the mind—her body and mind, and now mine too."[42]

As the relic/relict is the material remains of the dead, the trauma it articulates is physical, as dying itself is a physical process, whether slow or fast, whether by sickness, accident, or torture, whether painful or peaceful, whether experienced by saint or sinner. The sacred relic almost always speaks to religious or national martyrdom, a death painful in the extreme; the secular relic, to the process of dying itself, the ebbing of life, the bodily alterations that occur during the process, and the confusion caused by physical displacement as the dying person is shuffled between home, hospital, nursing home, trauma center, or hospice. The relic/relict also articulates the physical trauma of the bereaved, whose body responds to the dying and death of the beloved and the aftermath through physical means, such as tears, sighs, moans, chest pains, accelerated heart rate, numbness, and more, and who may also confront physical displacement and disorientation, with the loved one now permanently absent from her/his familiar haunts and with the bereaved possibly forced to find a new residence due to reduced monetary circumstances, inability to cope alone with the demands of home ownership, or unwillingness to be constantly confronted by the past. If the relict is a child, particularly one who has lost both parents, then she/he not only embodies the trauma of physical separation, but is (re)named ("orphan") and, often, physically and socially dislocated/relocated. The trauma that the relic/relict articulates is also psychical and emotional, as the dying individual must confront his mortality, her forthcoming absence from the lives of beloved survivors and the imagined impact of this absence upon them, and his legacy to the living; the survivor must experience the psychic pain of final separation, loneliness, grief, feelings of guilt or relief, wishes that she had done more (or less) or that he had handled things differently.

Both psychical and corporeal, trauma consists not in a specific event, but in its aftermath. Trauma, as Cathy Caruth explains, is:

> a response, sometimes delayed, to an overwhelming event or events, which takes the form of repeated, intrusive hallucinations, dreams, thoughts or behaviors stemming from the event, along with numbing that may have begun during or after the experience, and possibly also increased arousal to (and avoidance of) stimuli recalling the event. This simple definition belies a very peculiar fact: the pathology cannot be defined either by the event itself—which may or may not be catastrophic, and may not traumatize everyone equally—nor can it be defined in terms of a *distortion* of the event, achieving its haunting power as a result of distorting personal significances attached to it. The pathology consists, rather, solely in the *structure of its experience* or reception: the event is not assimilated or experienced fully at the time, but only belatedly, in its repeated *possession* of the one who experiences it. To be traumatized is precisely to be possessed by an image or event.[43]

Specifically, the traumatized individual is unable consciously to process the original event(s) and so must repeatedly experience the event(s) through dreams (nightmares), hallucinations (waking nightmares), or behavioral acts, the latter of which are most often metaphorically coded and unconsciously enacted. Trauma is the unconscious/unprocessed *remains* of the original event(s). The traumatized individual knows the event only through what remains of it, through its effects, through its repetition. Repetition allows the original event to be acknowledged until such time (if such a time does indeed come) that the traumatic event becomes consciously understood, interpreted, and assimilated.

It should be noted that in eighteenth-century Britain, the word "trauma" referred only to a bodily wound, and that madness of any sort was thought to originate in the body, not the mind. Nonetheless, our eighteenth-century predecessors acknowledged "wounds of the mind"—that is, they recognized the psychic damage and emotional hurt that individuals suffered upon moments of intense loss, particularly in regards to the death of loved ones. In addition, it was believed that *thought* could initiate madness; that is, by fixating on one idea, by studying too hard, by indulging in unrequited love, by allowing oneself to be carried away by fervor or enthusiasm (particularly of a religious nature), the nerves, bodily fibers, and viscous fluids of the body were adversely affected, engendering madness and/or melancholia. Thus, while the analysis of trauma in eighteenth-century British novels would seem inconsistent with historical reality, beliefs that individuals could suffer from wounds of the mind and that ideas could instigate madness and melancholia were in wide circulation. (A more detailed discussion of my use of psychoanalytic theory occurs in the introductory text for the "Persons" section of this book).

In sum, the relic/relict exists as the *remains* of the dead, of that which has been lost, just as trauma exists as the *remains* of an event, which itself has been lost to consciousness. As David L. Eng and David Kazanjian write, "loss is inseparable from what remains, for what is lost is known only by what remains of it, by how the remains are produced, read, and sustained."[44] The relic/relict bears witness: to the fact that someone/something is dead or missing, that something terrible has happened, that something traumatic has occurred, that something has been lost. As Derrida writes, "Mourning always follows a trauma,"[45] and the relic/relict functions both as sign of trauma and sign of mourning,[46] and because trauma naturally expresses itself through metaphor and repetition, it finds its way into literature, often in conjunction with the fictional relic/relict.

* * *

Michel de Certeau identifies the cultural disappearance of the dying and dead body—a disappearance that began in earnest during the eighteenth century—with our current inability to speak the painful interstice between dying and death itself, a space wherein "the dying person is prevented from saying this nothing that he is becoming, unable to do the act that would only produce his question,"[47] and de Certeau suggests that writing articulates this loss and seeks to remedy this silence. It does so because "writing has no meaning except outside itself, in a different place, that of the reader, which it produces as its own necessity by moving toward this presence it cannot reach," much in the way that we as a culture engage "in the illusion that localizes death elsewhere."[48] Like death, writing also "proceeds by successive abandonments of occupied places."[49] To restate, the act of writing locates meaning at a site other than itself, just as death is always located elsewhere than ourselves, and it "produce[s] sentences within the lexicon of the mortal, in proximity to and even within the space of death," as writing always involves "an impossible adequation between presence and the sign."[50] Words are "relics" of signifieds that language has stripped of presence.[51] Others theorists have similarly aligned language (both spoken and written) with death, albeit with slight variations. For instance, Michel Foucault writes, "It is quite likely that death—its sovereign gesture, its prominence within human memory—hollows out in the present and in existence the void toward which and from which we speak."[52] And Maurice Blanchot argues, "when I speak, death speaks in me," precisely because to name someone or something takes away its "flesh-and-blood reality" and causes it "to be absent, annihilate[d]"; further, "language is *the life that endures death and maintains itself in it.*"[53] Death may be found in language, and language speaks it, writes it, and survives it.

That said, texts attempt to create (artificial) life from these small deaths, and certain genres—novels in particular—fashion (fictional) lives through narrative. Yet, even if all texts partake of death to some extent, not all texts engage in mourning for things or persons loved and lost. In the past twenty or so years, increased scholarly attention has been given to the ways in which texts display mourning or engage with mourning, though the ways in which textual mourning is traced vary widely. Most studies center on modernist or postcolonial novels or on the elegy, though a few analyze a wide range of texts, from various cultures and time periods. Henry Staten's *Eros in Mourning* is one of the latter. Staten argues for a "dialectic of mourning" in texts as various as *The Iliad*, the Gospel of John, *Paradise Lost, Heart of Darkness*, as well as in the works of Lacan. According to Staten, the dialectic of mourning "begins with the process of attachment to, or cathexis of, an object, without which mourning would never arise, and includes all the moments of libidinal relation in general (the moments of libidinal approach, attachment, and loss), as well as the strategies of deferral, avoidance, or transcendence that arise in response to the threat of loss."[54] Staten's work on mourning recognizes and emphasizes the interrelatedness between desire (love) and loss. One cannot mourn for what one does not love, and love for an object is always accompanied by the knowledge of its possible loss. Further, Staten's work demonstrates that mourning involves movement toward and away from the lost beloved (just as trauma involves movement toward and away from the originary event), a point of significance in understanding how narrative mourning propels plot.

Nouri Gana's *Signifying Loss* owes a debt to Staten's work, productively employing Staten's "dialectic of mourning" and similarly deploying Freudian and Lacanian psychoanalytic theory. However, Gana also focuses on the literary use of specific figures of speech—primarily prosopopoeia, catachresis, and chiasmus—to identify and analyze narrative mourning. As Gana writes, "prosopopoeia (i.e., personification, apostrophe) figures as the master trope of mourning while catachresis (i.e., the figure of contextual abuse of, or improper, word use) and chiasmus (i.e., the figure of repetition and reversibility) as the master tropes of, respectively, melancholia and trauma. There are, of course, other supplementary tropes that hover in the gravitational pull of each of these master tropes; these include not only prolepsis, metaphor and aporia, but also allegory and metonymy."[55] As will be demonstrated in the course of my own analysis of narrative mourning in eighteenth-century novels, repetition, allegory, and metaphor are frequently deployed in displaying and articulating mourning; repetition and allegory, in particular, figure greatly in Sarah Fielding's *David Simple* novels, while repetition also marks Samuel Richardson's *The History of Sir Charles Grandison*.

More closely aligned to my own project are two works by Victorian scholars: Jolene Zigarovich's *Writing Death and Absence in the Victorian Novel: Engraved Narratives* and Deborah Lutz's *Relics of Death in Victorian Literature and Culture*. Zigarovich explores missing corpses in Victorian literature, arguing that "the absence of the corpse doubly signifies the unspeakable, the unknowable. As a result, mourning is suspended, burials are incomplete, and others must repeatedly tell the story of the corpse in order to attain some sense of narrative closure. In essence, missing corpses in fiction signify textual trauma and narrative hysterics."[56] I too am interested in the cultural disappearance of the dead or dying subject, but I would suggest that unlike the Victorian novel, the eighteenth-century novel does not suffer from a lack of dead bodies—indeed, some texts have an astonishing large number of them. In addition, whereas Zigarovich's project involves fictional characters whose deaths and dead bodies never make an appearance in their respective novels (think M. Paul's disappearance within the final pages of Charlotte Brontë's *Villette*), my project focuses on the way in which specific eighteenth-century novels replace dead or absent bodies with objects (relics) or people (relicts).

INTRODUCTION

Zigarovich also examines how the lack of ability to mourn in specific Victorian texts maps a cultural loss/lack, which translates into novelistic narrative: "With no knowledge of the grave, no body to venerate, and no relics to touch, survivors of the missing are left with the most fertile imaginations. And without the ability to enact the cultural insistence of mourning upon the corpse, the text itself becomes a manifestation of suspended mourning, while the absent figures become the 'floating signifiers' of the instability of language and representation. Without a corpse, most often a spectral metaphor must immediately replace the absent signifier."[57] In terms of analysis of narrative mourning, my own work differs from Zigarovich's in my argument that relics of the dead in works of fiction indicate the onset of narrative mourning, and that these fictional relics function as both symptoms and remedies. Specifically, relics express mourning, but they also, in many instances, provide its cure, as the relic offers itself as material compensation for loss. In addition, because the eighteenth century sees the earliest signs of the disappearing dying/dead body, the psychic and religious severance between body and soul, and the gradual acceptance of consciousness as the "soul" of both the living and the dead, boundaries between the living and the dead and between the relic and the real are often highly permeable, expressive of epistemological uncertainty. Relics replicate, replace, and displace disappearing bodies. Instead of the absence that marks the missing body in Victorian literature, the relic (thing or person) becomes the missing body, the material and metaphorical reliquary for the psychic essence of the dead or absent individual. In other words, the relic becomes the site wherein the consciousness of the dead resides.

My work also owes a debt to Deborah Lutz's *Relics of Death in Victorian Literature and Culture*, particularly her ingenuous re-imagining of "relic" in terms of literary theory. Regarding her work on relics within Victorian poetry and prose, Lutz writes, "Victorian relic culture sees death, and the body itself, as the beginning of stories rather than their end. Rather than denying death, the relic could help make apparent the terrible poignancy of the body becoming object; it could reenact that moment, again and again. Relic culture expressed a willingness to dwell with loss itself, to linger over the evidence of death's presence woven into the texture of life, giving that life one of its essential meanings."[58]

While I share a similar interest in relic culture, my project differs from Lutz's in several ways, other than the obvious one of time period. To begin, Lutz argues for "a steady and broad historical connectedness" between Victorian relic culture and "the relics of the Catholic cult of saints."[59] While not denying the English Protestant fascination with (and more than occasional repugnance toward) all things Catholic, it seems to me that England's history—specifically, the 1536 destruction of sacred relics, the prohibition against pilgrimages, and the desanctification of many English saints—made the sacred relic into an anomalous object, which, at best, became the subject of antiquarian study or, at worst, the material expression of superstition and of treasonous political beliefs. The Catholic sacred relic retains its ties to its medieval past, while the eighteenth-century secular relic articulates the changes that had occurred and were occurring in religious, philosophical, political, and scientific thought. (If a Catholic "saint" or relic does appear within an eighteenth-century novel, as happens in Samuel Richardson's *The History of Sir Charles Grandison*, a whiff of idolatry always accompanies her/it.) I also view the relic/relict as ambiguous in terms of cultural "willingness to dwell with loss itself," as the relic/relict exists as both evidence of and a form of compensation for loss. In addition, while Lutz examines "novels and poetry . . . as a means to understand the relic culture they elucidate,"[60] I read historical relics as a means to understand literature. Last, I am interested in reading fictional relics not just as material objects or beings, but also as narrative strategies that mourn fictional and/or cultural losses and/or as (fictional) reliquaries containing the consciousness of the (fictional) dead.

* * *

This book is arranged into three main sections: "Objects," "Persons," and "Ghosts."

"Objects" examines two novels: Samuel Richardson's *Clarissa* (1748) and Ann Radcliffe's *The Mysteries of Udolpho* (1794). In each novel, relics take their most predictable form: that of material objects. In Richardson's text, relics may be found in the form of commemorative hair jewelry; in Radcliffe's, as portraits and a waxen corpse. Notably, in the less than fifty years between the publication of the two novels, a significant change occurs in the fictional representation of relics, reflecting three things: the changing nature of the relic, from quasi-sacred to secular; the altered cultural relationship between the living and the dead; and acceptance of Locke's theory of consciousness. In the earlier novel, *Clarissa*, the relics take the form of locks of hair, which are then placed into crystal-covered ring bezels, reliquaries for the precious contents. The locks of hair come from the heroine's body; they are literally her remains. The commemorative hair jewelry—rings and brooch—fashioned from Clarissa's hair replicates Donne's "relic"—the bracelet woven from the beloved's hair—suggesting reunion in the (heavenly) future. In contrast, the portraits that function as relics in Radcliffe's *Udolpho* are determinedly secular in nature, akin to the ring, watch, and books left behind by Wollstonecraft, and they provide immediate connection between the lover and the absent beloved, while at the same time they recall the past (spent together). The two novels also highlight alterations in cultural attitudes toward the dead and dying. Clarissa dies a slow death, one for which she is fully prepared and eagerly anticipates. Her uncorrupted body lies in its coffin, which will be buried in a grave next to her grandfather; together, they will await resurrection. Clarissa dies the "tame death" that Philippe Ariès identified with an older, more intimate cultural relationship with death. Radcliffe's novel, however, displays two disparate types of dying/death. The first is the "tame death," wherein the dying are fully prepared for their fate, the dead are lovingly watched over until buried deep within the earth, and the bereaved remember the dead with melancholy fondness. The second is the "untamed death," wherein death comes suddenly, unexpectedly, and painfully, witnesses recoil in horror from the dying or already dead bodies, and the dead are all but forgotten.[61] Radcliffe also provides an elegiac love letter to the dead/dying body in the form of a waxen corpse, which functions as surrogate for the lost beloved that is death itself. Finally, Locke's theory of consciousness, while undoubtedly known to Richardson in the 1740s, demonstrates the bare minimum of cultural acceptance within *Clarissa*, as the relics function as extensions of the dead heroine—but nothing more. However, in *The Mysteries of Udolpho*, relics (portraits and waxen corpses) are highly animated and imbued with consciousness, so much so that they compete with the "real" (living or dead).

In "Persons," I examine three novels in which relics take the form of persons (relicts): Sarah Fielding's *David Simple* (1744) and *Volume the Last* (1753), and Samuel Richardson's *The History of Charles Grandison* (1753). Relicts are the persons left behind, such as widows, widowers, orphans, other family members, and friends. Within these fictions, relicts may also function as the remains or the residual effects of earlier narrative events or actions.

In Fielding's two novels, "friends" function as relicts. Yet, these "friends" disappear with disconcerting regularity. In *David Simple*, the disappearing friends have merely been "unfriended" by the titular character; in *Volume the Last*, they are innocent sufferers who join the ranks of the dead. Although *David Simple* focuses on the loss of living "friends," these friends whom the eponymous hero feels compelled to discard function as markers of narrative mourning; they are relicts of an originary friend, one who has betrayed David and discarded *him*. In *Volume the Last*, friends are relicts (both the causes and the effects) of the protagonist's original error in judgment, which leads to subsequent errors, all of which adversely affect his friends so that they suffer and then die, one after another after another. Repetition signals melancholia or trauma or both (the melancholic reaction to betrayal; the traumatized/melancholic response to suffering, loss, and death), and Fielding utilizes this repetition as a narrative strategy—a means to move the plot forward and to increase emotive responses on the part of readers.

The *David Simple* novels, particularly *Volume the Last*, render death as emptiness, as void, with bereaved and traumatized survivors all that remains of the dead. While *Volume the Last* does not present the dead in Lockean fashion—as free-floating consciousness—neither does it offer the comfort of a substantial soul or the joyous reunion of Resurrection Day. The only comfort offered is the oblivion of death itself. In her unusual (for the time) treatment of death—rejecting both the substantial soul and the Lockean conscious—Fielding nonetheless offers readers a depiction of the numbness and pain experienced by the bereaved, who must endure, despite watching one after another after another of their loved ones suffer and die. In the end, death itself becomes the best of all friends.

Richardson's *The History of Sir Grandison* presents a relict of an entirely different nature, as no one has died in that novel (at least no character whom the reader cares about). Yet, the eponymous hero and his Italian love interest (the Bolognese noblewoman, Clementina della Porretta) become textually positioned as widower and widow. Specifically, Sir Charles Grandison initially becomes the (missing) corpse to Clementina's widow; the roles then reverse, with Sir Charles playing the part of bachelor-widower and Clementina that of his dead first wife. Richardson's "madwoman in the attic," Clementina exists as Harriet Byron's dark double, as model for the innumerable lovelorn and lovesick characters found within the novel, and as a representative of and sometimes surrogate for death itself. Clementina's haunting of Harriet, which begins when Harriet first shows signs of amorous affection for Sir Charles, suggests the free-floating, unmoored nature of the Lockean dead, who, as mere spirit and consciousness, are free to mingle with the living—and haunt them.

Finally, "Ghosts" explores relics/relicts that have lost much, if not all, of their substantiality, yet whose "remains" may still be read and interpreted. Ghosts (at least the eighteenth-century versions of them) retain the outlines of their former bodies, wear the clothes they wore in life, speak as they did in life, and yet are shadows of their material selves. My study of "ghostly" relicts/relics focuses on Henry Mackenzie's *The Man of Feeling* (1771), arguing that Mackenzie's fiction is structurally founded upon (fictional) relics/relicts—a torn, partial manuscript; a protagonist, Harley, notably out of his place and time, who dies at the end of the novel and who may already be dead when the embedded narrative begins; and a shadowy "narrator" named The Ghost, who migrates easily between Harley's consciousness and his own. The manuscript, Harley, and The Ghost are relics/relicts of times past and/or of a type of people (empathetic, considerate, kind, sensitive) who are fast disappearing or may already have disappeared; these relics/relicts exist as the sole remains of an idyllic, idealized past, and they themselves are worn, torn, weak, and tattered—mere ghosts. Within the confines of Mackenzie's novel, those possessed of great sensibility live in the shadow lands, all spirit, all consciousness, lacking palpable earthly presence, while the so-called "men of the world" are all body, tethered to the earth by their lusts and pleasures. While remnants of the past haunt the landscape, few see them. Only the ghosts themselves—the mournful embodiments of Lockean consciousness—seem to know or care that something lovely and fragile has disappeared from modern life.

Objects

When in the form of a material object, the relic is most often small, portable, and incorruptible (or at least highly durable), affording its possessor ease of transport and, if necessary, the ability to secrete it, safe from the prying eyes and probing hands of others. If a sacred relic, associated with the bodily remains of a holy person or saint, then it possesses sentience (including the ability to "hear" the spoken words or unspoken thoughts of its possessor or petitioner), a measure of agency (as it can perform acts on behalf of those who believe in its numinous powers), and the property of beneficent contagion (sharing its powers with those who touch it or gaze upon it). Primary relics—the actual bodily remains of the decedent, his or her bones, teeth, hair, fingernails, or ashes—are the most potent of sacred relics because of their sentience and agency, because touching them provides access to and communion with the heavenly and the holy, and because they are agents of the miraculous and magical.

The secular relic operates in ways both similar and different. Unlike the sacred relic, which connects the possessor to the divine, the secular relic connects the survivor to the mortal, and, operating principally through memory, it vividly recalls one thing and one thing only: the decedent. That said, the secular relic's powers are such that the possessor feels connected to the beloved decedent when holding, wearing, or contemplating the relic, often so much so that the "consciousness" of the decedent appears to have taken residence within the relic, patiently listening, lovingly watching. And, like the sacred relic, the secular relic possesses a measure of agency, as it not only evokes the beloved decedent, but also commands the possessor to turn to it repeatedly, precisely because of its evocative powers; in other words, the secular relic offers itself to fetishization, as it recognizes loss and simultaneously compensates for it, in its materiality functioning as surrogate for the absent beloved.

In *Clarissa*, Samuel Richardson creates a set of primary relics—quasi-sacred ones—associated with the deceased heroine. In many crucial aspects, these relics operate in ways similar to those of medieval saints. Yet, they differ from them in ways that divorce them from the Catholic past. Specifically, the bequests of commemorative hair jewelry presented to certain of the heroine's mourners offer beneficent contagion, encouraging the wearers of the rings to acts of emulation; they conjure the memory of this dead saint and martyr; they pronounce moral judgment upon the living; they suggest reunion in the afterlife; and they offer the implication that from her heavenly abode, the heroine smiles upon the possessors of her relics (and frowns upon those who were denied them). Yet, although Richardson wants his readers to admire, even worship, his heroine as a Protestant saint, he stops short (barely) of making her relics truly sacred. In the end, they perform no miracles, and while the relics offer posthumous commendations or condemnations of the living, Clarissa and her soul remain in heaven (or awaiting heaven). Memory, materialized through the relics, connects the chosen recipients of her relics with Clarissa herself. Textually, these relics of the dead heroine extend and deepen the metaphor of her saintliness, and they allow the novel one means, among several, by which to extend the heroine's presence beyond death.

Ann Radcliffe's *Mysteries of Udolpho* offers readers several varieties of secular relics, including portraits and wax figures. Yet, these relics possess powers even medieval saints would find astonishing. Portraits of the dead and living vie for dominance with their subjects. They are animated, acute of hearing, and emotive. They are not mere extensions of their subjects, but rather have minds of their own, willing to take on/take over the lives of their subjects, albeit on their own terms. Similarly, a wax figure of a corpse becomes death in ways that the dying and dead can never be. In Radcliffe's fictive world, relics as objects possess consciousness and materiality, while persons (living and dead) exist as spectral beings, as sheer consciousness, as ideas rather than physical matter. In Radcliffe's novel, Locke's shape-shifting consciousness has left humans without the material anchor of the body, while material objects have become what humans once were in pre-Lockean times: entities in which body and soul are united. Textually, the relics exist as clues from the past, as well as active agents in the present, engendering memory and inciting action on the part of characters.

1

"WITH MY HAIR IN CRYSTAL"

Commemorative Hair Jewelry and the Entombed Saint in Samuel Richardson's *Clarissa* (1748)

NOTIFIED OF THE DEATH OF CLARISSA HARLOWE, Robert Lovelace insists that Belford send mementoes to him. These requested mementoes are primary relics—literally pieces of Clarissa's newly dead body: "But her dear heart and a lock of her hair I will have, let who will be the gainsayers!"[1] Yet, Clarissa's heart will be buried with her, and the "four charming ringlets" (8:128) cut from Clarissa's hair will be encased in mourning jewelry and bequeathed to a chosen few. Anna Howe and Mr. Hickman will each receive "a ring with my hair" (8:192), as will members of Lovelace's family. Colonel Morden claims one of Clarissa's tresses, "for a locket, which, he says, he will cause to be made, and wear next his heart in memory of his beloved Cousin" (8:128). A fifth and final ringlet is cut from Clarissa's hair, after Anna Howe pleads that she "might be allowed a lock of the dear creature's hair" (8:169), in addition to the ring that Clarissa has bequeathed her. No member of the Harlowe family will receive a lock of her hair, in any form, nor will Lovelace.

As Richardson's novel intimates, mourning jewelry that incorporates hair from the deceased was deemed a special gift—a material link to the beloved decedent. This chapter explores mourning jewelry as relic in *Clarissa*. The first section presents the historical background on mourning jewelry fashioned with human hair. The second section examines Clarissa's bestowals of mourning jewelry, exploring how these relics offer psychic compensation to the wearers and function through beneficent contagion, allowing access to the virtues associated with Clarissa, assuring her remembrance and enacting her judgment.

OBJECTS

"LONG, LONG WORN IN MEMORY": MOURNING JEWELRY

Mourning jewelry fashioned from or with human hair combines two forms of traditional jewelry: mourning jewelry and hair jewelry. Eighteenth-century mourning rings evolved from the medieval tradition of *memento mori*, as well as from "the tradition of bequeathing personal jewelry to family members and friends."[2] As Maureen DeLorme writes, "Mourning jewelry, originally designed with the ubiquitous *memento mori* individual reminder, changed in the 17th century to *memento illius*, or the commemorative remembrance of 'another'";[3] it is during this time period that mourning rings became a customary part of the funerary rites of the wealthy.

In the will, the decedent designated the recipients of the rings, which were most often distributed during funeral services, for wear immediately and during subsequent months of mourning. Often, several levels of mourning rings were distributed, determined by the social status of the mourner and the relationship between mourner and decedent. Inexpensive mourning rings might be inscribed with the decedent's initials, date of death, age at death, and some simple design elements. A more expensive ring might have a short "posie" or motto engraved into it, such as "prepared be to follow me" or "remember"; it might also be decorated with somber-colored gemstones, a sepia on ivory mourning scene, or even a miniature portrait of the decedent. A bequest of mourning jewelry to someone from the lower social stations was considered thoughtless because a ring was a luxury item, and more sensible bequests, such as clothing or money, would be judged more appropriate and thoughtful.[4] Yet, perhaps because mourning rings became *de rigueur* for members of the middle and upper classes, a certain impersonality attached itself to the custom. By the late seventeenth century, it was not uncommon for a hundred rings to be given away at a single funeral, nor was it rare for an individual to possess a collection of fifty or more mourning rings.[5]

In contrast, hair jewelry was extremely personal in nature, and it was not always associated with death. Instead, bracelets, necklaces, earrings, broaches, watch chains, and lockets made with human hair commemorated love (between family members, friends, lovers) or even successful business relationships.[6] A lock of hair was a token of high approbation. When the elderly Mary Delany was presented with "a lock of her Majesty's hair," she was informed that "it undoubtedly marks her [Queen Charlotte's] esteem and regard for you."[7] In Henry Fielding's *Amelia*, when Booth goes off to war, Amelia presents him with a casket, filled with medicines, foodstuffs, and remembrances, but according to Booth, the "most valuable of all to me was a lock of her dear hair, which I have from that time to this worn in my bosom."[8] Upon the death of King George IV, locks of hair counted among his possessions, material tokens of his numerous amours: "There was a prodigious quantity of hair—women's hair—of all colours and lengths, some locks with the powder and pomatum still sticking to them."[9] Because a lock of hair bespoke a high level of intimacy and affection between giver and receiver, requests for tokens of hair were often denied. Frances Burney refused a mutual friend's request to provide Sophia von La Roche with a lock of her hair: "thinking so little as I think of Madame de la Roche, it would be have been a species of falsehood to send such a gift."[10] When James Boswell requested a lock of the "charming auburn hair" of Anna Seward, she also refused, feeling that such a gift could suggests a willingness to provide other favors.[11] Thus, a present of hair designates both intimacy and approbation, highlighting the transgressive nature of the Baron's capture of Belinda's lock of hair in Alexander Pope's *The Rape of the Lock* and the inappropriateness of Marianne's gift to Willoughby in Jane Austen's *Sense and Sensibility*.

The most poignant use of hair was when a loved one died. For a mother, a lock clipped from the head of a newly deceased child preserved the love between child and mother long after the child had been buried. For friends, lovers, and family members, hair from the decedent, carefully preserved in a crystal-covered locket or ring bezel, also preserved remembrance, love, and grief. As Donne's "The Relique" testifies, in the seventeenth century and prior, a lock of hair from the deceased was believed to ensure reunion in the afterlife, and in the eighteenth century, presenting someone with a lock of hair was still presenting someone with a piece, in every sense of the word, of oneself, assuring (re)union of some sort, if only psychical. The two forms of jewelry—mourning and hair—had been combined "as early as 14th century Europe,"[12] yet not with any regularity until the late seventeenth century, and mourning jewelry worked from hair became highly fashionable only in the eighteenth and nineteenth centuries (see figure 1.1).

Mourning jewelry that incorporates hair from the deceased, then, exists as a historically specific phenomenon, prevalent only from the period of the late seventeenth century until the late nineteenth century; its popularity coincides with emerging industrialization, nascent consumerism, and transitional attitudes toward death. Initially, only the wealthy wore mourning jewelry or bequeathed it. However, mass production eventually allowed the less affluent to participate in the custom: "The local jeweler had only to put in the deceased's hair and engrave the pertinent information on the back of the broach or inside the shank of the ring."[13] Mourning rings and broaches became popular consumer objects, yet, paradoxically, once personalized with the hair, name, and death date of the decedent, resisted easy categorization as commodities, since the objects then held little value for anyone other than the intended recipients. In many respects, mourning jewelry

OBJECTS

Figure 1.1 An eighteenth-century Georgian mourning ring, with the decedent's hair "in crystal." Inscription reads "C. P. Galabin, ob 16 April 1812, at 38." Collection of K. M. Oliver. Photograph by Charles Parkhill, 2019.

incorporating human hair functions as fetish in the earliest (pre-1750) sense of the word, wherein a material object, the *fetisso*, is viewed by others as possessing little or no value, yet holds immense psychic, spiritual, and/or social value for the individual wearer.[14]

Much of the special nature of commemorative hair jewelry as relic resides in the potentially sentient nature of the hair itself. Memorial hairwork jewelry was at its most popular during the eighteenth and nineteenth centuries, when attitudes toward death were transforming. In the early to mid-eighteenth century, belief in the "sensibility of the cadaver"[15]—the corpse's ability to feel, listen, remember—still existed. As Ruth Richardson notes, a "transitional state" was posited "of a period between death and burial in which the human being was regarded as 'neither alive nor fully dead'"; in this liminal state, the corpse was believed to possess "both sentience and some sort of spiritual power."[16] Co-extant was the opposite belief that the "body without the soul is nothing,"[17] that nothing of the individual's essence remained within the corpse. Either way, people were interested in the corpse, in its dissection, exhibition, or preservation, whether because it could reveal scientific and medical secrets or because the corpse "retained a remnant of life that

[28]

on occasion was manifested."[18] Sometimes, corpses were preserved in their entirety, as was the case with Jeremy Bentham, whose will specified that his corpse serve both scientific and convivial purposes; more often, a portion of the dead body—usually a lock of hair—was preserved.[19] During the eighteenth century, the decedent's hair existed as "a commemorative monument, to be visited as one visits a friend living in the country"; during the nineteenth century, the lock of hair became merely "the vehicle of memory."[20] Commemorative hair jewelry, then, may be seen as a reaction against the increasingly dominant (purportedly, more rational) Lockean view of body and soul as separate entities, as well the increasingly clinical treatment of death. During the early to mid-eighteenth century, this reaction expresses itself as continued belief in the interconnectedness between body and soul, between the living and the dead, and during the latter part of the eighteenth century and into the nineteenth century, as a form of nostalgia.

Because commemorative hairwork jewelry contains a potentially sentient part of the decedent and it represents a final gift from the beloved, it is among the most personal of relics in eighteenth-century English culture. In Richardson's novel, commemorative hair jewelry partakes both of the medieval concept of sacred relic and the eighteenth-century concept of secular relic, neither fully one nor the other. Specifically, the potentially sentient nature of the locks of hair aligns Clarissa with the medieval saint, as does the "saintliness" that Richardson ascribes to his heroine. Further, the placement of the hair within the crystal ring bezel suggests a medieval saint's relic enclosed within a bejeweled reliquary. However, the rings with Clarissa's "hair in crystal" also hint at the secular relic's metaphorical encapsulation of the consciousness of the decedent, and Clarissa's bequests of rings "with my hair in crystal" are principally intended as vehicles of remembrance, as is the case with secular relics. As Charlotte Montague notes, the rings "will be long, long worn in memory" (8:207). In sum, the representation of commemorative hair jewelry in *Clarissa* is poised between the older view of the relic and the newer.

"WITH MY HAIR IN CRYSTAL": MOURNING CLARISSA

Being subject to decay, Clarissa's dead body needs burying no matter how lovely, and so for Clarissa's mourners, small pieces of this living/dead body must serve as substitutes for Clarissa herself. The locks of Clarissa's hair are taken from her corpse, not from the living woman. Yet, these bright ringlets appear invested with the living Clarissa's presence, and as noted previously, the newly dead corpse was often thought to possess both sentience and spiritual power. Several of the ringlets are designated for mourning rings, for enclosure within crystal-covered bezels. These rings function as reliquaries, as tiny coffins encasing an incorruptible piece of Clarissa, and they replicate in miniature the real coffin with the real body. In addition, the well-known iconography of Clarissa's "quite insanely appealing"[21] coffin—the broken lily, the winged hourglass, the coiled and crowned serpent, and other symbols and inscriptions—might easily be reproduced on the mourning rings, increasing their value as relics. The coffin exists within the novel as text, subject to exegesis and interpretation, its meaning determined by the individual reader/viewer, and just as the symbols on the coffin inspire "a veritable orgy of reading," so too will the mourning rings. As Terry Castle explains, "The coffin itself *says* nothing, but acts as a site for individual discoveries—of guilt, of compassion, of bitterness. It inspires as many interpretations as it has interpreters; readers read it according to subjective emotional states."[22] Similarly, the mourning rings act as "site[s] for individual discoveries," not only for the ring wearers, but also for those denied any such token of Clarissa's esteem.

As Raymond F. Hilliard writes, "The aggression implicit in Clarissa's posture as determined martyr is aimed at all her persecutors,"[23] and the stipulations of her will demonstrate this hostility, for neither her family nor Lovelace will receive one of the customary mourning rings, while Clarissa offers these rings to other individuals, many of whom she barely knows. Equally important, Clarissa assures that neither the Harlowes nor Lovelace will receive even the smallest part of her person; she denies them a single strand of her hair. Through her bequests, Clarissa reclaims her own body, refusing a piece of herself to those who sought to use—or who did use—this body for their own purposes, yet offering something of herself to select individuals. In death, Clarissa lives, conjured through the wearing of a ring with her "hair in crystal," offering solace to the chosen few and a bit of damnation to all the rest.

In her will, Clarissa bequeaths cash sums to certain individuals so that they may purchase mourning rings commemorating her death. Specifically, the will makes provisions for twelve individuals to receive plain mourning rings (plain only in that they lack Clarissa's hair as an element of the design) and seven individuals to receive mourning rings that contain her "hair in crystal." In addition, three individuals claim a lock of her hair, though only two—Colonel Morden and Anna Howe—will receive one, to encase in a locket or to preserve intact, respectively. At the very least, the mourning rings recall the living Clarissa yet acknowledge her absence; they act as mnemonic tokens, revivifying the dead. In addition, as Clarissa was remarkable for her virtue and patient suffering, a ring associated with Clarissa might act as a talisman by which the ring wearer could access those very attributes. In this respect, it is helpful to think of Clarissa as a Protestant saint, as many scholars have done: "Clarissa is a Christian saint, who by her probationary mortification assures herself of a reward in heaven."[24] According to Phillipe Ariès, "Saints were all thaumaturges (that is, miracle workers) and intercessors, and the faithful had to communicate directly with their relics, had to touch them in order to receive their magical emanations."[25] Thought of in this way, the mourning rings become reliquaries of the saintly Clarissa, allowing the ring wearer to summon aid and inspiration when required, and this would be particularly so if relics, as was believed by many, retained some measure of sensibility. (It should be noted, however, that although the *potential* for thaumaturgy exists, Richardson never allows these rings to become other than Protestant relics—that is, aids to remembrance and emulation.)

Through her bequests, Clarissa separates the living into two groups: the blessed and the damned. The rings provide a mark of her favor; they bind the wearers to Clarissa's memory and designate the wearers as acolytes and devotees of the cult of Clarissa. Aesthetically, the bequests create presence where least expected, as the rings momentarily bring minor characters to the forefront, and in doing so, Richardson renders palpable an absence associated with his villains: a figurative emptiness encircles the fingers of Clarissa's parents, uncles, brother, sister, and professed lover. If small kindnesses, such as Miss Biddulph and Mr. Goddard have rendered toward Clarissa, are worthy of a token of remembrance, then how great the unkindness of the Harlowes and Lovelace. In this way, the mourning rings encapsulate and stand for Richardson's didactic and moral message.

The intended recipients of the twelve mourning rings *sans* hair appear a disparate group, comprising four childhood friends, two clergymen, a physician, an apothecary, an executor, the acerbic Mrs. Howe, Aunt Hervey, and young Dolly Hervey. The amounts provided for the rings vary widely, from five to fifty guineas, though the amount of each does not necessarily correlate with the level of personal intimacy. The least expensive rings, at five guineas apiece, go to Clarissa's childhood friends: "Miss Biddy Lloyd, Miss Fanny Alston, Miss Rachel Biddulph, and Miss Cartwright Campbell" (8:193). Miss Alston and Campbell are mentioned only in the will, but Miss Biddulph and Miss Lloyd have expressed an avid interest in Clarissa's story since the beginning. They are mentioned as early as Anna Howe's second letter to Clarissa and appear in Anna Howe's correspondence with some regularity as neighbors of the Howes and Harlowes. Although extremely minor characters, they appear loyal to Clarissa, even after her elopement from Harlowe Place—an important point when considering Clarissa's distribution of rings. From a moral perspective, the bequests mark the young women as behavioral foils by which the conduct of Clarissa's family members and Lovelace may be measured.

Four other legatees receive bequests of mourning rings in recognition of services rendered during Clarissa's final days. All legatees are men, possessed of some

OBJECTS

measure of income and wealth, functioning in a professional capacity. None have known Clarissa for very long. To "the worthy Dr. H," in whom Clarissa "found a Physician, a Father and a Friend," twenty guineas is provided for a mourning ring; to "the kind and skilful Mr. Goddard," the apothecary, fifteen guineas for the same; to Mr. Belford, her executor, twenty guineas; and to "the reverend Mr.—, who frequently attended me, and prayed by me in my last stages" (8:197), fifteen guineas. All four men are mentioned with gratitude for services rendered or to be rendered, and if Samuel Pepys's will is any indication, the bequest of mourning rings to physicians, chirurgeons, apothecaries, lawyers, scriveners, and executors was common practice. (Of course, that famous literary law clerk, Charles Dickens's Wemmick, approvingly accepts mourning rings from Mr. Jaggers's deceased clients: "They're curiosities. And they're property. They may not be worth much, but, after all, they're property and portable."[26]) Some discernment has been made regarding the relative social status of the recipients, with the physician receiving more than the apothecary and the gentleman executor more than the clergyman. To those from the lower stations who have provided comparable levels of service, such as Mrs. Lovick, Mrs. Smith, the nurse Anne Shelburne, or Clarissa's landlord Mr. Smith, Clarissa bequeaths equivalent sums of cash rather than rings, suggesting that money is the more thoughtful provision for individuals (particularly women) from the working classes. In the case of Dr. H, Mr. Goddard, Belford, and the reverend, sums of cash might be deemed insulting, at odds with their social position or professional stature.

As with the bequests to Clarissa's childhood friends, the rings mark a disparity in moral behavior between these relative strangers and those with familial or amorous ties to Clarissa. These four characters stand as aesthetic and moral foils to the men in Clarissa's family: her father, two uncles, and brother. Clarissa expresses her gratitude toward the doctor and the apothecary in terms that suggest the fatherly nature of their treatment: "I am inexpressibly obliged to You, Sir, and to You, Sir . . . for your *more* than friendly, your *paternal* care and concern for me" (7: 243–244). Similarly, Belford now functions in a brotherly capacity. As talismans of good behavior, the rings indicate moral judgment on the part of Clarissa.

The remaining assignments for plain mourning rings are more personal in nature. The "reverend and learned Doctor Arthur Lewen" receives "Twenty guineas for a Ring." The amount, like the bequests to Belford and the others, is moderate. Yet, it recognizes "the instructions" by which the young Clarissa "equally delighted and benefited" during the thrice weekly "conversation-visits" (8:193, 306). The ring recognizes his sympathetic support of Clarissa. In his last letter to Clarissa, he writes: "I will only add, that the misfortunes which have befallen you, had they been the lot of a child of my own, could not have affected me *more*, than yours have done" (7:251). In the event that the elderly and "very ill" Dr. Lewen predeceases Clarissa, which indeed he does, Clarissa has thoughtfully arranged for Lewen's daughter to "have benefit of it" (8:248,193), with the twenty guineas rather than a ring provided directly to Lewen's daughter. Based on Dr. Lewen's age and the fact that his daughter lives with him, she is most probably a spinster, with few financial resources of her own and little hope of a substantial legacy from her clergyman father.

The acid-tongued Mrs. Howe also receives a bequest for "a ring of Twenty-five guineas price." In some ways, this bestowal is surprising after Mrs. Howe's prohibition of correspondence between her daughter and Clarissa, subsequent to Clarissa's elopement. Mrs. Howe writes to Clarissa about her daughter: "I have charged her over and over not to correspond with one who has made such a giddy step," labeling Clarissa's correspondence an "*Evil communication*" (6:108). Yet, the bequest to Mrs. Howe exists, first and foremost, as a gift to Anna herself, and most importantly, it acknowledges Mrs. Howe's almost immediate change of heart in allowing Anna to continue correspondence with Clarissa, out of love for her daughter, capitulation to Anna's "headstrong ways" (6:368), and from genuine compassion for Clarissa.

Only two mourning rings go to members of Clarissa's family—rings without her hair. Aunt Hervey receives a "sum of Fifty guineas for a ring" (8:190); Dolly Hervey, twenty-five guineas for the same. Yet, neither young Dolly nor her mother will receive a lock of Clarissa's hair to incorporate into the ring. The question is why? In Dolly's case, it is most probably because of her youth, and because Dolly does not need it, as Clarissa has provided "my kind and much-valued Cousin Miss Dolly Hervey" with other means of assuaging grief, diminishing loss, and asserting moral superiority through her bequests of "my watch and equipage, and best Mechlin and Brussels head-dresses and ruffles; also my gown and petticoat of flowered silver of my own work," "my harpsichord, my chamber-organ, and all my music-books," and "all my books in general, with the cases they are in." These items are meant for instruction and pleasure; they are intended to ensure that Dolly looks to the future, rather than the past, and that she will remember Clarissa with pleasure, rather than pain: "I know that she will take the greater pleasure in them (when her friendly grief is mellowed by time into a remembrance more sweet than painful) because they were mine" (8:190). The mourning ring provides Dolly with the customary means by which to negotiate Clarissa's death, but the other bequests allow Dolly, in a way, to become Clarissa herself, to enjoy those very things that gave Clarissa pleasure and informed Clarissa's mind, to become one with the deceased Clarissa in ways that others cannot. She will read Clarissa's books; she will play Clarissa's instruments; she will wear Clarissa's clothes. Through her bequests, Clarissa continues in Dolly's life, as instructor and educator, and Dolly's grief will be assuaged through her attempts to emulate her beloved cousin. The harpsichord and books offer continued communication with the deceased, initially engendering grief but, in the long term, providing countless hours of enjoyment. Pleasure and instruction are emphasized in Clarissa's bequests to Dolly.

The reason why Mrs. Hervey is denied a ring with Clarissa's hair is less clear. Mrs. Hervey has proven the most sympathetic of the Harlowes throughout Clarissa's ordeal (other than Dolly). Thus, she has merited a mourning ring. Clarissa writes of her aunt: "I beg of her to accept my thankful acknowledgements for all her goodness to me from my infancy; and particularly for her patience with me, in several altercations that happened between my Brother and Sister, and me, before my unhappy departure from Harlowe-Place" (8:190). Yet, all of Clarissa's thanks are reserved for the time prior to her "unhappy departure from Harlowe-Place"; none, after. Therein lies the probable cause behind Clarissa's refusal to provide Mrs. Hervey with a lock of hair: Clarissa twice requested Mrs. Hervey's intervention with her family, only to be refused on the grounds that Mrs. Hervey "dare not open my lips in your favour" (3:250). As Clarissa later writes to Mrs. Norton, "I did not doubt my Aunt's good-will to me. Her affection I did not doubt. But shall we wonder that Kings and Princes meet with so little control in their passions, be they ever so violent, when in a private family, an Aunt, nay, even a Mother in that family, shall chuse to give up a once favoured child against their own inclinations..." (8:266). Mrs. Hervey gave Clarissa up, against her own inclination. The stipulation appears intentionally ambivalent, representing both gratitude and hostility on the part of Clarissa. Also to go to Mrs. Hervey is Clarissa's "whole-length picture in the Vandyke taste, that used to hang in my own parlour" (8:192), a gift that seems highly fraught with emotional possibilities. Will the painted eyes of Clarissa smile benignly at Mrs. Hervey, or will they look at her with reproach and accusation?

The eleven plain mourning rings represent moral worth and, in this capacity, act as rejoinders to those denied such marks of esteem. The twelfth plain ring, Mrs. Hervey's ring, functions simultaneously as reward and punishment—a peculiarly purgatorial piece of jewelry. The remaining seven rings—all with Clarissa's hair in crystal—demonstrate Clarissa's desire to acknowledge love, to offer long-term solace, to diminish loss, and to exert her will over the future actions of the legatees. Because the rings contain a "relic" of the deceased (Clarissa's hair), the rings also offer beneficent contagion. Specifically, the hair encased within the crystal of the ring possesses the "potency" of the greater whole (Clarissa's entire living person).

It is no surprise that Anna Howe and Mr. Hickman receive rings "with my hair" (8:192). Anna has also asked for—and received—a lock of Clarissa's hair, which could be produced when the cold touch of hair in crystal is insufficient. For Anna, both ring and ringlet allow repeated reunion with the beloved decedent, invoking love, loss, and remembrance. Of the dead, Adam Smith commented, "It is miserable . . . to be no more thought of in this world, but to be obliterated, in a little time, from the affections, and almost from the memory, of their dearest friends and relations."[27] The mourning ring with Clarissa's hair ensures Anna's remembrance. The relationship between Clarissa and Anna Howe has been intensely close—"but one heart, but one soul, between us" (8:169)—and Anna functions as the most reliable witness and knowledgeable interpreter of Clarissa's behavior during her ordeal. Anna's role is that of principal living witness to the dead Clarissa's virtue, in return for which Clarissa offers Anna reunion on earth (through remembrance) and in heaven: "O my dear Anna Howe! . . . But we shall one day meet (and this hope must comfort us both) never to part again!" (8:70). By seeking prolonged union with Anna from beyond the grave, Clarissa seeks continued remembrance and in a way that sustains Clarissa's image as virtuous sufferer.

Anna has also received several other personal bequests from Clarissa, including a full-length portrait of Clarissa and Clarissa's "best diamond ring" (8:191). These bequests to Anna are meant to conjure Clarissa, to recall her physical presence. The full-length portrait assures that Clarissa's image never fades from Anna's memory; it exists as a stand-in for Clarissa. "Portrait gifts . . . not only represent people, they also stand in their stead."[28] Clarissa's best diamond ring becomes an engagement ring of sorts, pledging troth. The bequests to Mr. Hickman have equal resonance: the gift of a duplicate mourning ring, with Clarissa's hair enclosed within, provides a physical and psychical link between Anna and Hickman, with Clarissa as mediator. In addition, Clarissa symbolically gives Anna to Mr. Hickman, through the bestowal of her own locket containing a miniature portrait of Anna Howe. Clarissa's bequests to Mr. Hickman urge his suit with Anna by demonstrating Clarissa's approval of this "*mighty* sober man" (2:5).

The remaining five rings are designated for Lovelace's relatives, none of whom Clarissa has met in person. Unlike the other mourning rings, with or without her hair, Clarissa provides specific instructions as to their construction: "I bequeath to Lady Betty Lawrence, and to her Sister Lady Sarah Sadleir, and to the right honourable Lord M. and to their worthy Nieces Miss Charlotte and Miss Martha Montague, each an enameled ring, with a cipher Cl. H. with my hair in crystal, and round the inside of each, the day, month, and year of my death: each ring, with brilliants, to cost twenty guineas" (8:193). The rings would clearly be identified as mourning rings by their enameled surface and inscriptions. These rings seem intended to be like those bequeathed to Anna and Mr. Hickman, but the extra five guineas would ensure that "brilliants"—small multi-cut diamonds—surround the crystal bezel, as more befitting to adorn the aristocratic fingers of Lord M. and his relations.

These bequests to Lovelace's family show evidence of more than gratitude for their numerous kindnesses, which included offers of family, friendship, and "one hundred guineas *per* quarter" for life. Charlotte writes, "We each of us desire to be favoured with a place in your esteem; and to be considered upon the same foot of relationship, as if what once was so much our pleasure to hope *would* be, *had* been" (7:119). That is, they wish to be considered Clarissa's relations. The mourning rings offer forgiveness of sorts, an attempt to assuage the guilt they feel about their kinsman's rape of Clarissa. Yet, the rings with Clarissa's hair also bind Lovelace's family to Clarissa, and perhaps are intended to keep Lovelace outside the family circle, so to speak. By giving rings to Lovelace's family, she tries to bind their loyalty to her—not him. The distributions to Lovelace's family also serve as messages for the Harlowes, suggesting their faultiness toward their daughter, as Lovelace's relations are willing to treat Clarissa as a family member, whereas Clarissa's own relations are not.

The remaining lock of hair goes to Colonel Morden, at his request. In her will, Clarissa begs of "my worthy Cousin William Morden, Esq." (8:190) "to accept of two or three trifles, in remembrance of a Kinswoman who always honoured *him* as much as he loved *her*" (8:191). These "trifles" function doubly as fetishes, recalling Morden's deceased father, as well as Clarissa. One is a "rose diamond ring, which was a present from his good father; and will be the more valuable to him on that account" (8:191). Clarissa wore this same ring when escaping from Mrs. Sinclair's brothel the first time—"a rose diamond ring, supposed on her finger" (5:27)—the ring she wears when raped. Of course, Morden knows nothing of the ring's history. Nevertheless, it is significant that this ring is bequeathed to the man who will revenge Clarissa's rape and death. Although Clarissa has begged Morden not to be "my Avenger" (8:247), the bequest of this particular ring suggests the possibility that Clarissa desired such an end.

Another bequest to Morden is a "little miniature picture set in gold, which his worthy father made me sit for" (8:191).[29] As Susan Stewart writes, "the miniature allowed possession of the face of the other," and she argues that "the miniature projects an eternalized future-past upon the subject; the miniature image consoles in its status as an 'always there.'"[30] Uncle Morden had intended for this miniature portrait of Clarissa to be bestowed "upon the man whom I should one day be most inclined to favour" (8:191). The miniature should have gone to Lovelace.

Instead, Colonel Morden, the man most concerned with Clarissa's welfare and honor, receives it, as he has treated Clarissa with that respect, love, and affection that his father hoped Clarissa would find in a favored suitor and caring spouse. Colonel Morden also claims a lock of Clarissa's hair, "for a locket, which, he says, he will cause to be made, and wear next his heart in memory of his beloved Cousin" (8:128). Possibly, the miniature portrait of Clarissa might serve as exterior centerpiece for the locket, with Clarissa's hair enclosed within. If so, this piece of sentimental jewelry would increase its meaning as a relic: "When the miniature exists simply as a representation," Stewart notes, "it functions as sympathetic magic; when it is enclosed with a lock of hair, a piece of ribbon, or some other object that is 'part' of the other, it functions as contagious magic."[31] It is magic that conjures up the beloved decedent, allowing continued possession of the other and reunion even after death. Might Colonel Morden have been wearing this locket, "next his heart," when dueling with Lovelace?

Through the mourning rings, Clarissa recognizes the right of certain individuals to grieve her death, and she provides them with the means to negotiate and reconcile her loss. Yet, neither sister, brother, mother, father, nor either of her two uncles is offered any like solace. Instead, Clarissa provides them with those possessions that they long coveted, those buildings, plots of land, revenues, ancestral portraits, and silverware to which they long thought themselves entitled and for which they resented Clarissa's ownership. Clarissa determines that her family will receive what they have long desired—those material assets for which they sacrificed her happiness. Clarissa denies them any token of love, any sign of forgiveness, although, admittedly, her mother is offered the option of selecting "any one piece" of embroidery, as well as retaining Clarissa's Vandyke portrait, if she "should think fit to keep it herself" (8:192). With the exception of Dolly Hervey, Mrs. Hervey, and Mrs. Harlowe, the other Harlowes receive no personal items, which would express love, gratitude, respect, forgiveness, and desire on Clarissa's part to assuage their guilt and lessen their loss. Clarissa refuses them any token by which to palliate guilt and regret and, in doing so, denies them their right to grieve and, ultimately, to heal.

Lovelace, too, is denied any token of forgiveness, and, ironically, his insistence that he receive such a token results in a counterfeit relic being delivered to him. In response to Lovelace's urgent request for Clarissa's heart and a lock of her hair, Belford informs Mowbray, Lovelace's messenger: "As to the lock of hair, you may easily pacify him (as you once saw the angel) with hair near the colour, if he be intent upon it" (8:136). Because Lovelace could not distinguish Clarissa from other women—to him, "every woman is a Rake in her heart" (3:106)—his friends substitute the gold of Clarissa's hair with the dross of an impostor's. For Lovelace, mourning Clarissa will be without comfort, or perhaps one lock of hair will do as well as another, as his friend Mowbray asks, "What is there in one woman more than another, for matter of that?" (8:88).

CONCLUSION

In death, Clarissa administers her own brand of justice. Those who loved Clarissa and supported her throughout her ordeal, who offered some measure of comfort, no matter how small, will be provided with a relic by which to conjure Clarissa and, in doing so, receive temporary release from grief, vicarious access to Clarissa's virtue, and a sense of personal merit. Those whom Clarissa has deemed unworthy will come away with what all that they desired—antique silverware, plots of land, ancestral portraits—but nonetheless feel dissatisfied, the emptiness encircling their fingers weighing heavily in symbolic import. Similarly, through Clarissa's death, Richardson administers justice of sorts. For those readers who love Richardson's young heroine yet acknowledge the rightness of her death in terms of securing the novel's aesthetic, moral, and didactic aims, Richardson bequeaths metaphoric mourning rings in the form of moral missives and/or aesthetic gems embedded, enclosed, and encapsulated within the massive text, the former perhaps more important to eighteenth-century readers, the latter to twenty-first-century readers. Those deemed unworthy—that is, "the Story-Lovers and Amusement-Seekers"[32]—will receive precisely what they ask for, but will feel cheated nonetheless.

2

"YOU KNOW ME THEN"

The Relic versus the Real in Ann Radcliffe's
The Mysteries of Udolpho (1794)

AND, IF THE WEAK HAND, that has recorded this tale, has, by its scenes, beguiled the mourner of one hour of sorrow, or, by its moral, taught him to sustain it—the effort, however humble, has not been vain, nor is the writer unrewarded."[1] So reads the concluding line of Ann Radcliffe's classic Gothic tale, *The Mysteries of Udolpho*. After all mysteries have been solved, only then does the attentive reader—to her surprise—discover that this highly entertaining text is meant to assuage mourning, not to amuse or to help wile away the empty hours. Nonetheless, it is true that *Udolpho* is preoccupied with death and loss, as its heroine, Emily St. Aubert, endures the deaths of her entire immediate family (father, mother, brothers, and aunt); leaves her beloved childhood home against her wishes; undergoes forced separation from the man she loves; and uncovers a twenty-year-old murder and the murderess. However, the material world offers its compensation: letters, portraits, music, and landscapes conjure absent loved ones. For example, Emily's bereft lover, Valancourt, entreats Emily to think of him each evening as she watches the sunset: "You will then meet me in thought," he writes. "I shall constantly watch the sun-set, and I shall be happy in the belief, that your eyes are fixed upon the same object with mine, and that our minds are conversing." Emily believes that compliance with his request will "annihilate for a while the pain of absence" (163).

This chapter engages in paired readings of two anthropomorphous objects within *The Mysteries of Udolpho*: the portrait, in both in its miniature and life-size forms, and the wax effigy. It argues that the portraits of various characters and the effigy of the wax corpse function as relics of the lost, the absent, or the dead—or of death itself.

OBJECTS

PART I. THE SECRET LIFE OF PORTRAITS

Although mysteries abound within Radcliffe's novel, the central ones revolve around the past actions and subsequent fates of two presumably minor characters: Laurentini di Udolpho and the Marchioness de Villeroi. The marchioness never makes an appearance in the novel—she has been long dead—while Laurentini is believed dead, and once she does appear, she is unrecognizable even to her closest associates. However, life-size and miniaturized portraits exist of both women, and various characters treasure these relics of the dead, which are kept hidden in secret rooms, locked caskets, or under floorboards. Miniature portraits also exist of several other characters, which, like the portraits of the marchioness and of Laurentini, evoke their subjects so vividly and actively that they are treated by those who see them as the real.

This part of the chapter opens with an exploration of how portraits—life-size and miniature—served as relics that connected the living to the absent and to the dead, and how portraits functioned as highly evocative and effective surrogates. It then turns to portraits within *Udolpho*, focusing first on the miniatures of three living individuals—Emily St. Aubert, the Chevalier St. Foix, and the Marquis de Villeroi—and then on the life-size and miniature portraits of two dead individuals—the Marchioness di Villeroi and Laurentini di Udolpho.

"PIMPLES, WARTS AND EVERYTHING": PORTRAITS AND PEOPLE

In eighteenth-century England, portraiture production was "notably diverse," utilizing a variety of different mediums, such as drawing, painting, engraving, coinage, needlework, and waxwork.[2] However, our concern here is with two specific types: the life-size (or larger) portrait, usually painted in oil on canvas or wood, with the subject depicted in full-length, in half-length, or with just head and shoulders, sometimes alone and sometimes with others; and the miniature portrait, painted in watercolor on ivory or vellum or in enamel on metal, with the image usually that of a single subject's head and shoulders.

Most portraiture on a life-size or larger scale was meant to display wealth, power, and social status; assert social, political, or moral legitimacy; and document ancestral lineage.[3] Large-scale portraits provided messages about the individual and his/her society, through setting (battle scenes, estates, libraries, gardens, or salons), stance of the subject (standing, sitting, on horseback), gesture (hand raised, smiling or stern, eyes uplifted, downcast, or gazing afar), clothing (style, material, and decoration) and accoutrement (wigs, hats, gloves, jewelry, swords, fans), objects (orb and scepter, books, globes, flowers, animals, horses, skulls, weapons), colors, allegorical or symbolic imagery, and visual allusions to literary, theatrical, musical, or visual texts. To a greater or lesser extent, dependent upon aesthetic and artistic conventions of the time, large-scale portraits presented an idealized version of the subject. This is not to say that portraits did not look like the sitters—some did, some didn't—but rather that obvious flaws (wrinkles, warts, squints, bow-legs, etc.) were minimized or eliminated, and often facial features or bodily elements were rendered as a compromise between the subject's own looks and the cultural and aesthetic ideal. For instance, a square-shaped face might be softened to conform to the cultural preference for the oval, or square shoulders might be depicted as gently sloped to create the curved line so favored by eighteenth-century connoisseurs of beauty.[4] As Shearer West notes, "although portraits depict individuals, it is often the typical or conventional—rather than unique—qualities of the subject that are stressed by the artist. . . . Even though most portraits retain some degree of verisimilitude, they are nonetheless products of prevailing artistic fashions and favoured styles, techniques, and media."[5]

Miniature portraiture—or limning, as it is known—had been prized in England since Elizabethan times. Miniatures on ivory were only introduced in the early eighteenth century, after Rosalba Carrera, a Venetian painter, invented the process.[6] Prior to this, miniature portraits were almost exclusively painted on vellum glued onto the backs of playing cards or other heavy paper. Sizes of miniature portraits varied from the very small (one inch) to moderate (ten inches), dependent upon fashion trends and intended usage. However, most miniatures were in the range of one to two inches, particularly those used to decorate snuff boxes or those fashioned into jewelry. Although ivory was the preferred painting surface for miniatures during the eighteenth century, it initially proved a difficult medium, as it is oily in its natural state, making it difficult for water-based paints to adhere without extensive degreasing and sanding. One remedy was to work instead in enamel on metal, as some miniaturists did, but by the mid-eighteenth century, various techniques had been developed to roughen and degrease the surface of the ivory, rendering it an ideal surface for luminescent portraiture.

Miniature portraiture is "the most intimate of all portrait types";[7] it focuses on the head and shoulders of the sitter, usually to the exclusion of all else, with the background often a single color and with minimal attention given to clothing and accoutrement (see figure 2.1). Miniature portraiture is usually associated with more realistic portrayals of individuals. Richard Wendorf remarks, "the miniaturist must suggest the entire figure by depicting its most telling features as searchingly

Figure 2.1 Ozias Humphry, 1742–1812. *Portrait of a Lady*. Undated. Watercolor on ivory. Yale Center for British Art. Gift of Roger N. Radford. B2010.4.

as possible; and in the process, he will often isolate what is personally distinctive from what his subject shares with similar men or women"[8]—this in direct contrast to the strategy used by the painter of life-size images. Sometimes, the techniques used in miniature portraiture—brush stippling and facial outlining—might encourage a "tendency to prettify and flatter" the subject.[9] However, the fact that miniatures were meant for close family members, intimate friends, and lovers often led to more realistic depictions. As Marcia Pointon notes, with "imagery of rulers and powerful people . . . a degree of idealization (or air-brushing) is expected," but in "intimate small-scale portraits . . . likeness may be a more desired quality."[10] Notably, Oliver Cromwell's famous dictum to paint him "pimples, warts and everything" was not made in regards to his large-scale portraiture, which copied the iconography associated with Charles I and was meant for public display, but for a miniature portrait.[11]

Portraiture, both life-size and miniature, lends itself easily to surrogacy. As Shearer West notes, the "portrait . . . has a sort of power that allows it to be thought of as a substitute for the individual it represents. The use of portraits for marriage negotiations, gifts, and private contemplation grew from the power of the portrait not only to stand for the represented individual, but also to evoke the individual's presence in the minds of viewers."[12] With life-size portraits, the spectator sees an image that, in a skilled painter's hands, looks remarkably like the absent beloved—or at least the absent beloved at her best. Pointon writes, "The historical portrait assumes many of the characteristics of the fetish as anthropological and psychoanalytically defined: it is in the first place manufactured and in the second place it is that nothing-in-itself that constitutes a screen onto which fantasies are projected."[13] Often, portraits are also associated "with the past, with memory, and—by extension—with death. Portraiture almost magically retains the life of individuals who are dead, or the youth of individuals who have aged."[14] Portraiture vivifies the dead. Indeed, many bereaved family members in eighteenth-century England commissioned family portraits with the beloved decedent painted into them as if still alive.[15] In particular, because of its unique properties, the miniature portrait begs to be fetishized. As Marianne Koos notes, miniatures are "meant to be worn on the body, warmed (that is animated), kissed and touched. They allow the person depicted to be 'held in hand', and—viewed up close—to be contemplated in a concentrated 'private' act or concealed on intimate parts of the body, although not without the supporting ribbon demonstratively highlighting the personal connection or individual secret." Koos further comments that "the miniature comes to stand for the absent person. In the miniature portrait, framed by precious gemstones, given form by valuable pigments—that is, medially represented and embodied—the person . . . acquires immediate presence without any visible traces of the artist's hand."[16]

OBJECTS

Portraits—life-size and miniature—appear in many eighteenth-century English novels, such as Samuel Richardson's *Clarissa*, Henry Fielding's *Amelia*, Eliza Haywood's *The History of Miss Betsy Thoughtless*, Jane Austen's *Sense and Sensibility*, and Radcliffe's *The Italian*, to name but a few. However, to the best of my knowledge, *The Mysteries of Udolpho* contains the greatest number of portraits—six miniatures and two life-size portraits—of any literary text from this time period, and Radcliffe's usage of them demonstrates how, by century end, relics of the dead (or living) have become animated by the spirits of the real, so much so that they function as the real. Finally, while I include miniature portraits of the living in my analysis, I do so in order to demonstrate two things: the way in which portraits of the living compete with the real, while the portraits of the dead are the real; and how Lockean free-floating consciousness animates the portraits (relics) of both the living and the dead.

"I HAVE WORN IT NEXT MY HEART": MINIATURES OF THE LIVING IN *UDOLPHO*

Within Radcliffe's novel, the miniature portraits of living subjects (excluding Laurentini, who is presumed dead) include one of Emily St. Aubert, fashioned into a bracelet charm for her mother and stolen from the fishing shack at La Vallée by the love-stricken Du Pont; a somewhat larger, diamond-encrusted miniature of the Chevalier St. Foix, the fiancé of Blanche Beauveau, daughter of the Count de Villefort; and a miniature of the Marquis de Villeroi, at one time in the possession of his lover, Laurentini di Udolpho. All of the portraits offer themselves as potent relics (of the living), so much so that they not only conjure the absent individuals but also actively function as their surrogates. Each portrait is considered a remarkably accurate representation of the subject, evoking the same psychic and emotional response as its subject, and dependent upon the individual depicted in the miniature, the portrait is adored, caressed, avariciously eyed, wept over, or reproached. Yet, despite the fact that the miniatures act as surrogates for their subjects, they do not always perform the bidding of their subjects. At least two of the miniatures act in a way that their subjects would not: one offering its possessor hope, solace, and love, the other brazenly calling attention to itself and, by doing so, endangering the life of its subject. In sum, the miniatures are not merely surrogates for their subjects, simulacra of the real, but active agents in their own right. Notably, the miniatures and their respective subjects rarely appear simultaneously; if they do, the appearance of the subject forces the immediate disappearance of the miniature. Further, possession of the miniature is no guarantee of possession of the portrayed. In fact, it appears that one may possess the portrait *or* the person but never both simultaneously. In *Udolpho*, then, the miniature portrait exists as a highly satisfying substitute for the absent individual, so much so that in some instances (as we shall see), the portrait proves more satisfying than the original, as it is more malleable in serving the needs and fueling the desires of its possessor.

Early in the novel, a bracelet owned by Emily's ailing mother is stolen from the fishing house at La Vallée: "What made this bracelet valuable to her was a miniature of her daughter to which it was attached, esteemed a striking resemblance, and which had been painted only a few months before" (10). Other incidents at the fishing house—a love poem scratched into window glass, a plaintive song by an unseen musician—make it clear that whoever stole it was interested not in the bracelet, nor its monetary value, but in Emily's portrait: "When Emily was convinced that the bracelet was really gone, she blushed, and became thoughtful" (10). It is Du Pont who has stolen it, who has cherished it, as Emily later learns. Many months later, imprisoned within the Castle of Udolpho, Du Pont explains the importance of the miniature to Ludovico, Emily's servant: "Tell your lady . . . that this has been my companion, and only solace in all my misfortunes. Tell her, that I have worn it next my heart, and that I send it her as the pledge of an affection, which can never die; that I would not part with it, but to her, for the wealth of worlds, and that I now part with it, only in hope of soon receiving it from her hands" (443). He calls the miniature "a treasure, which was to me inestimable" (448).

The miniature has offered companionship, solace, love, and union with the absent beloved, Emily. It has conjured her for Du Pont, but more than that, it has become her; as her surrogate, it is clutched to Du Pont's heart, just as he would clutch the original, if available. The miniature, though, falsely offers hope, acting in a way inconsistent with Emily's own feelings. For Du Pont, to relinquish the miniature to Emily and, subsequently, for Emily to return it to him would signal her acceptance of his suit, her acknowledgement of and return of his love. It is her own self that she will give to him, when returning her surrogate; the surrogate, then, stands in place of the real, at least in Du Pont's eyes. Alas for this patient lover, Emily recoils from him, dismayed that the mysterious prisoner of Udolpho is not her beloved Valancourt nor, for that matter, anyone she knows; and she refuses to return the miniature to him, despite his urgent entreaties. He pleads with her, begging for the return of her double: "let me only supplicate from you forgiveness, and the picture, which I so unwarily returned. Your generosity will pardon the theft, and restore the prize. My crime has been my punishment; for the portrait I stole has contributed to nourish a passion, which must still be my torment" (448). However, relinquishing the miniature to Emily has resulted in its permanent loss, as Emily proves highly unwilling to indulge Du Pont's fantasies of possessing her, aware that her painted surrogate offers hope where none exists. In this instance, the miniature portrait has pleased more than its subject, as it has offered psychic and emotional compensation, and even now, after the potential for any union of subject and admirer has been denied by Emily, the double still offers a pleasurable delusion, though one not unmixed with pain nor without its own "torment." But why has the miniature acted the part of coquette, tantalizing Du Pont with dreams of future pleasures that will ever be denied? Why the separation between the simulacrum and the real? Perhaps the miniature *did* work in service of its mistress, as Du Pont provides Emily's means of escape from the castle, and his enamored infatuation with Emily, encouraged by her miniature surrogate, assures that he will do all that he can to secure her safe removal from Montoni's clutches. More realistically, however, the relic is by its very nature an object that encapsulates the essence of the absent beloved, but which does so only in conjunction with the desires of the worshiper. Specifically, a relic by its very nature must satisfy its possessor at the very same time that it recreates the absent beloved. Thus, no relic can fully represent the absent beloved, as it exists as an amalgamation of the absent beloved and the mourner/worshiper of the beloved. By refusing to return the purloined miniature to Du Pont, Emily seeks to break the hold that the miniature has upon him; he is denied any further opportunity to use the miniature to conjure up either the real (Emily) or the imaginary (the fulfilment of his desire). Once returned to her, Emily's miniature never appears again within the text. Valancourt may perhaps receive it on becoming Emily's husband, or Emily may wish to lock it away, as it possesses an energy and activity all its own, seeking to speak on her behalf yet not totally in accord with Emily's thoughts and wishes.

In an essay on the miniature portrait of the eponymous heroine of Henry Fielding's *Amelia*, Steven J. Gores argues, "Ultimately, *Amelia*'s narrative works to package its title character as an object that we, as readers, are asked to decide if Booth is worth possessing."[17] In this case, the real—that is, the subject of the portrait—becomes an object, a life-size version of the miniature. Allison Conway considers this interpretation of the miniature—of any miniature—as one that "underestimates the complexity that surrounds the miniature's relation to both the private and the particular, and to the world at large," suggesting that the miniature portrait is intimately associated with "women's emotional and economic lives."[18] Further, Conway argues that the "dynamics [that] surround the miniature portrait of a woman . . . differ from those surrounding the miniature portrait of a man"; specifically, "preoccupation with the representation of the female character governs the portrait's representation," whether the portrait be of a male or female subject.[19] This idea is expressed more fully in Conway's reading of the miniatures in Fielding's *Amelia* and Eliza Haywood's *The History of Miss Betsy Thoughtless*: "in *Amelia*, the miniature stands in a synechdochic and metaphoric relation to the heroine, representing both a part of and a likeness of her whole body"; in contrast, in "*Betsy Thoughtless* . . . the representation of Trueworth serves only as a means of accessing the spectacle of the heroine in her moments of private beholding. Because Trueworth, as a man, is not defined in relation to his objectness, his 'to-be-seen' aspect, his image is of little significance."[20] Thus, according to both Gores and Conway, the miniature and its female subject/female spectator possess equivalence: they are both objects. However, in her usage of miniature portraits, Radcliffe complicates and even dismantles completely this gendered dynamic, as her miniatures possess a subjectivity and agency that transforms them into something other than objects; in addition, the subject's gender appears to have little to no bearing on his/her objectification. In the case of Emily's portrait, the miniature cannot be considered an object (thus suggesting that Emily herself cannot be an object) because it possesses a measure of agency and because it exists as a material conjoining of the psychical essence of two individuals: the absent, longed-for individual and the yearning, desiring individual. The miniature becomes instead a third party, disruptive of binarism. Does Du Pont view Emily as an object? Perhaps. Perhaps not. But the miniature exists principally as the material expression of Du Pont's longing, and the reader interprets the miniature in terms of his beholding/holding of it, not in terms of Emily's "objectness."

The case of Chevalier St. Foix's miniature is more complex. It is the focus of both the male and the female gaze. It seems to objectify both him and the woman he loves. Yet, it also possesses a measure of independent agency. Upon her engagement to the Chevalier St. Foix, Blanche Beauveau, daughter of the Count de Villefort, is presented with a costly miniature of her fiancé, which she wears suspended around her neck by means of a ribbon, a chain, or a strand of pearls; the miniature nestles in the folds of her neckerchief, lying next to her heart. Described as "a large picture" (two to two-and-a-half inches would have been the standard size for lockets of this sort), it is considered a highly accurate depiction of the "young chevalier" (615); and as befits the chevalier's great wealth, the metal casing that surrounds the miniature is studded in its entirety with small diamonds. As Marcia Pointon notes, eighteenth-century "women of quality" were "known to have worn miniatures of their husbands; these were not hidden but placed facing outward as part of their apparel." These miniature portraits express "allegiance both to fashion and to a spouse who had almost total legal rights over a wife's person but, equally, considerable financial obligation, since under marriage law he was liable for her debts."[21] The locket worn by Blanche, then, not only physically depicts an image of her future husband, whom she apparently loves, but it also demonstrates his immense wealth, his "ownership" of her and her acceptance of this fact, and her subsequent obligations and duties toward him. By wearing the locket, Blanche indicates her ownership by St. Foix, which in turn suggests her objectification. But things are not so simple.

Blanche wears the locket on a journey to her future in-laws and on her return trip homeward to Chateau-le-Blanc, when she, her father, and St. Foix unwittingly enter the hideout of banditti. One of the banditti recognizes the chevalier from a previous encounter, in which St. Foix and his father had captured some of their band, who were subsequently hanged; the count is mis-recognized as the chevalier's father. Intent upon robbery, revenge, and murder, the banditti lead the count, the chevalier, and Blanche through a series of "long and ruinous passages" (611), under pretext of a warm fire and pleasant victuals. However, Blanche becomes separated from her father and lover, and, disoriented, she wanders toward an open door from which she hears voices. Standing outside, she overhears the banditti discussing plans to murder "the two chevaliers" (612). The banditti also discuss the miniature: "there is this picture; did you see that? . . . it hangs at her neck; if it had not sparkled so, I should not have found it out, for it was almost hid by her dress; those are diamonds too, and a rare many of them there must be, to go round such a large picture" (613). Alarmed, Blanche bravely attempts to find her father and lover (an act of subjectivity on her part), only to stumble in the dark, alerting the banditti to her presence. The banditti insist that she "surrender" the miniature, or they will "seize it" (614); she readily gives the locket to them. Once it is in their possession, they study it carefully, admiring the diamonds and the portrait itself, remarking upon the youthful charms of the chevalier: "faith; as handsome a young chevalier, as you would wish to see by a summer's sun" (615). When the banditti admire the miniature itself—remarking on the handsomeness of the painted chevalier and the number of diamonds that surround him—they are also admiring the real St. Foix's handsomeness and wealth. We see the miniature through their eyes, not through Blanche's eyes. It is their gaze that is important, as the banditti are now the possessors of the locket, and in this instance, St. Foix *is* objectified. From the banditti's perspective, the miniature represents the fulfillment of their latent desires: it materializes the riches of St. Foix, a wealth in which they believe they will now share; it objectifies his beauty, which they assess with connoisseur-like appreciation, perhaps sadistically considering its impending ruin. Possession of the miniature represents possession of St. Foix himself. For a time, St. Foix has become the miniature. The banditti intend to strip St. Foix of any riches that he has upon him, just as they intend to strip the locket of its diamonds and gold; and they intend to destroy him, just as they would the miniature portrait, as both body and portrait will become evidence of crime. (Interestingly, none of the banditti seem particularly interested in Blanche herself, though possibly this is due to the fact that, at least in their eyes, she appears as one of the chevalier's possessions, which they will soon own.) This strange interlude—a moment of admiration for the miniature and its subject conjoined with pleasurable contemplation of their attendant fantasies—is suddenly interrupted by sounds of "clashing of swords, mingled with voices of loud contention and heavy with groans" (615), which in turn force all of the banditti except one to rush to the defense of their fellows. The miniature disappears with the ruffians—for where it goes or with whom is never revealed—but almost simultaneously, a badly wounded St. Foix stumbles into the chamber, bloodied and chased by armed men, at which point Blanche faints. Previously, the miniature had taken the place of the real (St. Foix); the real has now taken the place of the relic.

The miniature and St. Foix never appear together within the novel, suggesting the ease by which one may replace the other, suggesting that they are indeed in some strange way the exact same thing. In addition, while the miniature is not solely responsible for the banditti's desire for murder—as mentioned, they wish to revenge themselves upon St. Foix and his father for an earlier encounter—it does offer itself as additional incentive and may be said to incite violence against St. Foix. On the one hand, the miniature has called attention to itself, sparkling in the dim light of the banditti's refuge and, by doing so, fueling the banditti's murderous desires. On the other hand, it may have saved St. Foix's life, as it has engaged the rapt attention of four of the banditti, separating them from their two remaining companions and allowing the count, St. Foix, and Ludovico to attack the latter. The miniature, then, exists initially as passive object, next as active "thing" and occasional subject. It seeks to render both its subject (St. Foix) and its owner (Blanche) as objects, which they reject through their own active agency, and for a time, it acts as a potent mediating object, articulating obvious outward elements of St. Foix's existence (his rank, his wealth, his handsome features) and the desires of the banditti for revenge and riches. Like many doppelgängers, it poses a danger to the original, and conflict over which will survive—the host or the visitant—ensues. Regardless, although his miniature has been lost, St. Foix has not, for though badly wounded, he will live. One has been sacrificed for the other. St. Foix will now take the place of the miniature, resting his head upon Blanche's bosom, where his surrogate had formerly laid.

The last miniature of a living person depicts the Marquis de Villeroi. Owned by a young Laurentini, the miniature has presumably been presented to her by the marquis, possibly in anticipation of their marriage, just as St. Foix had presented Blanche with his miniature. Yet, the marriage never occurs: "she, whom he had designed for a wife, afterwards became his mistress" (656), precisely because her sexual indiscretions with the marquis prompt a "minuter enquiry" into her past, wherein earlier sexual exploits are revealed. When the marquis leaves her, falsely promising to return and marry her, he leaves behind his miniature, which in turn becomes the relic of her thwarted affections. Repeatedly, she would "sigh and weep over" it (656), expressing her longing for the marquis. Yet, at some level, the miniature appears to convey the truth that the marquis withheld from her; it transmits the message that the marquis was too cowardly to express directly to her. It speaks for him, saying he is lost to her. Over the months of separation, she treats the miniature as if it were the marquis himself, "weeping over his picture, and speaking to it, for many hours, upbraiding, reproaching and caressing it alternately" (657). By leaving the miniature behind, the marquis, unintentionally or not, conveys ambiguous feelings toward his former lover—or at least Laurentini imbues the miniature with these ambiguous feelings. Because it exists as the material surrogate for the absent marquis, it allows Laurentini to conjure him, to commune with him, to reunite with him psychically on a daily basis. Because it offers its possessor the (temporary) assuagement of her desires, it keeps longing and hope alive. Thus, though she hears of the marquis's marriage, Laurentini clandestinely journeys to Languedoc to find him, certain perhaps that because the miniature is still hers, the marquis will also be hers. At that point in the narrative, the miniature of the marquis is heard of no more, as the subject of the portrait has taken the miniature's place. As with the miniature portrait of St. Foix, the miniature of the marquis and the person of the marquis never appear on stage at the same time, so to speak. The miniature only appears textually when the marquis is absent, suggesting its role as a surrogate and replacement for him, but it is also a surrogate that acts independently of him, one that has betrayed him, both in telling the truth and in offering continued hope—two things he wished to avoid revealing. Normally, the fact that the text focuses upon Laurentini gazing at the marquis's miniature would suggest her objectification were it not for two facts: the miniature spurs her into action, by fueling her passion; and the marquis himself linguistically becomes an object: "her whole heart being devoted to one object, life became hateful to her, when she believed that object lost" (657). Ambivalently, the miniature represents the real, as Laurentini weeps over it, caresses it, reproaches it, as she would the marquis himself; but it also stands as a relic of him, increasing her feelings of loss and demanding action on her part.

In a seminal essay, Terry Castle noted that "Characters in *Udolpho* mirror, or blur into one another" and distinctions between "subject and object, break down."[22] And so it would seem that the miniature portraits, originally mere objects, separate from their respective subjects at times of stress or crisis, sometimes acting the part of their subjects, other times acting with independence and agency. Thus, a certain level of conflict occurs between the miniature portraits and their subjects; and between the possessors of the portrait and the desires the portraits represent. Each miniature betrays the portrayed and the possessor alike, indulging, then thwarting, the desires of the possessor, acting as surrogate for, then as competitor against, the subject. In the end, the miniatures achieve reunion with their respective subjects, metaphorically reabsorbing themselves into the psyche of the subject and physically disappearing without a trace. In sum, the consciousness of the subject metaphorically splits into two—the subject and the miniature relic—allowing the relic to function on equal terms with the subject, as well as independently of the subject; re-absorption of the relic allows reunification of consciousness into a single entity.

"YOU KNOW ME THEN": PORTRAITS OF THE DEAD AND DYING

In *Udolpho*, the three miniature portraits of living personages exude "the discrete charm of second-order simulacra" in that each "double ends up being confused with the real thing," at least for a short period of time. That is to say, the miniature exists as "the map, the double, the mirror or the concept of the real," not as the real itself.[23] However, in the case of the large-scale portraits of the Marchioness de Villeroi and Laurentini di Udolpho, something different occurs: the portrait itself has become the real.[24] Each life-size portrait has, of necessity it seems, taken the place of the original, with little or no slippage between the portrait and the portrayed; each large portrait has, to all intents and purposes, become the original subject. The cause appears to be either that the portrayed is dead, as is the case with the marchioness, or that the portrayed is presumed dead and/or no longer resembles the painted self, as is the case with Laurentini. As regards the miniature portraits of the marchioness and Laurentini, they—like the miniatures of the living subjects—function in dual fashion as material relics and psychic embodiments of their respective subject's personality and of their respective possessor's needs and desires. Furthermore, these small portraits also possess independence and agency, though unlike the miniatures of living individuals (Emily, the Chevalier St. Foix, and the Marquis De Villeroi), no conflict occurs between the miniatures and their subjects—their allegiance is always to the real, whatever form and shape the real may take.

Two miniatures and one life-size portrait of the Marchioness de Villeroi appear within Radcliffe's novel. The two miniatures are near duplicates, one "the exact resemblance" of the other (645); both are kept in secret places. The miniature cherished by Monsieur St. Aubert is enclosed within an ivory case (not necessarily

[51]

OBJECTS

painted on ivory), then carefully wrapped in "paper after paper," and stashed within a "purse of louis" (103), the latter of which is then deposited in a secret hollow beneath the floorboards of his private closet. Thus, it is encased and enclosed within at least four separate, protective materials, some with multiple layers, suggesting the high value that it holds for its owner, St. Aubert, but also its taboo nature, as the coverings not only protect but also deliberately conceal or shroud. Its subject is a woman "of uncommon beauty," whose face is "characterized by an expression of sweetness, shaded with sorrow, and tempered by resignation" (104). Later conversations between Emily and Dorothée suggest that the miniature was painted during the short period of the marchioness's marriage, thus accounting for the sorrowful looks, as the marriage was an unhappy one on numerous counts, largely because both parties were in love with someone other than their spouse.

At this point in its career, the "real" to which the miniature portrait aligns itself is still the marchioness, as she lives in St. Aubert's memories; he still grieves for her. The secretiveness with which St. Aubert's miniature is hidden and the special care that is given it, nestled as it is among layers and layers of papers, suggests its nature as a treasured relic of his sister: "St. Aubert gazed earnestly and tenderly upon this portrait, put it to his lips, and then to his heart, and sighed with convulsive force" (26). It functions as surrogate for the late marchioness—in kissing it, he kisses her; in placing it next his heart, he places her next his heart—but St. Aubert's excessive grief when viewing it (excessive when one considers that the deaths of his wife and two young sons are met with melancholic resignation) suggests that the purpose of the relic is not simply to connect psychically with his deceased and well-loved sister, but also to relive her grotesque death, which he further emphasizes by rereading "the last pathetic letters of the Marchioness" (660). Both miniature and letters function as relics and surrogates for the late marchioness; the miniature replicates the physical presence, while the letters replicate her voice and thoughts. The miniature's association with death—a particular kind of death—is what renders it taboo to others and perhaps a source of shame to St. Aubert, as the miniature forces him to confront death in its ugliest manifestation as murder, at a time when death itself—in all its various guises—was beginning to be shunned. Although Emily has only spied her father weeping over the miniature once, a suggestion exists that at least since the death of his wife, Monsieur St. Aubert has repeatedly engaged in viewing the small portrait of the marchioness and rereading her letters. Past midnight, Emily looks for her father in his study, where, "since the death of Madame St. Aubert, it had been frequently his custom to rise from his restless bed, and go thither to compose his mind" (25). The closet where St. Aubert weeps, sobs, prays, and sighs over the miniature and the letters—the hiding place wherein he secretes the miniature and the letters—belongs to that study.

Repetitiveness is characteristic of trauma and of narrative mourning. The trauma survivor re-enacts the original event (usually on an unconscious level), in order to understand it, to find meaning in it, and to strategize ways of surviving it. As Freud notes, "It is clear that in their play children repeat everything that has made a great impression on them in real life, and that in doing so they abreact the strength of the impression and, as one might put it, make themselves master of the situation."[25] In other words, activity in the form of re-enactment is preferable to passivity, as the former allows for some measure of control and offers the means to process the event, to provide it with meaning. For St. Aubert, the pain associated with the marchioness's mysterious death is unbearable, yet must be born over and over again, particularly as his own time on earth is fast nearing its end. The relic thus conjures the beloved marchioness herself and her unnatural death, and so the miniature of the marchioness may be said to evoke both her presence and the presence of death, to bring comfort as well as unbearable pain. On a journey that will be his last, St. Aubert leaves behind the miniature (simulacrum/relic); he will soon lie next to the marchioness (the real) in the cold earth.

Once the miniature becomes Emily's possession, she keeps it locked in "a little box, which contained some letters of Valancourt, with some drawings she had sketched, during her stay in Tuscany" (496). At this point, with St. Aubert dead, the miniature aligns itself with a new real—its life-size counterpart at the Chateau-le-Blanc. Curiously, once the miniature has come, along with Emily, to Chateau-le-Blanc, it takes on a more active role. Somehow unwrapping itself from its layer-upon-layer of paper cushioning and freeing itself from its ivory case, it escapes from Emily's little box, slipping from its place among the letters and falling to the floor at the feet of Dorothée, one of the few living persons able to identify the subject and lead Emily to the life-size portrait. The miniature seemingly wishes to be recognized for what it—a surrogate for the real—and it can only do so by reuniting with the real. By thrusting itself into Dorothée's sight, it brings forth revelations that lead Dorothée to disclose the marchioness's story to Emily, as well as to show her the life-size portrait of the marchioness. Like the miniature portraits of living individuals, the miniature of the marchioness textually disappears when the real—the life-size portrait—appears.

This large-scale portrait of the marchioness hangs in oriel—the windowed recess that functions as closet—in the marchioness's abandoned suite of rooms in the North Wing of Chateau-le-Blanc; the suite has been sealed by order of the marquis immediately following the death of his wife. The portrait shows a young woman "all blooming" with youth, but with a look of "pensive melancholy" (533) on her face; the portrait was "drawn . . . before she was married" (349). For twenty years, only the housekeeper of Chateau-le-Blanc, Dorothée, and her husband have had access to the suite of rooms. Yet, they choose not to enter due to the sad and sinister circumstances surrounding the marchioness's death. The isolation of the portrait of the marchioness, locked in an abandoned set of rooms, replicates the isolation that the marchioness experienced during her marriage, when the cruelty of the marquis would make her "go to her own room, and cry so!" (524). In the oriel where the portrait hangs, the possessions of the former marchioness lay strewn about as if the portrait continues to use them. Black satin slippers, black gloves, a long black veil, and a robe are "scattered," "as if they had just been thrown off" (533). A silver crucifix and an open prayer book lie on the table, as if the marchioness had just finished her prayers. A large Spanish lute lies "on a corner of the table, as if it had been carelessly placed there by the hand, that had so often awakened it" (534). The portrait, then, has become the dead marchioness, seemingly wearing her clothes, playing her lute, and reading her prayer book. The portrait is the real. As Dorothée notes, "there she is, ma'amselle . . . there is her very self!" (533).

Like the life-size portrait of the marchioness, the one of Laurentini also hangs in an area where it receives few visitors. It has become the real, not because Laurentini is physically dead but because Laurentini no longer resembles her portrait and because she herself is no longer Laurentini, but rather Sister Agnes, another thing altogether. Covered "with dust and cobweb" (278), Laurentini's portrait hangs "in an obscure chamber, adjoining that part of the castle, allotted to the servants," presumably viewed only by Old Carlo and his wife during the many years of Montoni's absence. With the Castle of Udolpho again inhabited, the portrait is viewed only by other servants, who are curious about the woman who disappeared so many years ago (279). The portrait "represented a lady in the flower of youth and beauty; her features were handsome and noble, full of strong expression. . . . It was a countenance, which spoke the language of passion, rather than that of sentiment; a haughty impatience of misfortune—not the placid melancholy of a spirit injured, yet resigned" (278). Of course, the "placid melancholy of a spirit injured, yet resigned" belongs to the marchioness, so that Laurentini's portrait simultaneously evokes that of the marchioness by its very difference. As it is highly unlikely that the haughty, proud Laurentini would choose such an obscure site for her portrait—a place where it would be "little seen" (279) and then only by the "vulgar"—it suggests that Montoni himself has relegated the portrait to this ignominious place, perhaps hoping to disgrace and humble the surrogate of the woman who rejected him and his love: "She was rich and beautiful; I wooed her; but her heart was fixed upon another, and she rejected me"

(289). Instead of being admired by courtiers, the portrait is gawked at by curious servants. Although the portrait is "mute"—there are no accompanying letters or statements as in the case of the marchioness—its story is nonetheless told by gossiping servants and by Montoni himself, the latter of whom provides a reasonably truthful account (289–290), though he believes Laurentini to be dead. The portrait is treated in ways identical to how Laurentini herself would be treated, if present: it is the object of pointing fingers and salacious gossip; it is shunned by polite society, though recognized as the former mistress of Udolpho; it is placed in a location intended to disgrace and humiliate; and it is associated with death, not only through associated gossip (Montoni suggests she has killed herself; the servants believe Montoni has killed her), but also through the constant conflation and confusion between the life-size portrait and the waxen corpse that hides behind the black pall in a recess at Udolpho. Equally significantly, when Emily later sees the miniature portrait of Laurentini, it is not Laurentini herself whom she recognizes, but the life-size portrait of Laurentini at Udolpho. Laurentini is no longer the subject of the life-size portrait; that woman no longer exists, either visually or psychically. The life-size portrait, then, has become the subject, the real.

Laurentini, now Sister Agnes, has in her possession two miniature portraits—one of her former self and one of the marchioness—that she keeps in a locked casket (or box) at the convent of St. Clair. The miniature of the marchioness lies within the main compartment of the locked casket; the miniature of Laurentini lies within "a secret drawer" (646) of the casket, suggesting the need for this latter portrait to be doubly hidden. As it is unlikely that the marchioness had gifted her miniature to Laurentini—after all, they had never met—then it must be the marquis himself, Laurentini's lover and co-murderer of the marchioness, who has given it to Laurentini, no doubt to punish her for a deed in which he himself was complicit. As for the miniature of Laurentini, it would seem logical that it was once part of a pair of miniatures exchanged by the lovers Laurentini and the marquis. The fact that Laurentini possesses it now suggests that the marquis returned it to her, signaling his disgust with and renunciation of her. But what do these miniatures—as relics of the past, as relics of the dead—represent to Laurentini as Sister Agnes?

Both miniatures may be penitential in nature, used to conjure remorse. Taking the miniature of the marchioness into her hands, Sister Agnes/Laurentini studies it: she "gazed upon it earnestly for some moments in silence; and then, with a countenance of deep despair, threw up her eyes to Heaven, and prayed inwardly" (645). For Laurentini/Sister Agnes, the miniature recreates the marchioness's death—and in gazing upon it, she is forced to confront the fact that in killing the marchioness, she lost her lover (as the marquis "curse[s] her as the instigator of his crime" [659]), her own self (as she was forced into the convent by the marquis), and what innocence she yet possessed. The miniature makes present "that most abhorred deed!" (644)—an act "for which whole years of prayer and penitence cannot atone!" (646). To dwell upon the miniature of the marchioness is to revisit that period in time when Laurentini's passion for the marquis raged like "a fiend" (646). Yet, unlike the wax figure behind the black pall, which offers Laurentini's ancestor the hope of "pardon for all his sins" (662), the small portrait of the marchioness offers no such hope. The miniature, then, reconnects Laurentini with the criminal deed and its unsatisfactory results, but in doing so, she enters a personal hell, "where peace / And rest can never dwell, hope never comes / That comes to all."[26] The miniature of Laurentini may also offer itself as a cruel remembrance of who and what Laurentini once was and of the "crime, which whole years of repentance and of the severest penance had not been able to obliterate from her conscience" (664). Like the portrait of Dorian Gray—but in reverse—Sister Agnes's hideous ruined looks reveal the true ugliness of Laurentini's soul, while the miniature retains the outward marks of innocence. "Look at me well, and see what guilt has made me" (646), Sister Agnes commands Emily.

However, it is equally likely that the miniatures of the two women—one victim, one murderer—also speak to the fact that Sister Agnes is no longer Laurentini, but rather an uneasy admixture of Laurentini and the marchioness. Specifically, since her murder of the marchioness, Laurentini has attempted to become the marchioness, taking the marchioness's history as her own (577), singing haunting music while playing the lute at night, just as the marchioness sang and strummed her lute each evening, wearing a black veil (albeit a nun's veil) in place of the marchioness's black veil. The placement of the miniature of the marchioness within the body of the locked casket suggests that this relic is meant to connect Sister Agnes to the marchioness, whose mildness, meekness, and quiet resignation Sister Agnes hopes to emulate. The placement of the miniature of Laurentini within the secret compartment of the locked casket, in contrast, suggests that which must be shunned and avoided. But Sister Agnes cannot shed herself entirely of Laurentini, just as she cannot rid herself of her miniature portrait; the passions of Laurentini remain in Sister Agnes, even if hidden deep. As Sister Agnes, she is and is not Laurentini; she is the marchioness and Laurentini, victim and murderer, saint and sinner. Thus, when Emily receives the miniature of Laurentini from Sister Agnes, she is only able to connect the miniature with "the portrait of Signora Laurentini, which she had formerly seen in the castle of Udolpho—the lady, who had disappeared in so mysterious a manner, and whom Montoni had been suspected of having caused to be murdered" (646). The miniature functions as the surrogate of the life-size portrait, not of Sister Agnes: "In silent astonishment, Emily continued to gaze alternately upon the picture and the dying nun, endeavoring to trace a resemblance between them, which no longer existed" (646). When Sister Agnes says to Emily, "You know me then," it is not entirely true, as Emily only knows Laurentini, the former mistress of Udolpho, not the half-mad nun who shrieks in terror on her deathbed.

CONCLUSION

Radcliffe's novel raises several important epistemological questions about images—painted or drawn portraits, photographs, videos, tattoos, holographs—and their efficacy as relics able to conjure the spirit of the absent, the missing, and the dead. No one doubts their highly evocative nature and their ability to bring the absent or the dead to momentary life. However, images, even moving ones, tend to be static and stable in that they are relegated to a particular place and time from which they cannot escape. As such, they always represent the past, whether it be a recent past or a long-ago one. But the subjects of those images possess a mutability that alters them, minute by minute, creating an ever-widening distance between the past self as captured in an image and the present self in biological form. The image captures a moment in the life of the real, but does that mean it is equivalent to the real, a form of the real? In addition, memory lends meaning to images, but memory is elusive, subject to fading and revision.[27] Is the image, then, "hyper-real," alluding to something that never truly existed, something the beholder imbues with his or her own (accurate or not) memories, meanings, desires, and longing?

On a similar note, Radcliffe's novel also confronts readers with the uneasy truth that objects are sometimes more pleasing than their subjects—no matter how beloved the subject (individual) might be or have been. Objects bend to our memories and desires, whereas people rarely do. Du Pont learns this when Emily's miniature offers him greater consolation than Emily herself ever will. This, then, is the true magic of the relic, as it freezes the lost beloved at a particular point in time and thus stabilizes the longed-for individual within the mourner's imagination, where she will never grow old, where she will always look upon him or her with fond eyes and a gentle smile; and it bends to the mourner's desires, offering pleasing illusions, perhaps even to the point of altering memory itself.

PART II. DEATH AS THE LOST BELOVED

"Oh! I would not tell you what is behind the black veil for the world! Are not you wild to know?" So asks Isabella Thorpe of Catherine Morland, the susceptible heroine of Jane Austen's *Northanger Abbey*. Catherine replies, "Oh! yes; quite; what can it be?—But do not tell me—I would not be told upon any account. I know it must be a skeleton, I am sure it is Laurentina's [sic] skeleton."[28] Despite the misspelling of Laurentini's name, Austen nonetheless highlights what is perhaps the most memorable, most talked about, and alternately revered and ridiculed aspect of Radcliffe's novel: the object behind the black veil. Of course, it turns out not to be Laurentini's skeleton. Indeed, it is not a skeleton at all, but rather a wax figure sculpted to mimic a decaying corpse. Expecting the partly decomposed body of an actual murder victim, readers instead encounter its waxy surrogate. An imposter has taken death's place, and many readers feel cheated. As Sir Walter Scott noted, "some such feeling of disappointment and displeasure attends most readers, when they read for the first time the unsatisfactory solution of the mysteries of the black pall and the wax figure," and he concludes that "the incidents of the black veil and the waxen figure, may be considered as instances where the explanation falls short of expectation, and disappoints the reader entirely."[29] Nonetheless, the wax figure functions as the abject representative of death—its handmaid, so to speak—at a time when death was becoming culturally unrepresentable. By the end of the eighteenth century, as both Philippe Ariès and Thomas W. Laqueur have separately demonstrated, death was no longer considered the natural end to life and the dead body evidence of the deep sleep of the soul, but rather death had become "a symptom of failure and the dead body a site for understanding what went wrong."[30] The corpse became the scapegoat for the loss of faith in the supernatural.[31] Instead, the dead would be served by "the new gods of memory and history: secular gods."[32]

But if this is so, then why does the wax figure of a corpse disappoint? Is it because readers expect Gothic texts to reveal the culturally unspeakable, unrepresentable, and unthinkable, and thus only a real corpse will do (not the simulacrum of one)? Is it because no wax figure can possess the abjectness of a real corpse, its stench, its ooze, and its maggot-eaten rot? Is it because the wax figure inherently lacks human identity—that is, it cannot be recognized as Laurentini di Udolpho or Madame Montoni or the Marchioness de Villeroi—and thus lacks relevancy to the plot? Or is it because death itself disappoints—or, shall I say, death as it began to be re-imagined in the eighteenth century? I believe all of these to be true. However, I also believe that in many ways, the wax figure does not disappoint at all, as its very ambiguity, its ghastly waxen depiction of bodily decay and corruption, allows it to be molded and shaped into a reflection of each reader's imagination.

This part of the chapter examines the wax figure of a corpse, arguing for its centrality to a novel that seemingly dismisses death yet which also repeatedly invokes it. As wax figures were strangely commonplace in late eighteenth-century London, I provide a brief history of waxworks and examine their problematic potential as relics. I then turn to the wax figure itself, arguing that it stands for the lost beloved, which, in this novel, is death itself.

WAXWORK FIGURES; OR THE STRANGE AFTERLIFE OF WILLIAM CONGREVE

In the 1790s, wax figures of human beings and wax models of human body parts were common enough sights for London residents and visitors, as well as for travelers to continental locales, particularly cities where major waxwork studios and collections were housed, such as Amsterdam, Paris, Venice, Bologna, Florence, Vienna, and St. Petersburg.[33] For centuries, Londoners could view waxwork (and wooden) effigies of important personages in the chantry over King Henry VII's Lady Chapel in Westminster Abbey.[34] In 1769, the waxwork figures, dressed in the decedent's finery and bearing her/his accoutrements of office or life, included Queen Elizabeth I, King Charles II, King William III and Queen Mary, Queen Anne, General Monck, the Duchess of Richmond (with her parrot), and the Duke and Duchess of Buckingham with their son, the Marquess of Normanby, who died at the age of three.[35]

In addition, for the price of one shilling, visitors could also examine the various wax figures at Mrs. Salmon's Royal Wax-work, originally located near St. Martin's, Aldergate, and later at its long-time location on Fleet Street. Since its opening in the 1690s, Mrs. Salmon's Royal Wax-work exhibited 140–200 life-size wax figures with glass eyes, and Mrs. Salmon herself offered classes in wax modeling. After Mrs. Salmon's death in 1760 at the venerable age of ninety, a Chancery Lane surgeon and his wife, Mr. and Mrs. Clark, continued exhibiting the wax figures until 1812.[36] (Madame Tussaud's opened in London in 1802 and displayed more than 200 figures of a more sensational nature than Mrs. Salmon's;[37] attendance at Mrs. Salmon's had apparently tapered off prior to this time, possibly because Mrs. Salmon was no longer around to sculpt new figures.) Among the wax figures displayed over the years at Mrs. Salmon's were various members of English royalty (Henry VII, Henry VIII, Anne Boleyn, Queen Elizabeth, Queen Anne), star-crossed legendary and/or historical lovers (Arthur and Guinevere, Marc Antony and Cleopatra), mythological beings (Andromeda, mermaids), Biblical characters (e.g., the "chaste Susanna and the Two Elders"), folk characters (Peter, the wild boy; the British giant), certain generic character types (a sailor and his sweetheart, an old maid), figures engaged in scenes of pleasure (a masquerade, a Dutch

[59]

christening, and "Dutch merry-making"), and busts of Mrs. Salmon herself and three of her children.[38] A figure of Mother Shipton gave the visitor "a kick as you are going out" the door.[39] The Lyceum also appears to have regularly offered visiting waxwork exhibitions as a lure to London customers. In 1785 (or thereabouts), an "Entire New Exhibition Just Arrived from Paris, Containing a Cabinet of Royal Figures" offered visitors the opportunity to view wax figures of European royalty, as well as a "SLEEPING VENUS" and a figure of Voltaire;[40] another "Entire New Exhibition Just Arrived from Constantinople" contained almost the exact same figures, with the addition of a "SERAGLIO," consisting of the "*GRAND SIGNIOR*, [and] many of the most *BEAUTIFUL TURKISH* and *ARMENIAN LADIES*, his own mistresses, all richly dressed." All this for a shilling. In each instance, "Ladies and Gentlemen may have their Portraits taken in either Wax or Miniature," by the respective artist, for an additional fee.[41]

Anatomical wax models were also available for public viewing during this time period. In 1790, Rackstrow's Museum in London displayed twenty-six cases filled with anatomical figures or body parts in wax, all made by the "late celebrated Mons. *Denoue*, Professor of ANATOMY to the Academy of Sciences at *Paris*." Because the anatomical models were nude and because of the lifelike, sometimes gruesome depiction of bodily organs and parts, "*A proper Person to attend to the Ladies*" was recommended.[42] For medical students and scientists, anatomical models offered an alternative to dissection, during a time when the public viewed dissection with suspicion and when the number of corpses available for medical instruction was strictly limited.[43] The anatomical model offered a stable, odorless, and often aesthetically pleasing substitution for the decomposing, malodorous corpse, as Joan B. Landes notes: "Models in wax, being highly realistic imitations, superb artificial contrivances, managed to cleave a deep chasm between death's horrid aspects and the student."[44] A major problem with dissection is that while a corpse is "lifeless," it is "not really atemporal": "With each passing moment the dead body becomes less comprehensible to the observer. Insofar as a corpse may be said to have a life, it is a temporary, ever-changing one. As early modern anatomists learned, the cadaver's secrets were too often the surprises represented by decaying matter."[45] The varied anatomical models shown at Rackstrow's Museum included several heads, torsos, and/or full bodies of men and women, a waxy "skin" covering certain of their parts, but with the remaining sections flayed or "skinless" in order to reveal nerves, muscles, brain tissue, organs, and more. Several models of anatomical oddities were also displayed—for instance, a "new born Child with one Eye in the middle of the Forehead," conjoined twins, and "a Child with two Eyes close together in one Orbit, which is placed in the Middle of the

Forehead"—presumably cast using real individuals.[46] One specimen case was dedicated to the display of a variety of separate body parts, such as a spine, liver, lungs, heart, gall bladder, and more. A few of the models conjoined wax modeling with human bones or other body parts from corpses.[47]

Like the waxwork figures at Mrs. Salmon's or at Madame Tussaud's, most anatomical models were exquisitely and skillfully wrought, with glass eyes and human or animal hair, and most utilized "an idealized [visual] language of representation . . . to depict normative human anatomy"[48]—the perfect hand, the perfect uterus, the ideal musculature—though anatomical abnormalities were also captured in wax. Some wax anatomical figures, such as the *Venus de' Medici* figure produced by the workshop of Clemente Susini and Giuseppe Ferrini, depicted the prone, passive female figure in an "unsettling erotic" fashion,[49] engaged in "a scarcely concealed orgasm,"[50] her glassy eyes rolled back in dreamy ecstasy, lips slightly parted, nipples erect, luxurious hair spread about her shoulders; opening a lid that spans from her curling pubic hair to her pearl necklace, her inner organs are revealed, including a fetus curled tightly within her uterus.[51] The anatomical models possessed an eerie luminescence of skin, with rosy cheeks and reddened lips; their glass eyes, tiny red veins showing in the whites, rendered them bright-eyed, seemingly alert, and ever watchful. After the eighteenth century, anatomical models became sequestered within medical schools,[52] but during Radcliffe's time, those able to afford the shilling entrance fee could view these anatomical *exempla*.

Humans and their waxen counterparts share numerous commonalities, not the least of which is the ability of wax to mimic the color and touch of human flesh. Wax is easily dyed or tinted to match skin tones; its luminescence and opaque transparency mimic the fragility and transparency of flesh, and, like human flesh, the coolness of wax warms and yields to human touch. As Roberta Panzanelli writes, "its material flexibility has secured its place in artistic production over four millennia of Western history, particularly as a simulacrum—whole or partial—of the human body. Wax is indeed the ultimate simulacrum of flesh, indexical to skin, *negative of its negative.*"[53] By referring to wax as a "negative" of human skin, Panzanelli obliquely refers to the lost-wax process or *cire perdue*, wherein a wax impression or model is made of an object (such as a human face or hand), which is then encased in some harder material, such as plaster, which makes a mold; hot molten liquid (such as bronze or, in the case of wax figures, more wax) is poured into the mold, which burns the wax away. This method captures fine details of the original object, and it was used to create death masks, waxwork figures, and anatomical models. Madame Tussaud purportedly used this method—or one quite similar (using plaster for the initial impression)—to cast the heads of guillotine victims, which she later displayed in her Chamber of Horrors. As Uta Kornmeier notes, "the portrait based on a face cast is a representation of a person's face not because of its resemblance to the face but because it is part of the face—as its usually unnoticed negative equivalent."[54] Similarly, anatomical models used real human bodies (alive or dead) as their reference point, as Beth Kowaleski Wallace notes: "To make a wax image of the human heart, for instance, one begins with a heart itself that leaves its exact impression in a plaster mold."[55] Landes notes that "at the ceroplastic workshop of La Specola in Florence . . . modelers used the astounding number of some two hundred corpses to create a single wax figure."[56] Horror films such as *The Mystery at the Wax Museum* (1933) and *House of Wax* (1953) exploit the intimate relationship between wax figures and human figures, as does the use of wax dolls in voodoo (*vodou*) and witchcraft.[57]

Once molded into human form, wax in a skilled sculptor's hands can mimic the real individual so closely as to create cognitive dissonance.[58] Kornmeier notes, "A well-made wax figure can exude such a strong corporeal presence that we are convinced, against our better judgment, that we are in the company of a fellow human being rather than a lifeless image."[59] Unlike a sculpture chiseled from marble or cast in bronze, the lifelike coloring and softness of the waxwork's "skin," the human or animal hair that adorns its head, face, and body, and the clothing (often the sitter's own clothes) creates a disjunction in perception on the part of the viewer. Instead of viewing the waxwork as a work of art, the viewer instead responds as if "to another person."[60] As Georges Didi-Huberman writes, "wax *goes too far* where resemblance is concerned,"[61] and indeed, waxwork sculpture tends to be judged not on its aesthetic qualities, but rather on its degree of verisimilitude. In the case of anatomical models of corpses, such as the ones shown in figures 2.2 and 2.3, we might say, as Sir John Pringle did to the wax sculptor Marie Marguerite Biheron: "Mademoiselle, there is nothing lacking except the stench!"[62] Indeed, many contemporary viewers of wax corpses complained of the "unbearable stench," exhibiting a "form of olfactory hallucination, that is, the false sense of a putrid smell."[63]

Can a wax figure of the deceased function as relic? Yes and no. It is possible, though somewhat problematic, precisely because a waxwork figure may so closely resemble the person who has been lost. After William Congreve's death in 1729, Henrietta Godolphin, 2nd Duchess of Marlborough, the close friend and probable mistress of the deceased playwright, commissioned a wax replica of him at a cost of 200*l*., which was delivered to her home in June 1730.[64] According to reports, the waxwork Congreve was placed each day "at her toilet-table, to which she would talk as to the living Mr. Congreve, with all the freedom of the most polite and

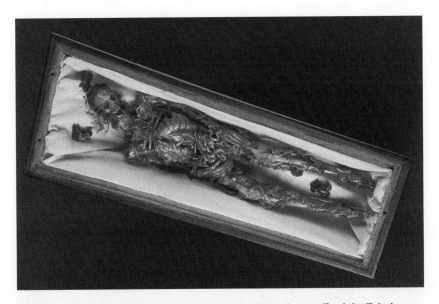

Figure 2.2 Wax model of a decomposing body in a walnut coffin, lid off. Italy, 1774–1800. Photograph by H. C. Koch. Science Museum Group Collection Online, London. Loan: Wellcome Trust. A128411.

unreserved conversation."[65] Rumor may have exaggerated the Duchess's engagement with the wax figure—or not: "Common fame reports, that she had his figure made in wax after his death, talked to it as if it had been alive, placed it at table with her, took care to help it with different sorts of food, had an imaginary sore on its leg regularly dressed; and to compleat all, consulted Physicians with relation to its health."[66] With a waxwork that closely resembles the lost beloved, the potential for slippage between the real and the simulacrum is high, allowing for the possibility of sustained misrecognition. If misrecognition becomes permanent, then the waxwork object no longer functions as relic because the waxwork *is* now the beloved. It is also possible that even though the waxy surrogate may conjure up the lost beloved in vivid fashion, its still, unmoving, and unresponsive demeanor may suggest that the beloved has just died anew. Either way, the wax figure of Congreve was fated to an early demise. In July 1732, it "was broke to Pieces by the Carelessness of a Servant in bringing it down Stairs."[67] By October 1733, the Duchess herself was dead. A waxwork of the dead beloved, then, can function as a relic of the deceased, but it can also potentially become the dead beloved in the eyes of the mourner; it is merely a matter of degree.

OBJECTS

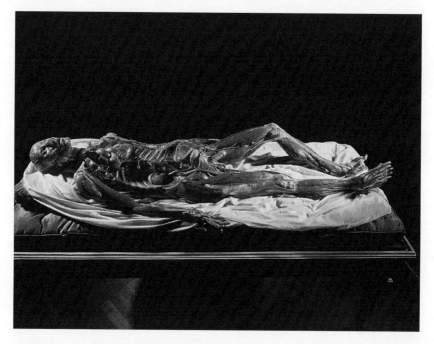

Figure 2.3 Reclining figure of a man showing muscles, tendons, and inner organs, 1785. Institut für die Geschichte der Medizin (Josefinium), Vienna. ART96857. Photo Credit: Erich Lessing/Art Resource.

"A HUMAN FIGURE OF GHASTLY PALENESS": DEATH AS THE LOST BELOVED

If a wax model depicting a living or once living person can be misrecognized as the person himself or herself, then what about a wax model of a corpse? In *The Mysteries of Udolpho*, Emily St. Aubert mistakes the "so horribly natural" wax corpse for a real one (663), and certainly may be excused for doing so if it was skillfully wrought as the ones shown in figures 2.2 and 2.3. But can a generic waxen corpse function as a relic? The answer is yes, but only if it is a relic of death itself.

As noted in the introduction to this book, cultural attitudes toward death—more specifically, cultural attitudes toward both the act of dying and the dying/dead body—changed, slowly yet radically and irrevocably over the course of the eighteenth century. Terry Castle's 1987 essay, "The Spectralization of the Other in *The Mysteries of Udolpho*," recognizes that Radcliffe's novel articulates the new attitude toward death and toward the dead body, wherein the topic of death itself is avoided and the dead body abhorred and shunned. Castle is most concerned with how, in *Udolpho*, both the dead and/or absent live more fully in imagination and memory than they ever did or can do in person, how the "internalized images" of loved ones are preferred over their material presence.[68] Castle notes that "To be a Radcliffean hero or heroine in one sense means just this: to be 'haunted,' to find oneself obsessed with spectral images of those one loves. One sees in the mind's eye those who are absent; one is befriended and consoled by phantoms of the beloved."[69] Castle argues that, in Radcliffe's novel, "we sense both a new anxiety about death, and a new reactive absorption in mental pictures," and she notes "the fervor with which the finality of death is denied."[70] According to Castle, "there is no such thing as a real corpse" within the novel: "many moments in the novel traditionally adduced by critics as classically 'Radcliffean' have to do with supposed deaths that have not really taken place, or with corpses that turn out not to be corpses at all."[71]

I agree with Castle's assertion that Radcliffe's novel subscribes to the new attitude toward death, with the dead or absent constantly made present through memory. However, I also think the novel a death-haunted one, which embeds both older and newer attitudes toward death and which not only hides the dead/dying bodies, but desperately seeks to recover them.[72] Death possesses two distinct visages within Radcliffe's novel—that of the older "tame" form of death and that of the newer "untamed" death[73]—and, in consequence, it betrays conflicting impulses toward death. Specifically, *Udolpho* exhibits "nostalgia for the simple and familiar death of yesterday";[74] a fascinated horror at the erotic conjoining of sex, death, and violence that characterizes death as re-envisioned during the late eighteenth century; and both repulsion and compulsion toward the dead and dying body. The novel lovingly lingers on the "tame" death and mourns its loss; at the same time, it seeks to compensate for this lack by supplying a relic—the wax figure of a corpse—to stand in place of the lost beloved, to conjure it in its most abject form. The bodies that are missing—those of the dying (Madame Montoni), the dead (the Marchioness de Villeroi), and the presumed dead (Laurentini di Udolpho)—are those associated with "untamed" deaths; the circumstances surrounding the discovery of each of these bodies replicates the circumstances surrounding Emily's discovery of the wax figure behind its veil. Although the identity of the "figure behind the veil" is not revealed until the concluding chapters of the novel, its presence reverberates throughout the novel, retroactively imposing meaning on every death, tame and untamed, real or presumed. Thus, the wax figure makes present the absent bodies until such time as they can be (physically or spectrally) recovered; it conjures the lost beloved, by functioning both as simulacrum (for death itself) and as relic (what death has left behind); and it mediates between the older and newer forms of death.

The wax figure behind the black veil is a *transi*—that is, a decomposing corpse, almost always depicted with maggots, worms, toads, and flies feasting on the remains; it was the subject of the *memento mori* of the fifteenth and sixteenth centuries. Radcliffe's wax figure is described as "a human figure of ghastly paleness, stretched at its length, and dressed in the habiliments of the grave. What added to the horror of the spectacle, was, that the face appeared partly decayed and disfigured by worms, which were visible on the features and hands" (662). The wax figure is "so horribly natural" (663), as to make it appear at first glance to be real. For the original owner, an ancestor of Laurentini's, it is a penitential fetish, meant to convey the "humiliating moral" (662) that all humans are destined to die, their bodies doomed to corruption and decay, and that earthly desires are inevitably short-lived, as life itself is short-lived. However, the wax figure also offers gratification, as the ancestor believes that regular contemplation of the waxen corpse will "obtain a pardon for all his sins" (662) and assure him a pleasant stay in the afterlife. Notably, the ancestor's descendants do not feel the same way about it—the figure possesses no magic for them; they are the ones who choose to cover the recess in which the figure lies with the black pall, an act that may be "interpreted in two ways: their iconodulic veneration turned into fear or simply iconoclast contempt."[75] As Ya-Feng Wu astutely points out, whatever messages the waxwork held in the past or even in the present are lost on Emily, as the "recalibrated horizon of knowledge" provided to readers "remains 'unperceived' by Emily."[76] For her, it remains a real body, real death, not a waxy imitation of it.

But why should death take the form of the *transi*—the decomposing corpse—within Radcliffe's novel, particularly when most early Gothic literature employs ghosts and skeletons as the principal representatives of the dead? The skeleton or *morte secca*, scoured clean of corruption, its bones a crisp, gleaming ivory, its teeth in a perpetual grin, became the favored representative of bodily death from the seventeenth century onward. As Ariès writes, the "skeleton is neither so frightening nor so wicked" as the *transi*. Instead, "It was the dark, disembodied shadow or the shrouded ghost, rather than the skeleton, that inspired fear after the seventeenth century."[77] The skeleton and the ghost are two complementary aspects of death: the skeleton represents the body, albeit the body stripped of stench, ooze, and rot, without maggots and flies; the ghost represents the spirit. The skeleton is the dead body purged of its abjectness and pollution; in this respect, it becomes a fitting representative of death during this time period. However, the skeleton possesses no sentience, unlike the unhappy or avenging ghost; the skeleton exists merely to provide physical evidence of some past wrongdoing. The skeleton, then, holds no real horrors in and of itself; it is the ghost that bears the burden of the past. Notably, the ghost retains everything individual about its former self—its personality, its human shape, even its former clothing, albeit in shadowy form—everything except a material body, that is. The ghost is the spectral individual, desperately clutching the remnants of what made the person unique in life. In contrast, the skeleton, the purified bodily remains, is scrubbed clean of individuality, sexuality, gender, race, ethnicity, and class, of corruption, abjection, and pollution.[78] This, then, is how death is portrayed in the majority of early Gothic novels, such as Horace Walpole's *The Castle of Otranto* and Clara Reeve's *The Old English Baron*.[79]

In contrast, the *transi* makes the abject body present, a body only recently abandoned by the soul. The *transi* exists in a liminal state, poised somewhere between subjecthood/individuality and objecthood/anonymity. It is the most powerful material representation of death precisely because, unlike the skeleton that is wiped clean of individuality, it exhibits particularity (the remains of a specific individual) and generality (the rot and decay to which all human flesh is subject); it exists as evidence of a particular life and of that life's dissolution, of every life and of every life's dissolution. The decaying, rotting corpse is both static and in motion: despite its lack of animation, it is nonetheless always in the process of transformation, suggesting movement not only in the writhing of worms and the buzzing of flies upon the flesh, but also in its incessant decay and in its transformation from personhood to objecthood to dust to nothingness. The *transi* exists as a set of paradoxes: static yet in constant motion; individualized yet generalized; clearly dead yet holding on to rotting remnants of life; abhorrent, yet once beloved. Not least, the *transi* represents the body at its most vulnerable, its most abject, its most repulsive and least loved, and so it is this stage that most clearly represents death itself as the opposite of life.[80] Significantly, unlike the skeleton that abstracts death by rendering it distant, by relegating death to some long-ago past, the *transi* emphasizes both the immediacy and the finality of death through the melting dissolution of the body into itself; unlike the ghost, the *transi* is no (spectral) Lazarus that will rise from the grave. In a novel where the dead have the potential to live forever in memory as spectral beings, there is a need to have something "real," some material evidence that demonstrates death's finality, that marks the individual's earthly passing, and this is what the *transi* provides.

Within the novel, the waxen *transi* mediates the ever-widening distances between life and death during the eighteenth century, between older and newer attitudes toward death, and between "tame" and "untamed" deaths. Its physical presence marks the absence of (real) death and (real) dead bodies in eighteenth-century culture; the physical, psychical, and emotional voids created when a particular individual has died; and the erasures that occur when a person is forgotten by, unremembered by, or outcast from human society and lost to human knowledge. The wax figure cannot be death itself—as death is the absent beloved—but, as relic, it can remind us of the absent beloved, connect us temporarily to it, and perhaps even be it for a short period of time. Robert Miles, obliquely referring to the wax figure, suggests that "Radcliffe's so-called explained supernatural is best thought of as a means of keeping antithetical possibilities in solution," and so, following that idea, we might easily see the waxen corpse as both denying death and confirming its existence.[81] In other words, the wax figure embodies paradox.

Furthermore, the wax corpse offers itself as a truer representation of death than a real decomposing body in two specific ways. First, the decomposing corpse of, say, Laurentini or the marchioness represents only that person, while the waxen figure is an everyman/everywoman of death, specific to none yet applicable to all. Second, unlike a real decaying body, the wax figure abides in unchanging form if not subjected to intense heat or fire (or cast down the stairs by a careless footman!). To repeat what Joan Landes wrote, in speaking of a human cadaver, "With each passing moment the dead body becomes less comprehensible to the observer. Insofar as a corpse may be said to have a life, it is a temporary, ever-changing one. As early modern anatomists learned, the cadaver's secrets were too often the surprises represented by decaying matter."[82] The wax figure offers a stable, comprehensible image of death—revolting, yes, but allowing death to be apprehended and contemplated; it offers itself as a gateway to understanding that ineffable state of nonbeing that is death. As Gary Farnell writes, the wax figure refers "to the ultimate physicality and deathliness of the human body at the level of the Real, but at an artificial remove from It that makes this image a false god referring, for entirely cultural purposes, to a condition that is invisible even to observers of a real dead body: that of the unrepresentable Thing behind even the signs of death."[83] Put simply, the wax figure makes present the unrepresentable and the unnameable Thing that is death, as least in as far as such a Thing can be made present.

The waxen *transi* unifies all deaths within the novel, as traces of it appear in the faces and bodies of those who are dying, whether they experience an untamed death or not, as it is meant to unite the newer form of death—the "untamed" death—to the older. Many of the novel's characters—Monsieur St. Aubert, Madame Montoni, the Marchioness de Villeroi, Laurentini di Udolpho, and an unnamed *condittieri*—all show evidence of bodily decomposition, as they lay dying. Even before these characters gasp their final breath—and die they do—death has already overtaken and altered them, sinking the eyes, discoloring the skin, revealing the skeleton beneath the skin. Toward the end of the prolonged illness of Monsieur St. Aubert, "the lines of death [are] beginning to prevail" (81);

the "damps of death" have "settled" on his forehead (82); his countenance is "emaciated"; his "sunk eyes . . . their heavy lids pressing close" are "heavy and dull" (81) and soon "his sight" has "failed him" (82). Dying slowly from starvation and fever, Madame Montoni already shows signs of the grave when Emily discovers her lying in a curtained bed "in a dusky and silent chamber." Madame Montoni has "a hollow voice," "a pale and emaciated face," "heavy eyes," and a "skeleton hand." Emily doubts that her aunt still lives: "Do you indeed live or is this but a terrible apparition?" Grabbing her aunt's hand, Emily cries, "This is substance . . . but it is cold—cold as marble!" (364). The poison that courses through the veins of the Marchioness de Villeroi alters her looks, making her already one with death. As the housekeeper at Chateau-le-Blanc, Dorothée, recalls, "How well I remember her look at the time—death was in it!" (535), and she remarks on how "I was shocked to see her countenance—it was so changed!" (527). At the moment of death, "a frightful blackness spread all over her face" (528); the blackness is evidence of the poison, but it also prescient of the alterations to the flesh once the corpse begins to decay. Her impending union with death also alters the features of Laurentini: her countenance is "ghastly"; her "heavy" eyes are "dim and hollow" (643). She reaches out "her cold, damp hand" (646). Death enters the living though ailing body, altering the physical appearance of its host, and once it holds sway, it marks its territory by the rapid decomposition of the body, as occurs in the case of the unnamed *condittieri*: "The features, deformed by death, were ghastly and horrible" (348).

Dark curtains, black veils, or black palls are also associated with almost all of the dead or dying bodies, further strengthening the relationship between these individuals and the wax figure.[84] Admittedly, no veil shrouds the dying or dead Monsieur St. Aubert from view, but Emily views her father's corpse, "when the gloom of the evening obscured the chamber, and almost veiled from her eyes the object of her distress" (83); as she accompanies the coffin to the burial ground, "her face [is] partly shaded by a thin black veil" (87). Madame Montoni's dying body is discovered behind a curtained bed (364); when Emily watches as the body of her aunt being lowered into its grave, her face is "shaded by a thin veil" (377). The dead *condittieri*'s body is hidden behind "a dark curtain," which descends "from the ceiling to the floor" (348). The bed where the Marchioness de Villeroi died is covered by "a counter-pane, or pall, of black velvet, that hung down to the floor" (532); the servant Dorothée takes a black veil worn by the late marchioness and throws "it suddenly over Emily, who shuddered to find it wrapped round her" (534). Emily visits the dying Laurentini in the deep evening; the former murderer wears the black veil of a nun, and Laurentini's revelations of her past bring to Emily's mind "the terrible spectacle" (648) of the wax figure at Udolpho.

OBJECTS

The image of the veil, pall, or curtain hiding death is consistent with the new cultural attitude toward death—death must not be seen—yet also consistent with this new attitude is Emily's overwhelming compulsion to look, even though the sight repeatedly causes her to faint in horror. Death is both taboo and mysterious. Time and again, Emily gazes "with an eager, frenzied eye" (348) at death, compelled by curiosity and a need to know. The novel, then, betrays competing impulses: the desire to rid itself of death, by hiding or veiling the dying or dead body from view; and the desire to confront death, by pulling aside the veil. It is trite, perhaps, to consider death in *Udolpho* a "return of the repressed." However, it is true that death is portrayed in the novel in ways that demonstrate how *unheimlich*, how uncanny it has become by Radcliffe's time. The repetitiveness associated with the discovery of each dead or dying body; "the unintended recurrence of the same situation . . . result[ing] in the same feeling of helplessness"; and the way in which what "ought to have remained hidden and secret" nonetheless "comes to light"[85]—all speak to death as something that was once familiar but has now become unfamiliar. Notably, Freud remarks that the uncanny is often felt in "the highest degree in relation to death and dead bodies,"[86] and he also identified "wax-work figures, ingeniously constructed dolls and automata" as decidedly *unheimlich*.[87]

As mentioned previously, the deaths within Radcliffe's novel are separated into two groups: "tame" deaths and "untamed" deaths. Associated with older attitudes toward death, the "tame death" is characterized by "advanced warning," allowing the dying individual a measure of time—no matter how small—in which to make "the necessary arrangements" and to gather loved ones about him or her. The dying person also experiences a "simple acceptance of imminent death" and "resignation to the inevitable," even though "the dying man feels sad about the loss of his life, the things he has possessed, and the people he has loved."[88] The deaths of Emily's parents represent the tame death, the good death. Despite the physician's inability to determine if Emily's mother will survive her illness, Madame St. Aubert knows that she is going to die, and she is prepared for it. She gently informs the physician of her fate: "Do not attempt to deceive me. . . . I feel that I cannot long survive. I am prepared for the event, I have long, I hope, been preparing for it. Since I have not long to live, do not suffer a mistaken compassion to induce you to flatter my family with false hopes. If you do, their affliction will only be the heavier when it arrives: I will endeavor to teach them resignation by my example" (18). Similarly, Monsieur St. Aubert receives physical/psychical warning that he is about to die, and he uses that time to prepare for it, by confessing his sins and receiving last rites, by informing his daughter of the arrangements he has made for her future, and by providing his daughter, his only remaining care, with words of advice and caution and a father's blessing. His final moments are calm: "St. Aubert lingered till about three o'clock in the afternoon, and, thus, gradually sinking into death, he expired without a struggle, or a sigh" (82). This, the novel suggests, is how death should be. Despite the physical corruption and decay accompanying St. Aubert's dying moments, his death is viewed as natural, peaceful; and Emily sits in the room with the corpse for a day and two nights, before relinquishing it for burial. The body of her deceased father, while an object of "awful astonishment" (83), is neither abject nor repulsive; though he is dead, she tenderly kisses his lips. His final place of rest is known; there is no mystery surrounding his death. Because his death is "tame" and natural, his daughter is able to remember him lovingly, to render him a "spectral Other," to use Terry Castle's expression.

For Madame Montoni, the Marchioness de Villeroi, and Laurentini di Udolpho, death is "untamed" due to "unnatural causes" such as imposed starvation, murder, or the madness of excessive guilt; the act of dying is emotionally, psychically, or physically violent; and each woman is, at one point, forgotten or forsaken—if alive, the physical body is missing; if dead, the spectral body is shunned by memory.[89] Not least, sex is almost always implicated as a root cause of the death. As to the last point, from its inception, Gothic literature has always been preoccupied with death and sex. As Yael Shapira notes, "Sex, torture, rape, and death were ever-present in the Gothic, whether they actually occurred or only hovered as ominous possibilities,"[90] and it is surely no coincidence that the first Gothic texts in England appear when death itself had become the unwanted, the unmentionable guest and when sexual practice and gendered identity were becoming increasingly circumscribed.[91] When death was no longer treated with "the traditional intimacy" that distinguished it in the past, it entered the imaginative realm of the mysterious, the unmentionable, and the forbidden, as Ariès writes: "A connection has been made between death and sex; the one has become as fascinating and obsessive as the other. These are signs of fundamental anxiety that does not yet have a name. . . . When the fear of death appeared, it was first confined to the realm where love had so long been kept under cover and at a distance, the world from which only poets, novelists, and artists dared to lead it forth: the world of imagination."[92] Sex, death, and violence become the unholy trinity of the new realm of the dead.

Like Charon ferrying the dead across the river Styx, the aptly named Madame Cheron ferries Emily across the Alps, to the Castle of Udolpho, where Emily encounters this new mode of death for the first time. Motivated by vanity and avarice to marry again, the middle-aged Madame Montoni (neé Cheron) soon engages in passionate battle with her new husband, jealously protesting his interest in other women and adamantly refusing to sign over her estates to him. Impatient with her constant refusals to comply with his demands, Montoni threatens his wife with removal to "the east turret" (305) of the castle; the threat alone makes her suffer prolonged, exceedingly violent, and debilitating convulsions. Nonetheless, convinced that his wife has attempted to poison him, Montoni sends her to the turret, where, imprisoned, she wastes away to skeleton-like thinness brought about by fever, starvation, and neglect: "without pity or remorse, [Montoni] had suffered her to live, forlorn and neglected, under a raging fever" (365). For a period of more than a week—for possibly several weeks—Emily attempts to find the body of her aunt, sometimes convinced that her aunt is already dead, sometimes hopeful that she yet lives. Once Emily finds her, Madame Montoni reproaches her: "I thought you had forsaken me" (364). Restored by Emily's intervention to her former chambers, the dying Madame Montoni and her husband once again engage in "obstinate dispute" (372), until Madame becomes "exhausted," "unintelligible," and, finally, "insensible" (372). Soon thereafter she dies, never having ceded to her husband's will.

For the Marchioness de Villeroi, the poison administered by her husband and his lover over several months culminates in an excruciatingly painful death: "she was seized with such terrible pains! O, I never shall forget her shriek!" (527). Not only is her death a violent one, as any murder must be, but its cause is shrouded in secrecy and surrounded by mystery, as befits the new mode of death. Suspecting that the marchioness has died from poison, the doctor sends "the attendants out of the room" (528); the housekeeper's husband bids her to "hold her tongue" (528); and the doctor himself is paid for his silence. Although rumors abound, "nobody dared to make any stir about them" (528). And while Monsieur St. Aubert posthumously lives in his daughter's fond memories, the marchioness has been so completely obliterated from spoken memory that her niece is unaware that she once existed. St. Aubert forbids mention of the Marchioness de Villeroi: "he never could hear her named, or mention her himself after her death, except to Madame St. Aubert" (660), as her violent death precludes pleasant memories, even to the point of eradicating earlier ones.

More than any character, Laurentini di Udolpho enacts the new form of death, with its absent bodies, its mystery, its passion and violence, its toxic sexuality, and its secretive, hidden, and vengeful nature. She exists as the living counterpart to the waxen *transi*, but also as that which the *transi* attempts to correct. The long-ago disappearance of Laurentini—a death in which no body was found—replicates the new type of death, wherein the corpse is absent from view. In addition, the "thrill" (278) that Annette and the other servants experience when hearing and speaking about the taboo topic of Laurentini's disappearance reproduces the new reaction to the dead, wherein the dead have become an object both of abhorrence and of fascination. Sex is integral to Laurentini's story, as her previous sexual indiscretions stop the marquis from marrying her (656); her continuing passion for the marquis turns her into a murderess.

Laurentini is intimately associated with death. The peasants view the haunting music that Laurentini makes as a harbinger of death, and the mysterious maker of the music makes death itself a mystery as she haunts the night forests around Chateau-le-Blanc. Notably, Laurentini and the wax corpse are constantly confused. As Ya-Feng Wu notes, Emily "conflates the *memento mori* (death in the future) with Montoni's amorous trophy (death in the past)—the corpse of Laurentini di Udolpho."[93] Twice, Emily asks Annette if Laurentini's portrait is "veiled" (277), mistaking portrait for wax figure, and Annette herself suggests that Laurentini's portrait should be placed "in the great apartment, where the veiled picture hangs" (279). Aptly, Laurentini is a murderess, administering "untame" death in small doses of poison, and, like the wax figure behind the black pall, Laurentini hides behind Sister Agnes's black veil. And her final moments are "untamed" in the extreme: the unhappy results of Laurentini's uncontrollable passion for another woman's husband render her own death a nightmare of the mind as her guilty conscience conjures the ghostly visages of her innocent victim and her perfidious lover, and she screams, groans, and shrieks as she departs to she knows not where. Finally, as the new death is characterized by memorial, it is appropriate that when Sister Agnes/Laurentini dies, Radcliffe provides readers with her detailed history, set apart from the rest of the text with her full name in capital letters; it is an obituary of sorts, a memorial to an "untamed" life and an "untamed" death.[94]

Catherine Morland was partially right, for the figure behind the black veil *is* Laurentini, at least symbolically so. And Sir Walter Scott was partially wrong, as the figure behind the black veil functions as the central symbol of the novel, offering itself as the relic by which death may be conjured and its mysteries revealed.

CONCLUSION

We consider death as absence, as loss, as negative, as void, because it is the opposite of life, because it takes away the people we love, because, as hard as we try, we cannot comprehend its ineffable nature. But since the eighteenth century, death has become a murderer, stalking its victims, hiding in dark corners, menacing the weak and strong alike. Only constant vigilance against it—on the part of scientists, medical practitioners, and ourselves—can keep it at bay, forcing it back into the shadows. However, its disappearance from physical view, its relegation to the remotest corners of our consciousness, creates another type of emptiness, another form of longing, another category of fear. Whether we know it or not, death—the "tame" death of our ancestors—is the lost beloved of all of us, of our culture and our time. Death not as failure but as fate; the dead body not as abject horror but as the corporeal remnants of a lost loved one, still containing the soul of the deceased. Death not necessarily as friend but as well-known companion, who comes for us not out of hate but simply because it must.

Persons

Considered a legal part of her husband's person, a *feme covert* under the law, the married woman, when widowed, became his relict, that is, his remains, with the words "relict" and "widow" used interchangeably to describe both her person and her status. Although most often used in reference to widows, the word "relict" also applied to any surviving member of a decedent's family. In the two chapters that follow, my use of the word "relict" refers to the following: any character that functions/exists within the text as the remains of something else (another character, an act, or an idea). Usually, though not always, the character as "relict" replaces another character, functioning as its double or surrogate; and this act of replacement can occur indefinitely, with character replacing character replacing character and so on, until the narrative exhausts itself. In other instances, however, the character as "relict" exists as the residue of some earlier act or idea that the narrative has yet to resolve and so dwells upon this single relict until such time as a narrative resolution of sorts is achieved. In both instances, the "relict" functions as the narrative marker of melancholia (a non-normative form of mourning) and/or trauma. Both disorders speak to unprocessed/unresolved issues or events, and within the confines of the novel, these unprocessed/unresolved issues or events complicate narrative, engender pathos and suspense, stall and propel plot, and signify the onset of narrative mourning.

Nouri Gana identifies "prosopopoeia (i.e., personification, apostrophe) . . . as the master trope of mourning," "catachresis (i.e., the figure of contextual abuse of, or improper, word use) and chiasmus (i.e., the figure of repetition and reversibility) as the master tropes of, respectively, melancholia and trauma," and prolepsis, metaphor, aporia, allegory, and metonymy as "supplementary tropes."[1] Within the three novels examined in this section, chiasmus, in the form of repetition, and allegory prove the most prevalent; these are markers of melancholia and trauma, in both fiction and reality. However, in combination with these two tropes, the characters themselves—the "relicts"—also possess attributes that align them with melancholia, trauma, and death.

Repetition of a negative experience, both in reality and in fiction, suggests the presence of trauma and/or melancholia. Although trauma and melancholia represent two separate pathologies, they may often be found together; in other words, trauma may co-exist with melancholia, and melancholia with trauma. Both disorders involve (un)knowing, as the melancholic knows not what she mourns (the refusal to acknowledge a loss on the conscious level), while the trauma survivor knows not (consciously) the source of his trauma. Furthermore, repetition of the originary event occurs in both cases: revisited through dreams and hallucinations in the case of the trauma survivor and through metaphorically inspired physical actions in the case of both the trauma survivor and the melancholic. Allegory also functions as a rhetorical marker of melancholic mourning and trauma, which it performs through abstraction and displacement, mirroring the metaphoric (and unconscious) re-enactments that the melancholic and the trauma survivor stage. While allegory only imperfectly re-enacts the originary event (because it avoids direct confrontation with the "real" event), it nonetheless offers a means by which this event may be safely (re)visited, and thus, in its own way, allegory exists as a form of repetition or doubling. Finally, fictional "relicts" may also bear the rhetorical marks of melancholia and trauma, their authors having invested them with traits or experiences that present them as somehow damaged, either psychically or physically; symbolically, they bear scars.

A question, then, arises as regards melancholia and trauma as rhetorically performed within works of fiction, particularly eighteenth-century fiction: is psychoanalytical theory anachronistic or incompatible with historical texts or historicism as practice? The answer is yes and no. In eighteenth-century England, madness was still considered a disorder of the body not the mind. Nonetheless, it was understood that chronic mental activity of one type could cause madness by adversely affecting the nerves and nervous system. For instance, melancholia was considered to be caused by incessant dwelling upon a certain idea or experience. Attempts to understand and interpret melancholia have a long history within early modern British thought, including, though not limited to, Robert Burton's *The Anatomy of Melancholy* (1621) and Dr. George Cheyne's *The English Malady* (1733), and expressions of melancholia appear prominently in early modern British literature as well, including such well-known texts as Shakespeare's *Hamlet* (1599–1602) and Milton's *Il Penseroso* (1645/1646). In addition, while the word "trauma" (from the Greek word for "wound") as used in eighteenth-century England always meant a bodily wound not a mental one, the notion of "wounds of the mind" did exist. For instance, *The Annual Register* of 1759 recounts the death of General Wolfe in the taking of Quebec and provides this description of his mother's sorrow: "the public wound pierced her mind with a particular affliction," particularly as "Within a few months she had lost her husband; she now lost this son, her only child."[2] In *All for Love*, John Dryden's version of the story of Antony and Cleopatra, the playwright has Ventidius speak the following lines to Antony, after Antony has ignominiously retreated at the battle of Actium: "I would bring Balm, and pour it in your Wounds, / Cure your distemper'd mind."[3] In sum, while psychic and emotional wounds may not have been identified under the rubric of trauma in the eighteenth century, the idea that the mind could suffer from non-physical wounds was extant.

As regards the compatibility of historicism and psychoanalytical theory, I would argue—as do many scholars—that the two practices *can* complement each other, particularly if the psychoanalytical analyses of texts acknowledge historical notions regarding the nature of melancholia, mourning, madness, and "wounds of the mind." In addition, as Carla Mazzio and Douglas Trevor write, "the methodologies of historicism and psychoanalysis often operate by means of the same constellation of terms: *anxiety, alienation, desire, otherness, fetish,* and *symptom,* to name a few." Mazzio and Trevor continue: "While there is no doubt a series of vexed relations at stake in the intersection of particular narratives of history and psyche, it is important to note that when these methodologies are divorced from each other they can offer quite limited models and vocabularies of experience. In early modern studies, for example, while psychoanalytic criticism has been taken to task for its historical belatedness and its reductive articulations of states of subjective experience, historicist work has often been criticized for leaving its own lexicon of interiority and phenomenology undertheorized and overgeneralized."[4] Or, as Cynthia Marshall writes, "historicism has been advanced as a theory in itself rather than one important aspect of a fully articulated practice," and she argues that psychoanalytical theory represents "an evolving body of ideas that provides techniques for reading."[5]

It should further be noted that the eighteenth century saw the rude and raw beginnings of modern psychological practice. During this time period, physicians such as William Battie, William Tuke, and Francis Willis experimented with new (and old) methods for the treatment of madness, and asylums and sanitariums for the insane, such as St. Luke's Hospital, the York Asylum, and others, were established. In sum, psychoanalysis, in conjunction with historicism, offers a "technique for reading" relicts (in this instance, fictional personages) within Fielding's *David Simple* novels and Richardson's *Grandison*, particularly as these novels utilize rhetorical structures (repetition and allegory) that we now associate with trauma and melancholia and which, within these texts, occur in relation to fictional situations that engender psychic or emotional stress on the part of characters. In particular, in the case of *Grandison*, the relict in question is a madwoman whose symptoms and attendant treatments are rhetorically (and quite deliberately) represented by the author in the form of a medical case study.[6]

* * *

Sarah Fielding's *David Simple* and its sequel, *Volume the Last*, are among the most mournful, melancholic novels of the eighteenth century, with elevated body counts in both. In *David Simple*, innumerable false friends replicate and replace another, with Daniel replaced by Fanny who is replaced by Orgueil who is replaced by Splatter and so on; in *Volume the Last*, nine characters die, one after another. In the former novel, the loss of each false friend replicates the original loss of David's first friend, Daniel; the repetition of loss signals melancholia, which the novel utilizes as narrative strategy for plot movement, and, in oblique manner, the discarded bodies represent the (textual) death of specific characters (though one discarded character will be resurrected in *Volume the Last*). In the latter novel, the death of each true friend replicates the loss of David's first-born son, not from death (though the child later dies) but because the boy has been given away prior to birth, pledged to another family in return for promised monetary and social rewards. This is David Simple's original sin. Relicts of this original loss takes the form of suffering bodies (children and relatives), who exist as both the causes and effects of David's moral failures. In the two *David Simple* novels, the repetitive narrative gestures—in *David Simple*, the replacement of discarded living bodies with other (soon-to-be-discarded) living bodies; in *Volume the Last*, the replacement of suffering bodies with other suffering bodies, of dead bodies with soon-to-be-dead bodies, of dead bodies with more dead bodies—generate the expected and required pathos of the novel of sensibility while testing the reader's own ability to sympathize with a flawed protagonist and allowing the reader to experience vicariously the pain that the relict—as sufferer or as witness of suffering—endures. The extensive use of allegory in *Volume the Last* also provides an additional layer of meaning: it too functions as another narrative expression of mourning and melancholia, and it offers a key to the author's didactic intent.

In Samuel Richardson's *The History of Sir Charles Grandison*, readers are confronted with two heroines: one English, Protestant, and rational; the other Italian, Catholic, and mad. In one of the most curious narrative moves in an eighteenth-century British novel, Richardson positions Sir Charles and Clementina della Porretta, his Italian co-heroine, as metaphoric wife and husband—albeit always with one or the other of them "dead." Specifically, Clementina functions as Sir Charles's relict, his widow, dressing in black and mourning his loss, while he becomes the spectral dead spouse. Later, the roles are reversed, with Sir Charles playing the role of "bachelor-widower" to Clementina's deceased first wife, the latter of whom textually haunts Sir Charles's new love, the English girl, Harriet Byron. By examining a series of repetitive events within the novel, Clementina's malady can be traced to an originary traumatic event: her silencing by Sir Charles, accompanied by his inexplicable disappearance. Clementina's (fictional) body may also be read for evidence of trauma, as Richardson imbues the symptoms and treatments of her malady with potent symbolism.

Although Fielding's *The Adventures of David Simple* does not deal directly with death (or rather it does so only tangentially), it *is* engaged with loss and with discarded persons/bodies that disappear without a (textual) trace. *Volume the Last* exists as an extended monody to death and loss, though death itself offers a welcome release from earthly travails; it is the suffering inflicted upon the living (the relicts of David Simple's original sin) that the novel mourns most deeply. Fielding's *David Simple* novels reject the substantial soul of earlier times *and* the free-floating conscious associated with Locke's view of the afterlife. Indeed, no promise of an afterlife appears within these two novels, and as such, they may be viewed as intermediary texts, falling into the breach between one belief system and the other. Richardson's *Grandison* also engages with death, but not the type of death that Clarissa Harlowe undergoes, wherein her soul patiently awaits Resurrection Day. Instead, death is intimately entwined with madness, and two members of the living exist as the (metaphoric) dead, one of whom, like death itself, is "other."

3

"ALL THE HORRORS OF FRIENDSHIP"

Counting the Bodies in Sarah Fielding's *The Adventures of David Simple* (1744) and *Volume the Last* (1753)

IN A CURIOUS YET HIGHLY revealing conversation between the eponymous hero of *The Adventures of David Simple* and his newfound friends—Cynthia, Camilla, and Valentine—the four vie to determine who "had suffered the most," with David and Valentine ultimately ceding the figurative crown of thorns to their respective love interests: "The two Gentlemen agreed, that *Cynthia* and *Camilla*'s Sufferings had exceeded theirs; but *David* said, 'He thought *Camilla*'s were infinitely beyond any thing he had ever heard.' *Lysander* [Valentine] replied, 'That, indeed, he could not but own her Afflictions were in some respects more violent than *Cynthia*'s; but then, she had enjoyed some Pleasures in her Life.'"[1] Cynthia and Camilla readily admit that their sufferings have been great, but still they acknowledge that another woman, a French acquaintance of Cynthia's, has endured much worse: "That, indeed, they had always thought their *own Misfortunes* as great as human Nature could bear, till they had heard poor *Isabelle*'s story" (196).

This conversation is notable in several respects. First, it encapsulates the essence, as well as the elegiac undertones, of *David Simple* and its sequel, *Volume the Last*, both of which center on the incessant personal disappointments and disasters encountered by the protagonist, David Simple. Second, it suggests that suffering is viewed as valuable in and of itself, a commodity of sorts that may be weighed, measured, and exchanged; suffering functions as a form of currency, which accrues wealth in terms of moral authority to both sufferer and empathetic listener/viewer. Third, it concedes that women suffer more than men (or at least that the female characters within the novel have suffered more than the male characters). And fourth, it highlights a disparity between the two novels. In *David Simple*, the sufferings encountered by David and his three true friends appear light in comparison to those experienced by the same characters in *Volume the Last*. Specifically, *David Simple* focuses largely on problems relative to betrayal, misrepresentation, and

[81]

economic fraud or disinheritance, with comic resolution in the form of restored wealth and multiple marriages. In contrast, *Volume the Last* depicts continuing problems of betrayal, misrepresentation, and economic fraud, but adds to these woes bankruptcy and penury, loss of home and all worldly possessions, relentless and ruthless cruelty toward the innocent, and death upon death upon death. Needless to say, *Volume the Last* ends tragically.

In this chapter, I explore the ways in which narrative mourning is enacted within these two novels, with a particular focus on narrative representations of melancholia and trauma, and how "friends" function either as relics of earlier discarded "friends," replicating or replacing those who came before them, or as relics of earlier actions, the latter of which bear bitter consequences. The chapter is in two sections. Part I explicates the melancholic nature of *David Simple*, arguing that the melancholia experienced by the protagonist is expressive of mourning, albeit of an inconsolable and self-wounding nature. It should be noted that the characters in *David Simple* who do die (father and uncle) are not mourned; only betrayal by friends inspires emotional outpourings of deep grief and despair on the part of the titular character. In this novel, death is erasure, a return to primal dust, with the living expunging the dead from memory; only the living require metaphorical burial, as certain individuals become "dead" to David Simple. Part II examines allegory in *Volume the Last* and its function as a means of expressing trauma. Allegory provides the key to understanding David Simple's suddenly flawed character, his moral weakness and passivity; through allegory—and perhaps only through allegory—is Fielding's didactic intent revealed. In *Volume the Last*, the dying and the dead become objects of the reader's sympathy—though not of the protagonist's; for David Simple, death exists as a welcome release from earthly suffering. Death comes as a friend, offering the ultimate eternal rest—a sleep without dreaming, a sweet nothingness, the total and complete annihilation of spiritual and conscious being. By viewing death as "friend," Fielding's *Volume the Last* engages with earlier cultural notions of death, though it resists any sense of an afterlife, whether in the form of a substantial soul or as Lockean consciousness.

PART I. THE SORROWS OF YOUNG DAVID: MELANCHOLIA

I begin Part I with an in-depth examination of melancholia, as it fashions the narrative structure and plot of *David Simple*, not only by utilizing the malady's repetitive stagings of an originary loss, but also through the principle character's preoccupation with suffering, the novel's concern with poverty, and more. In addition, as the "relicts" in *David Simple* are "friends" who are no friends at all, the pathology of melancholia suggests why. Specifically, these "non-friends" exist as "relicts" or doubles of David's brother, Daniel, the object of David's ambivalent love.

* * *

Published in 1917, Sigmund Freud's influential essay "Mourning and Melancholia" has shaped subsequent discussions of the two psychological conditions/processes and, to some extent, retroactively rewritten or at the very least colored prior articulations and depictions of them. As Juliana Schiesari notes, this essay has "come, in fact, to occupy—whether correctly or incorrectly—the pivotal position for discussions of melancholia not only in psychoanalysis but also in contemporary literary analysis, feminist theory, and cultural criticism. No study of melancholia can begin without a reconsideration of Freud's essay."[2] And so I too begin with a discussion of Freud's essay, supplementing my summary and analysis with insights from psychoanalysts Nicolas Abraham and Maria Torok and from literary scholars Juliana Schiesari and E. L. McCallum.[3]

Despite the authority given to "Freud's beautiful and difficult essay,"[4] "Mourning and Melancholia" remains highly ambiguous on some issues and self-contradictory in regards to others. Nonetheless, it provides intriguing ideas about the nature of melancholia and mourning that hold, so I believe, particular relevance for reading Sarah Fielding's *David Simple*. In Freud's essay, melancholia and mourning appear symptomatically similar, each involving "a profoundly painful dejection, cessation of interest in the outside world, loss of the capacity to love, inhibition of all activity." In other words, mourning and melancholia provoke "the same painful frame of mind."[5] However, Freud then teases out some (not-always-distinct) differences between the two processes. In the discussion that follows, I focus on five aspects of melancholia that hold particular relevance in terms of Fielding's novel:[6] ambivalence toward the mourned object, repetition of originary loss, feelings of moral superiority, masculine gendering, and fear of poverty.

To begin, mourning and melancholia diverge as regards the conscious or unconscious nature of the loss. Whereas the mourner consciously mourns a lost beloved, knows who or what he, she, or it was, the melancholic remains unconscious of exactly what or whom he or she mourns. A "loved object" has been lost, but the object of loss is obscure, even to the melancholic. As Freud writes, "one feels justified in maintaining the belief that a loss of this kind [of a beloved object] has occurred, but one cannot see clearly what it is that has been lost, and it is all the more reasonable to suppose that the patient cannot consciously perceive what he has lost either."[7] Other times, "there is a loss of a more ideal kind. The object has not perhaps actually died, but has been lost as an object of love (e.g. in the case of a betrothed girl who has been jilted)."[8] In this latter instance, the lost object elicits an ambiguous response from the melancholic subject, which makes mourning difficult, if not impossible. However, blurring the distinctions that he himself has drawn, Freud notes that (normative) mourning may also involve a loss of an abstract ideal or an ambiguous relationship to the lost object, and thus a more important distinction may be drawn from the fact that even in the case where a (material or abstract) loss can be identified, the melancholic "knows *whom* he has lost but not *what* he has lost in him."[9] As Schiesari writes, "it is this 'what' absorbing the melancholic so thoroughly that signals a difference from mourning, by the tell-tale sign of something repressed."[10] The melancholic, then, is unable consciously to mourn the lost object or represses the loss so thoroughly, burying it and entombing it within his/her psyche, that he/she remains unable to recognize it as a loss at the conscious level. In sum, a mourner and a melancholic may have the same object of loss—an individual, say—yet the melancholic resists full or even partial conscious acknowledgement of the loss. To understand why this is so, it is important to turn to how loss is processed by the mourner and the melancholic, respectively.

The process of normative mourning appears relatively transparent, no matter how painful. A love object (person, object, or ideal) has been irretrievably lost, and the bereaved must learn to live without her, him, or it—a process that requires both hypercathexis and decathexis over an extended period of time. Specifically, the mourner paradoxically disengages his/her libido from the lost beloved by psychically reconnecting with the lost beloved through intense remembrance or, as Schiesari writes, through an extended "ritual of commemoration and farewell,"[11] which also serves at the same time to remind the mourner of the reality, the finality, of the loss. Ultimately, accepting the reality that the mourner continues to live though the mourned does not, the mourner's ego detaches its emotional investment from the lost beloved, as Freud explains: "Every single one of the memories and situations of expectancy which demonstrate the libido's attachment to the lost object is met by the verdict of reality that the object no longer exists; and the ego, confronted as it were with the question whether it shall share this fate, is persuaded by the sum of the narcissistic satisfactions it derives from being alive to sever its attachment to the object that has been abolished."[12] Perhaps unwittingly, Freud makes it appear that "successful" mourning ultimately requires complete emotional severance from the once beloved object. However, Schiesari provides what I consider a more accurate depiction of a "successful" conclusion to the mourning process: "the work of mourning might be better understood as a *refiguring* of the ego's relation to the object rather than as a simple dismissal or disavowal of it. Far from being insensitive to the lost object after mourning is completed, the ego still remains sensitive to it, but the affective relation is *different* from what it was."[13] The relationship with the love object remains, as does the love felt for it, but both exist in altered form. The mourner does not forget the loved object or stop loving it, but rather he/she recognizes the reality of the love object's absence and accordingly, over time, reconfigures his/her relationship to the lost beloved.

The process of melancholia, however, follows a different trajectory. While "a strong fixation to the loved object must have been present . . . the object-cathexis must have had little power of resistance,"[14] Freud writes. That is, the actual love object is given up, viewed perhaps as no longer worthy, yet the melancholic is unwilling to surrender "the love-relation" associated with the love object.[15] In other words, the melancholic retains the love relation through "an *identification* of the ego with the abandoned object." Narcissistically regressing, the melancholic maintains the love relation by incorporating the once loved (no longer loved?) object into his/her own ego and thus "in spite of the conflict with the loved person the love-relation need not be given up."[16] Incorporation allows for the love object and love relation to be maintained, as Abraham and Torok explain, "The magical 'cure' by incorporation exempts the subject from the painful process of reorganization [after loss]. When, in the form of imaginary or real nourishment, we ingest the love object we miss, this means that *we refuse to mourn* and that we shun the consequences of mourning even though our psyche is fully bereaved. Incorporation is the refusal to reclaim as our own the part of ourselves that we placed in what we lost; incorporation is the refusal to acknowledge the full import of the loss, a loss that, if recognized as such, would effectively transform us."[17] To return, then, to Freud's assertion that the melancholic "knows *whom* he has lost but not *what* he has lost in him,"[18] the "*what*" that is lost "was really self-love to begin with."[19] Furthermore, "The loss of self-esteem in melancholia (so great that it may even produce a desire for and expectation of punishment) thus occurs *in addition* to the loss of a lost object."[20] By incorporating the lost/loved-hated object into his/ her own psyche, the melancholic denies the slight to the ego, the psychic wounding and loss of self-esteem that has occurred, as a portion of the ego has now been altered to function as surrogate for the lost object.

Avoidance and denial of loss are meant to bolster the ego and yet insure the opposite, as the ambivalence—the love and the hatred—toward the object is retained within the ego, as the incorporated surrogate object, and the traumatic or troubling aspect associated with the lost object becomes the source of the melancholic's own self-loathing: "If the love for the object—a love which cannot be given up though the object itself is given up—takes refuge in narcissistic identification, then the hate comes into operation on this substitutive object, abusing it, debasing it, making it suffer and deriving sadistic satisfaction from its suffering."[21] The ego becomes split in two, with one part—the critical aspect of the ego—standing in judgment over the incorporated "other." Freud notes, "one part of the ego sets itself over against the other, judges it critically, and, as it were, takes it as its object."[22] Suffering thus becomes valuable to the melancholic for three interrelated reasons. First, it punishes the substitutive "other" for whatever perceived slight or crime it committed. Second, it allows the critical part of the ego to prove its moral superiority over the loved-hated "other" and, in doing so, recover some measure of self-esteem. Third, it allows the now debased part of ego a means of representation, as Schiesari remarks: "The melancholic ego . . . is dependent on loss as a means through which it can represent itself. In doing so, however, it derealizes or devalues any *object* of loss for the sake of loss itself."[23] Instead, "it is the condition of loss *as* loss that is privileged and not the loss of any particular object."[24] Repetitive suffering, then, becomes a means of representation for the surrogate "other" incorporated within the ego, and through re-enactment, it allows the psyche to come to terms, albeit in veiled fashion, with the ambivalent feelings toward the original object of loss, as well as stage scenarios wherein self-esteem—through the mechanism of the critical part of the ego—is fed and nourished.

By incorporating this less-than-loved object into the psyche, the melancholic—through the critical aspect of the ego—assumes a moral superiority that (apparently) renders him/her a superior judge of human behavior, or so Freud would have it. For Freud, the melancholic "has a keener eye for the truth than other people who are not melancholic."[25] However, this moral authority requires repeated suffering and loss, until such time (which may be never) the ego expels the incorporated other. With the incorporated other still abiding within the psyche of the melancholic, both the critical part of the ego and the incorporated other must continue to act their respective parts, as Schiesari articulates: "The melancholic display of loss paradoxically increases the value (hence accumulating the gain) of the subject of loss. As such, the melancholic model can be understood not simply as the 'incorporation' of a lost object of desire, but also as an introjection of loss that needs to be endlessly reproduced as loss to sustain its myth. In other words, the greater the loss, the greater the wisdom or 'truth' claimed by the loser, who then profits from this turn of psychic events by gaining from the loss."[26] Schiesari uses Abraham and Torok's concept of introjection, which Nicholas T. Rand describes as "the idea that the psyche is in a constant state of acquisition, involving the active expansion of our potential to open onto our own emerging desires and feelings as well as the external world"; it is the "enrichments and disturbances in the process of self-fashioning," "the unhindered activity of perpetual self-creation."[27] In other words, introjection represents the processing of experience and emotion by the psyche, while incorporation represents its unprocessed "traumas, obstacles, or near deaths."[28] Thus, to return to Schiesari's assertion, the melancholic's originary loss—the loss that he/she refuses to acknowledge consciously—and the subsequent split of the ego encourages the hyper-critical aspect of the ego to gain from the loss and to require repeated losses in order to sustain the psychic gains associated with its evident moral superiority—and perhaps eventually to come to terms with the loss. To restate, melancholic incorporation of the lost object signals unprocessed and unconscious loss and/or trauma, while melancholic introjection of loss—in the form of repetitive encounters with loss—indicates the need of the critical part of the ego to assert continuously its superiority over the incorporated object and afford it opportunities to restage (and perhaps process, acknowledge, and subsequently move on from) the original loss.

Normative mourning over the lost object eventually ends in time—that is, the grief experienced at the loss of the beloved eventually lessens, with the loss then becoming something that the mourner is capable of "living with." Mourning promises a cessation of grief; the only question is when. Melancholia, however, presents multiple possible terminal outcomes. Sometimes, melancholia "passes off after a certain time has elapsed,"[29] in a manner nearly identical to that of mourning. Other times, the melancholia changes into mania, triggering a bout of "high spirits," which are displayed by a "discharge of joyful emotion and by increased readiness for all kinds of action,"[30] a burst of creative output generally associated with artistic genius. In other instances, mania may revert back to melancholia, or melancholia and mania may present themselves in cyclical fashion: "Some cases run their course in periodic relapses, during the intervals between which signs of mania may be entirely absent or only very slight. Others show the regular alternation of melancholic and manic phases."[31] In worst-case scenarios, melancholia ends in suicide, when the ego becomes overwhelmed by the surrogate object choice and reacts with sadistic revenge.[32] The manic outcome—the triumphal state in which the melancholic releases himself or herself from the grasp of the internalized ego object and expels it, so to speak—"calls for an extraordinarily high anti-cathexis," perhaps based on the ego's ultimate "satisfaction of knowing itself the better of the two, as superior to the object."[33] In other words, the critical aspect of the ego—the part that enjoys moral superiority—finally recognizes the unworthiness of the incorporated object and summarily sends it on its way.

Before turning to the relationship between melancholia and fear of poverty, I would like to address the gendering of melancholia and mourning—a point of particular relevance in terms of Sarah Fielding's *David Simple*. As most feminist scholars have noted, including Luce Irigaray, Julia Kristeva, and others, melancholia has historically been perceived as a masculine phenomenon and, as such, has been privileged over mourning, which in Western culture has largely been viewed as the purview of women.[34] As E. L. McCallum writes, "Melancholia was a special quality that not only elevated a man above the vulgar masses, but also separated out the man of genius from the common woman whose grief came to be coded as her natural role rather than as a culturally valuable expression."[35] This is not to say that women can't be melancholic or that men can't mourn, but rather that "Melancholia could be understood as a particular discourse that encodes male subjectivity in terms of the history of great men and great deeds."[36] Specifically, male melancholia, particularly when interspersed with bursts of manic output, translates culturally into "inspired artistry and genius," into "individual triumph in the guise of moral conscience, artistic creativity, or heightened sensitivity."[37] In contrast, female melancholia—frequently denigrated or dismissed under the appellations of "depression" or "hysteria"—is "expressed by less flattering allusions to widow's weeds, inarticulate weeping, or other signs of ritualistic (but intellectually and artistically unaccredited) mourning."[38] Although the male melancholic is "feminized" in his grief and suffering, he is able to employ this feminization to his advantage—an advantage that the female melancholic is denied—as this feminization through suffering provides a platform for the masculine display of moral superiority, artistic genius, or sensitivity (or sensibility, as the case may be—a point particularly worth noting as relates to *David Simple*). In addition, if normative mourning is based on a recognizable and acknowledged loss rather than on the refusal to recognize and acknowledge loss (because of the threat to self-esteem), and if mourning is culturally gendered as a feminine ritual function and melancholia as a masculine aesthetic discourse, then it appears that melancholia employs the signs of feminine mourning for its own gain.[39] As McCallum notes, "melancholia is a drag version of mourning."[40] The male melancholic appropriates the sighs, the sorrow, the gloomy thoughts associated with mourning as outward signs of inward depth.

Finally, the melancholic fears poverty: "fears and asseverations of becoming poor . . . occupy a prominent position" in the melancholic's thoughts, which Freud presumes derives "from anal eroticism which has been torn out of its context and altered in a regressive state."[41] This is the sum total of Freud's remarks on this peculiar symptom of melancholia in "Mourning and Melancholia," but an earlier essay from 1908 discusses anal eroticism and its relationship to money. In "Character and Anal Eroticism," Freud notes how the infant's body possesses numerous sites of erotic pleasure—or as Freud terms it "erotogenic zones"— including the anus.[42] As the child matures and develops, he/she learns that certain zones—the anus among them—are viewed negatively, and thus for a child who is particularly invested in the activities of his/her anus, sublimation of his/her feelings into orderliness (or cleanliness), obstinacy, and, most particularly, parsimoniousness occur. The love of money or niggardliness comes from the metaphoric association of money with filth or excrement: "filthy rich," "dirty money," and the like. But what has this to do with melancholia? Why does the melancholic regress to a state of anal eroticism, and what does Freud mean by the fact that this act of "anal eroticism . . . has been torn out of its context and altered"? Since Freud doesn't say, I must make an educated guess. Elsewhere in "Mourning and Melancholia," Freud notes that in extreme cases of melancholia, the melancholic will refuse food or other sustenance.[43] He traces this rejection of real sustenance to the desire to devour the lost object, taking it into the body through incorporation. Abraham and Torok argue that "the fantasy of incorporation merely simulates profound psychic transformation through magic; it does so by implementing literally something that has only figurative meaning. So in order not to have to 'swallow' a loss, we fantasize swallowing (or having swallowed) that which has been lost, as if it were some kind of thing."[44] Perhaps anal eroticism, then, works on a similar metaphoric level for the melancholic. While in the ordinary course of events the "debased love object . . . will be 'fecalized,' that is, actually rendered excremental,"[45] the melancholic subject is unwilling or unable to "shit" the incorporated other out of his/her system, taking anal eroticism out of its original context and altering it to accommodate the newly incorporated "other." Abraham and Torok note that incorporation involves "Introducing all or part of a love object or a thing into one's own body, possessing, expelling or alternately acquiring, keeping, losing it."[46] And, since money and excrement are linked at a metaphoric/cultural level, the melancholic's fear of poverty relates to his/her fear of expelling the incorporated "other."

In *The Poetry of Mourning,* Jahan Ramazani "recast[s] the classical distinction between mourning and melancholia, shading it as a difference between modes of mourning: the normative (i.e., restitutive, idealizing) and the melancholic (violent, recalcitrant)." He further asserts that "melancholic mourning . . . tends not to achieve but resist consolation, not to override but to sustain anger, not to heal but to reopen the wounds of loss."[47] Ramazani's nuanced reframing of melancholia complements Freud's original essay, and it suggests that violence and anger underlie the melancholy suffered by Sarah Fielding's protagonist, David Simple.

* * *

The Adventures of David Simple tells the story of a young man, only eighteen when his sorrows begin, whose younger brother, Daniel, contrives to cheat him out of his portion of inheritance after the death of their father. The young man, David, finds refuge with an uncle, who helps David recover his portion of the bequest—indeed, a bit more than his portion[48]—and, when the uncle dies, David is his principal heir. Allowing his brother an annuity yet still in despair over his sibling's betrayal, David sets forth to London "to seek out one capable of being a real Friend" (21)—a friend akin to the one he once thought he had found in his brother. Yet, David's search for a friend initially proves futile. His love interest, Nanny Johnson, proves fickle, torn between genuine affection for David and genuine fondness for money, and a parade of unworthy men—with dubious sounding names such as Orgueil, Spatter, and Varnish—prove less than satisfactory as friends. Over and over, David finds himself bitterly disappointed in his quest for true friendship until, at last, David meets Cynthia, then Camilla and Valentine. After reciting their respective stories of woe, the foursome become fast friends, with David marrying Camilla and Valentine marrying Cynthia.

To understand David's melancholia, it is necessary to return to the beginning of *David Simple* and compare David's reactions to the deaths of two true friends—his father and his uncle—against his response to Daniel's betrayal. Interestingly, the deaths of David's father and uncle appear to make little claim upon him emotionally (or at least the text makes relatively light of these losses). David's first real loss—the death of his father—occurs at the end of chapter 1. Yet, David handles his father's death with a fair degree of equanimity: "The Loss of so good a Father was sensibly felt by the tender-hearted *David*; he was in the utmost Affliction, till by Philosophical Considerations, assisted by a natural Calmness he had in his own Temper, he was enabled to overcome his Grief, and began again to enjoy his former Serenity of Mind" (8). What these "Philosophical Considerations" might be, the narrator does not share. However, without a doubt, the textual period allotted to David's mourning is minimal (a sentence only); his brother Daniel's period of mourning is even shorter (a single, short phrase), as Daniel, being "much more gay, soon recovered his Spirits" (8). In sum, David philosophically accepts the death of his father and moves on.

Later, after Daniel's betrayal of David, David turns to his uncle, who takes David in, nurses him, recovers his inheritance, and makes him heir to his entire fortune. Although David had intended to live out his life with his uncle, "that he might take care of him in his old Age; and make as much Return as possible of his generous, good-natured Treatment of him" (19–20), his uncle's death meets with little grief and minimal mourning on the part of David:

> This was a fresh Disturbance to the Ease he had proposed; for *David* had so much Tenderness, he could not possibly part with so good a Friend, without being moved: tho' he abated his Concern as fast as possible, with

the Consideration that he [the uncle] was arrived to an Age, wherein to breathe was all could be expected, and that Diseases and Pains must have filled up the rest of his Life. At last, he [David] began to reflect, even with pleasure, that the Man whom he had so much reason to esteem and value, had escaped the most miserable part of human Life. (20)

Strangely enough, once the uncle is dead and buried, the narrator informs us that he was not quite the type of friend that David truly valued, as the uncle was "void of those Delicacies, and strong Sensations of the Mind, which make both the Happiness and Misery of whoever is possessed of them" (20). That is the sum of David's mourning for his uncle; instead, David's thoughts immediately turn to his brother, whose betrayal continues to haunt David obsessively: "When *David* saw himself in the possession of a very easy comfortable Fortune, instead of being over-joyed, as is usual on such occasions, he was first the more unhappy; the Consideration of the Pleasure he should have had to share this Fortune with his Brother, continually brought to his Remembrance his cruel Usage, which made him feel all his old Troubles over again" (20). As Shawn Lisa Maurer notes, "In possession of two fortunes—the restored legacy from his father, and his uncle's nearly comparable estate—David feels not joy but a deep sense of emptiness resulting from his loss of faith."[49] But is his loss of faith in Daniel, in the notion of friendship, or in himself? I would suggest all three.

As Freud notes, in melancholia, ambiguity exists toward the once beloved object, perhaps because of "all those situations of being slighted, neglected or disappointed,"[50] and David Simple's feelings regarding his brother display extreme ambiguity. David feels slighted, neglected, and disappointed all at once. Daniel's initial maltreatment of David "threw *David* into that inconsistent Behaviour, which must always be produced in a Mind torn at once by Tenderness and Rage. That sincere Love and Friendship he had always felt for his Brother, made his Resentment the higher, and he alternately broke into Reproaches, and melted into Softness" (13). Upset, David seeks the refuge of his room: "It would be impossible to describe what he felt when he was alone; all the Scenes of Pleasure he had ever enjoyed in his Brother's Company rushed at once into his Memory. . . . He was sometimes ready to blame himself," but then "several little Slights came into his head, which he had overlooked at the time of their happening" (14). His hurt feelings war with his desire for reconciliation: "Sometimes in the Confusion of his Thoughts, the Joy of being again well with his Brother, appeared so strong to his Imagination, he could hardly refrain going to him" (14).

While I don't necessarily agree with George Haggerty that "*David Simple* is a novel about family"—after all, older family members are dispatched to the grave or countryside without much ado or even a backward glance—I do agree that "David *feels* this loss because he has been betrayed where he most has trusted."[51] The opening paragraph of the novel insists that others remark upon the "strict Friendship" that David and Daniel initially possess (7). Obviously, this is David's earliest and closest relationship with another human being. By Daniel rejecting this relationship—by suggesting through his subsequent behavior that this relationship did not exist in reality—he leaves David with the impossible task not only of reinterpreting his idealized and lived notion of friendship, but also of confronting the knowledge that David himself is not considered a worthy object of Daniel's love. David cannot interject the experience—that is, his ego rejects accepting the severe psychic wounding that has occurred—and yet he has no choice other than to reject Daniel himself as love object. Thus, he begins the unpleasant task of incorporation in order to retain the love relationship and, with it, salvage some semblance of self-worth. And so David's sufferings begin in earnest.

Like Freud's melancholic, David knows "*whom* he has lost but not *what* he has lost in him." The "whom" is Daniel, of course, but the "what" is David's own self-esteem and self-love, which have been severely damaged due to Daniel's rejection of David. Abraham and Torok speak of the act of incorporation as one of antimetaphor, by which subjects "annul the humiliation [which incited their melancholia] by secretly or openly adopting the literal meaning of the words causing the humiliation."[52] What has humiliated David is his brother's devaluation of David's friendship and of the word "friend" itself, and so "friend" becomes the literalized word by which David re-enacts his humiliation, his loss, his sorrow, over and over again, in variations of this theme. He offers himself as friend, only to find his friendship dismissed or devalued, or to discover the object of his friendship unworthy.

With thoughts of Daniel fresh in his mind, David determines to "seek out one capable of being a real Friend, and to assist all those, who had been thrown into Misfortunes by the ill Usage of others" (21). Due to the split in ego—between the incorporated "other" and the critical aspect of the ego—the melancholic must act in ways that satisfy the demands of both. The incorporated "other" must suffer not only in order to obtain its punishment, but also to articulate itself, to have its presence known. The critical aspect of the ego encourages suffering, as it revels in punishing the incorporated "other," making it suffer for the real or perceived slights, the hurts, the betrayal, and because suffering demonstrates the critical aspect of the ego's moral superiority over the incorporated "other" through comparison and through patiently enduring the suffering. Thus, suffering and loss prove compensatory to the melancholic ego, requiring repetition of acts of loss similar to the originary event in order to sustain this compensatory satisfaction. And so it goes with David Simple. Although he purportedly sets out to find a true friend, it is clear by his initial way of going about it that what he seeks is the repetition of his originary loss, not friendship.

As Betty Schellenberg notes, "David's continual disappointments . . . soon transform the quest into a seemingly endless oscillation of hope and hopelessness with an ever-diminishing possibility of success."[53] David begins his search for a friend in a place where he is highly unlikely to find one: the Royal Exchange. Liz Bellamy suggests that "It is perhaps a sign of David's innocence and ignorance that he chooses to begin his journey with a visit to the Royal Exchange. A cursory knowledge of the literature of commerce would have told him that this was unlikely to be the place where he would find a real friend, but David is undeterred."[54] Even the narrator notes, "he could not have gone any where to have seen a more melancholy Prospect, or more likelihood of being disappointed of his Design" (22), and true to expectations, David finds men engaged in acts of "Villainy" (23) and is shocked and outraged. But what did David expect to find there? I suggest he found what he was looking for: loss, disappointment, suffering.

On his way out of the Exchange, David meets a jeweler by the name of Johnson, who knew David through his uncle and knows that David is his heir. Johnson has two eligible daughters at home, and so he invites David to come reside with them, and without hesitation, David accepts the offer. He soon finds himself attracted to the younger daughter—Miss Nanny—who in turn willingly encourages David's attentions. Yet, as David's preference for Miss Nanny originates in her beauty, his chances for finding a real friend in Miss Nanny are suspect. As expected, David's ill fortune continues when Miss Nanny is introduced to the "immensely rich" (26) Mr. Nokes and finds herself conflicted over whether to choose the elderly and ugly Nokes over the young and charming David. Overhearing Nanny debate the relative merits of both suitors with her maid, David takes any semblance of choice away from her when he urges her to marry Nokes and then summarily moves out of her father's house. Curiously, the narrator assures readers that Nanny could have made a good wife for David—that her affection for him, upon marriage, would have grown. Ostensibly, David leaves Nanny to her ugly old suitor and "her beloved Grandeur" (30) because he wishes her well. Yet, he does enact his revenge by feigning indifference about the loss, suggesting the anger and violence underlying the presumed self-sacrifice. Nonetheless, David's own vanity has been punctured, "when he found the Woman he so tenderly loved, and who he thought returned that Love, was in the highest Perplexity to determine, whether she should take him with a Competency, or the Monster they had described with great Riches" (30). Once again, David's friendship has been devalued, and once again, he repeats a scene of intense suffering similar to the one he experienced with the loss of Daniel's friendship.

David now finds himself "in the same Condition as when he discovered his Brother's Treachery" (35). He expresses "great Contempt" for "his Mistress's Conduct" (35); he weeps "to think that Vanity should prevent such a Creature from being perfect" (35); he believes that "if she could have such Faults, no Woman was ever truly good" (35). But, a moment later, "he was ready to go back, throw himself at her Feet, and ask ten thousand Pardons for believing his own Senses; confess himself highly to blame, and unworthy of her Favour, for having left her" (35). Through his relationship with Nanny, David replicates the same experience of trust and love, followed by devastating loss of and betrayal by the once beloved object, and indeed, the narrator links the two relationships and experiences: he "had been used ill, by both the Man and the Woman he loved" (35).

Once he recovers from this second loss, David steps up his efforts to find "a valuable Friend," taking new lodgings "every Week," yet finding "all the Women tearing one another from Envy, and the Men sacrificing each other for every trifling Interest" (36). After repeated efforts, he begins "now utterly to despair that he should ever meet with any Persons who would *give him leave* to have a good Opinion of them a Week together; for he found such a Mixture of bad in all those he had yet met with, that as soon as he began to think well of any one, they were sure to do something to shock him, and overthrow his Esteem" (38). Eventually, though, a man "whose Conversation Mr. *Simple* was mightily charmed with" appears—a Mr. Orgueil—and "*David* imagined such a Companion, if he was not again deceived in his Opinion, would be the greatest Blessing this World could afford" (44). His newfound friend takes David around London, introducing him here, accompanying him there. Mr. Orgueil appears the perfect friend—intelligent, personable, free of vices, and desirous of doing good—with the possible exception of "too severe Condemnation of others Actions" (45). Yet, David is content in the friendship, until he learns that Mr. Orgueil believes "Compassion . . . to be a very great Weakness"—a revelation that causes David great consternation: "he began to be frighten'd, lest he should have no more reason to esteem Mr. *Orgueil*" (55). Indeed, Adam Smith notes, "But whatever may be the cause of sympathy, or however it may be excited, nothing pleases us more than to observe in other men a fellow-feeling with all the emotions of our own breast; nor are we ever so much shocked as by the appearance of the contrary."[55] Compassion ranks chief among the sympathetic emotions, so Smith argues, and Orgueil's lack of compassion argues for his inherent villainy, as the "greatest ruffian, the most hardened violator of the laws of society, is not altogether without it."[56] Mr. Spatter—an acquaintance of both men—confirms David's altered opinion of Orgueil, and David, in despair, sets off with Spatter, desolate over the impossibility of meeting a real friend. This pattern—initial esteem of the object on the part of David, followed by feelings of disappointment, even betrayal—continues with Mr. Spatter and Mr. Varnish. Spatter ultimately disappoints David with his constant mockery of others, and when David finds himself the butt of Spatter's jokes (76), so Mr. Varnish informs him, the friendship ends. He continues on with Varnish, but the relationship is "but of small duration" once it becomes clear that Varnish was "not at all affected with others Sufferings" (97).

David's disappointments and sufferings highlight his superior claim to virtues and attributes most esteemed within a culture of sensibility. The values that David embraces—sympathy, empathy, charitableness, kindness, compassion—are those values that we as readers are intended to embrace, and the fact that other characters do not possess them displays their unworthiness. Suffering—whether it be sympathetic suffering or self-experiential suffering—performs moral superiority in several ways. It singles the melancholic sufferer out as the possessor of "the most exquisite sensibility,"[57] demonstrating that he/she alone displays—nay, *feels*—human emotions to the fullest. This, in turn, argues for the sufferer's innate physical and mental superiority, as George Cheyne theorized: "there are as many and as different Degrees of *Sensibility* or of *Feeling* as there are Degrees of *Intelligence* and *Perception*. . . . One shall suffer more from the Prick of a *Pin*, or *Needle*, from their extreme Sensibility, than others from being run thro' the Body: and the *first* sort, seem to be of the *Class* of . . . *Quick-Thinkers*."[58] As G. J. Barker-Benfield notes, "Degrees of sensibility, then, betokened both social and moral status. Paradoxically, however, an innate refinement of nerves was also identifiable with greater suffering."[59] Suffering becomes both the mark of and the result of sensibility. In a similar vein, Joseph Bartolomeo notes, "Suffering is symptomatic of the novel of sensibility. Narratives generally, and novels of sensibility in particular, are impelled by ongoing conflict and often by suffering."[60] As is no doubt clear by this point, "*David Simple* is . . . the first out-and-out novel of sensibility,"[61] and, in "David Simple, Sarah Fielding creates perhaps the first man of feeling."[62] The fact that Fielding's novel is also satiric does not undermine is sentimental moralism, for, as Sara Gadeken notes, "Satire and sentimentality, both unstable and complicated, intersect at a number of points but in none so obviously as their common insistence on the moral natures of their respective genres."[63] Although moral superiority and scenes of suffering are inherent in the novel of sensibility, this does not mean that they are not evidence of melancholic display—they most certainly are. The novel of sensibility is melancholic by nature, as the sorrows of Werther, the sufferings of Harley, and the pains of David Simple make clear.

Up to this point in the novel, "real Friend" has translated into repeated disappointment, feelings of personal betrayal, personal slights and insults, and, upon occasion, physical illness. Yet, once David meets Cynthia, "real Friend" becomes synonymous with loss and suffering on the part of others—in particular on the part of women. Upon David's initial encounter with the intelligent, resourceful Cynthia, whose "Countenance" attracts him because of its "fix'd Melancholy" (78), the novel shifts to a series of "feminine fictions—that is, Camilla's story, Cynthia's story (with Livia's history contained within Cynthia's), and Isabelle de Stainville's history. These 'histories' record the accepted, standard tale of the eighteenth-century woman and her plight of harassment, exploitation, and seduction."[64] In some ways, these stories replicate David's own history of loss. Regarding "Cynthia, Camilla, and Valentine," Butt remarks, "Their merits are defined for us in a context of victimization; they have all suffered from the effects of gross misrepresentation by those who have had the means to exert power over them."[65] In other ways, however, the women's stories are decidedly different from David's, precisely because they are women's stories, documenting events and experiences that—while not necessarily an ordinary part of every eighteenth-century woman's life—were by no means unusual or extraordinary. Cynthia is considered too intelligent, something of which no man was accused, and when she refuses to marry the nondescript gentleman whom her father has chosen for her, her father alters his will, leaving her nothing and forcing her to work as a "Toad-Eater" (89) or lady's companion. A stepmother alienates the affections of Camilla's father from his daughter, viciously destroying Camilla's reputation by hinting at incest between Camilla and her brother Valentine, which results in Camilla and Valentine becoming social pariahs, without any means of economic support. A male might recover more easily from such slander than a woman, perhaps starting life anew in a distant country, and he would also possess economic opportunities denied to women. Camilla's reputation is her entire surety against a cruel world, and once she has lost that, she is destitute and scorned. And Isabelle's sad tale is caused by her sister-in-law's too-early marriage and fatal attraction to the man whom Isabelle loves. Again, it is a story of the suffering caused specifically by a woman's place within society. As Norman Simms notes: "Each [female] narrator exposes domestic crises in the relations between parents and children, brothers and sisters, and daughters and suitors; these are crises set in motion by patriarchal authority clashing with the female's attempts to protect her physical and psychological integrity . . . a lack of symmetry in human experience and rational order as aesthetic ideal is revealed not just for correction and ridicule but as a fact of life—something women have to live with, defend themselves against, and run away from, physically and psychologically."[66] Valentine has no story of his own to tell, and indeed, his role in his own history is determinedly intertwined with that of his sibling, Camilla, and once David meets Cynthia, he has no more stories of his own to tell. Although both Valentine and David are feminized,[67] the narrative has shifted to "real" female suffering rather than male suffering, and it has done so because (male) melancholia must now appropriate (female) mourning in order to sustain itself.

What I suggest is this: David's melancholia no longer has sufficient impetus with which to feed itself—after all, any more false friends would not only strain the reader's patience, but also label David a mere fool, not a suffering saint. Instead, his melancholia and his moral superiority need fresh fuel, and where better for David to get it than from women, who (presumably) do not suffer from melancholia themselves, but whose sufferings are surely equal to or greater than David's own, as David himself acknowledges. If, as E. L. McCallum suggests, melancholia is mourning in drag, then David's melancholia appropriates these women's mourning and makes it his own. Their stories become part of his story—quite literally, in fact, if we consider that these women's stories are incorporated within David's adventures. While one of David's stated goals is "to assist all those, who had been thrown into Misfortunes by the ill Usage of others" (21), he nonetheless is attracted by suffering. Every instance of his burning desire to hear these women's respective stories is prefaced by the idea that he wants to do good, but an urgency exists behind his words to hear—and by hearing, vicariously experience—their suffering.

When David first sees Cynthia's melancholic countenance, he becomes "uneasy" (78), and later, he seeks to meet her privately, saying to her, "That he saw by her Look and Manner she was very unhappy, and begg'd, if it was any way in his power to serve her, she would let him know it; for nothing in the World was capable of giving him so much Pleasure, as relieving the Distress'd" (79). When he meets Camilla and the desperately ill Valentine, David "longed to know their Story" (103) and, getting Camilla alone, urges her "to let him into her History" (104), which she does. What he wants from each woman, in return for his assistance, is "the History of her Life" (79), which he listens to with avidity, exclaiming, sighing, weeping as each story unfolds. Through the women's stories, he vicariously experiences their sufferings and, in doing so, claims these stories as his own. As James Kim argues, "The virtuous interiority of the female subject thus turns out to be the final repository of true value in the novel."[68] However, this value derives not only from the "virtuous interiority of the female subject," from her inner morality, but also from the quality and depth of female suffering.

This is particularly true when David and his newfound friends encounter Isabelle, a former acquaintance of Cynthia's. Seeing the mournful look on Isabelle's face, Cynthia worries that "Company would be troublesome to her" (152). Nonetheless, David insists that Cynthia visit her, ostensibly to "find out, if possible, if there was any Method could be thought on for her Relief" (152). As they wait, the foursome spends its time "in Conjectures on Isabelle's Circumstances" (152), each person overlaying her/his own plight over Isabelle's. David insists that Cynthia renew her acquaintance with Isabelle, even though "*Cynthia* would not so far transgress the Rules of Good Breeding, as to ask her any Questions concerning her own Affairs" (152): "*David* waited with great Impatience while *Cynthia* was with *Isabelle*, in hopes at her Return to learn, whether or not it would be in his power to gratify his favourite Passion (of doing Good) on this Occasion: but when *Cynthia* informed him, it was impossible as yet, without exceeding all Bounds of Good Manners, to know any Occurences that had happened to *Isabelle*, he grew very uneasy, and could not forbear reflecting on the Tyranny of Custom" (152). Interestingly, David's passion "of doing Good" is placed as a parenthetic qualifier, as if some doubt existed as to what his favorite passion might be, not only on the reader's part but on the narrator's as well. In addition, there is that word "uneasy" again. David becomes "uneasy" every time he suspects that a woman has suffered, and his unease is not assuaged until he has heard her full story. His unease is not caused by their suffering, but by his inability to access that suffering. Finally, after "several Days," Isabelle succumbs to their repeated entreaties: "At last, by their continual Importunities, and the Uneasiness she was convinced she gave to People, who so much deserved her Esteem, she resolved, whatever Pain it would occasion her, to comply with their Requests, and relate the History of her Life" (153). Although Isabelle's story renders David sleepless, weeping, and sighing, neither he nor his friends can aid her. Nonetheless, Isabelle's story has served its purpose, providing fuel for the group's vicarious suffering: "This tragical Story left very melancholy Impressions on all their Minds, and was continually the Subject of their Conversation" (195).

Notably, Cynthia, Camilla, and even Isabelle endure suffering more stoically than their highly sensitive male counterparts, David and Valentine, and they do so despite the fact that the magnitude of their sorrows is as great, if not greater, than those of the men. These behaviors, I suggest, are symptomatic, respectively, of female mourning and male melancholia. When cut from her father's will, Cynthia actively seeks employment, and though that employment is none too pleasant, she nonetheless endures it. Once David offers her an escape from her servitude, she accepts his largesse only with the caveat that her behavior not be misinterpreted.

Camilla too, once cast out of her relatives' houses, seeks employment and, when denied that, begs on the London streets for enough money to feed herself and her brother. And Isabelle, mourning the deaths of her lover and brother, has come to England from France, at her aunt's request. When the aunt dies of small pox, Isabelle has presence of mind left to settle the estate, prior to returning to France and a life confined to a nunnery. The female characters are active, not passive.

In contrast, the men—David and Valentine—are often rendered ill or incapable of action when encountering the same or lesser ills. Upon being dismissed from his aunt's house, Valentine immediately falls "into a Violent fever" (129), much like David did upon Daniel's treachery. Carolyn Woodward comments, "Valentine, a shadow figure who is rarely onstage, is plagued with recurrent illness and passive melancholy."[69] Similarly, Shawn Lisa Maurer notes that Valentine is "Frequently ill, persistently passive, and often silent"[70] (see figure 3.1). The sensitive male characters indulge in melancholic inaction, which paradoxically renders them morally superior. When insulted, they can summon no response other than sickness. Presumably rage and reason will prove equally ineffective in combating the injustices and indignities that they endure; illness alone can express the full magnitude of the insult. In contrast, sensitive female characters must "soldier on," so to speak, despite severe economic hardships, ill-treatment from others, and loss of reputation, because this is women's cultural lot, at least in eighteenth-century England. Women may have reason to mourn, but indulgence in grief will only render their lot worse by making them ever more vulnerable, economically, socially, and even sexually. In contrast, male melancholia performs grief in the extreme, with the assurance that no loss in status (economic, social, or sexual) will occur, but rather the opposite.

The last point regarding melancholia in *David Simple* involves the correlation between economics and morals—one of the more frequently commented-upon aspects of the novel. As Janet Todd notes, "Feeling and money, cash and compassion become weirdly interchangeable" in *David Simple*.[71] As noted earlier, one of the more unusual symptoms displayed by the melancholic is concern over money, and both Fielding as author and the characters within the novel express extreme anxiety over financial issues. Fielding's "Advertisement to the Reader" claims that her *"venturing to write"* the book is due to *"Distress in her Circumstances, which she could not so well remove by any other Means in her Power."* As Simon Stern notes, this, "a despondent woman's foray into commerce, suggests that for Fielding this venture is fraught with anxiety."[72] Sara Gadeken concurs, saying, "This is a voice of apology, pleading inadequacy, economic distress, victimization, and the potential for inciting sympathy."[73] In addition, the vast majority of suffering that

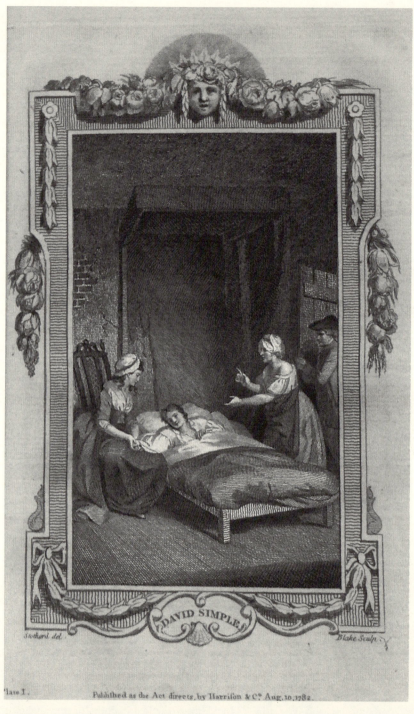

Figure 3.1 *David Simple*. Etching by William Blake, based on an illustration by Thomas Stothard. From *Novelist's Magazine*, No. 18 (1782). Camilla attends Valentine on his sickbed, with landlady and David Simple entering the room. Collection of K. M. Oliver. Photograph by Charles Parkhill, 2017.

occurs within both *David Simple* and *Volume the Last* initiates from economic want or economic fraud. Gillian Skinner explains:

> The problems encountered by David Simple and his community of friends are essentially financial: the question is not *how* to avert disaster (the answer is, money) but whether or not the means to avert disaster will be forthcoming, which in turn depends upon the arrival of a sufficiently monied individual. In Volumes I and II, David himself is that individual and his reaction to the tragic story of Isabelle, which will not admit of any material reparation, reveals clearly how far the benevolence of sensibility relies on economic solutions. . . . The degree of generosity is directed related to the degree of sensibility; as the latter increases, so does the former.[74]

David's initial sufferings—Daniel's betrayal and Miss Nanny's betrayal—hinge upon economics. Daniel has defrauded David of his share of his father's estate; Miss Nanny imagines finer coaches if she marries Nokes instead of David. Cynthia's plight is clearly economic. Cut from her father's will, she must work as a lady's maid to earn her keep. While Camilla and Valentine suffer a loss of reputation, the most immediate impact is economic—they have no family or friends to support them, nor can they easily support themselves. Later, in *Volume the Last*, the beginnings—and the ends—of David's sorrows and those of his friends are similarly economic, as the need for money makes the little community of friends dependent upon the largesse of others, which ultimately is not forthcoming. Sarah Fielding personally understood economic privation of the sort that her characters endure, and it is surely no surprise that her characters display a similar attitude toward money. However, combined with all the other elements (the incessant pursuit of loss, the sense of moral superiority, the use of feminine suffering as a means to display masculine sensibility), the pervasive economic anxiety confirms the melancholic nature of *David Simple* and its protagonist.

Within her fictive world, Fielding uses repetition in *David Simple* to explicate David's original trauma of betrayed friendship, racking up the discarded bodies of so-called friends with unseemly frequency. These false friends exist as textual relicts of David's brother Daniel, and they serve to propel the plot forward, with each new false friend offering (at least temporarily) a species of narrative compensation for earlier losses. Repetition also occurs in terms of the set of "true" friends that David finds in Cynthia, Camilla, Valentine, and Isabelle and in their respective stories of suffering, but in this instance, these suffering relicts exist as textual replicants of David himself. To put it another way, each and every "false" friend is a relict/replicant of Daniel; each and every "true" friend is a relict/replicant of David. These friends—false and true—exist as the textual *remains* of the original twosome. The novel moves, then, from the trauma of Daniel's perfidy, repeated until textually exhausted, to David's internal (re)valuation of self, repeated through the surrogacy of the female or feminized characters, ultimately resulting in David's melancholic "cure." Notably, one "false" friend follows another "false" friend, each new one replacing a former one, while the "true" friends accumulate, with Cynthia, Camilla, and Valentine all becoming lifelong friends and permanent additions to the story. Thus, despite the melancholic repetitiveness of the first part of *David Simple*, the second part signals a move into normative mourning, wherein David begins to understand his own worth as well as the unworthiness of his brother. It should also be noted that narrative repetitiveness is intimately related to the episodic nature of the novel of sensibility, wherein "plot is displaced because all external action is subordinated to the responses created in a physiologically imagined interior landscape"[75]— that is, in engendering physiological and emotional responses in readers. Finally, in *David Simple*, death is neither dreaded nor is it mourned; it is the living who bring dread and suffering—or, if one is fortunate enough, happiness and emotional consolation. But if *David Simple* is not interested in death per se, it *is* interested in bodies, with characters introduced and dispatched with alarming frequency, leaving no textual presence behind except for their replacements.

CONCLUSION

David Simple ends happily enough, with Camilla and Valentine reconciled with their father and with marriages between David and Camilla and between Cynthia and Valentine. Money abounds, as Camilla's father divides his remaining fortune between his two children, leaving his own maintenance to their and David's largesse. And Daniel dies, repentant on his deathbed, and with his death, David's melancholic suffering appears to die for good. Sarah Fielding's *Familiar Letters between the Principal Characters in David Simple*, published in 1747, three years after *David Simple* and six years prior to *Volume the Last*, confirms that the four friends are happy, but as we shall see, that happiness doesn't last long.

PART II. DOUBLE VISION: ALLEGORY

Sarah Fielding's *Volume the Last* is a gloomy affair from start to finish. Published nine years after *David Simple*, the sequel no doubt owes a large part of its despairing world view to events in Fielding's own life, as many scholars have noted. Two years prior to its publication, Fielding lost her three sisters—Catharine, Ursula, and Beatrice—with whom she lived, as well as her eight-year-old nephew, her brother Henry's eldest son, within a period of less than eight months, most probably due to an epidemic of jail fever, a form of typhus.[76] During the same time period, Fielding was sued for debt by the owner of her childhood home at East Stour, a debt that Henry apparently repaid for her, or at least assisted her in repaying.[77] However, if the economic anxiety that Fielding experienced in her personal life was acute, that experienced by David Simple and his extended family exceeds it, as they lose literally everything they own, including their most meager possessions. And if the death count in Fielding's own life was notably high, the death count in *Volume the Last* surpasses it. As Butt notes, "The mortality, indeed, is frightful, and would do credit to a Jacobean tragedy: only Cynthia and one of David's children survive."[78] More humorously, Petit remarks, "Fielding might as well have titled the last book of *Volume the Last* 'Containing Eight Deaths, and Consequently the Conclusion of the Sequel.'"[79] Clearly, *Volume the Last* exhibits narrative mourning in terms of plot—but it also does so through allegory and repetition.

Allegory performs trauma through displacement and abstraction, which in turn allows for an articulation of that which is otherwise inexpressible. If death is always "elsewhere," always experienced by someone other than one's self, then allegory places the trauma associated with this loss "elsewhere." Richard Stamelman writes, "Allegorical discourse . . . is always incomplete and imperfect because it evokes some meaning, some image, some figure lying beyond the horizon of its signification," much as death itself lies beyond signification. Further, he notes, "Allegory could be called the trope of death, the language of fragmentation, decay and erosion that death speaks."[80] As Ros Ballaster notes, Sarah Fielding and Jane Collier employ allegory in their 1754 "dramatic fable" *The Cry*,[81] but Fielding's most intensive application of allegory appears within the *David Simple* novels, coincidentally the most autobiographical of her works.

To interpret the allegory that underlies *David Simple* and *Volume the Last*, we must turn to Sarah Fielding's "A Vision,"[82] itself part of the *David Simple* oeuvre, appended to the end of the final volume of *Familiar Letters between the Principal Characters in David Simple*, published in 1747, three years after *David Simple* and six years prior to *Volume the Last*. "A Vision" begins in Bunyan-esque fashion: "METHOUGHT I was conveyed into a large Plain, amongst such Multitudes of Men and Women, that I could have no other Idea, than that all Mankind were assembled together." The unnamed narrator—more spectator than participant—spies the multitudes gathering at "the End of this Plain," where "four prodigious large high Gates" are erected: "On the First was written, *The Way to Wealth*; on the Second, *The Way to Power*; on the Third, *The Way to Pleasure*; and on the Fourth, *The Way to Virtue*."[83] However, each gate also has written, in miniscule lettering above the larger inscription, the true nature of the path—the fine print so to speak—and so the way to Wealth is really the way to Avarice; Power, to Ambition; Pleasure, to Disappointment; and Virtue, to Pride. Because the narrator is not blinded by any of these vices, she finds herself able to travel with the various "pilgrims," scrutinize their behaviors, recognize the respective guides to each pathway for what they truly are, and visit the court of each of the various sovereigns, identifying their consorts and companions and inspecting the dubious rewards conferred upon their devotees.

In *David Simple*, we are introduced to individuals, specific "types," who fit the profiles of devotees of Avarice, Ambition, Pleasure, or Pride. Daniel represents the individual, of whom there are many, who first stops by the court of Avarice, gathering as much money as possible, before wending his way to the Palace of Pleasure, where "these Bags" of money provide "a very good Passport" (359). After years of dissipation in the Court of Pleasure, he ends his days with Disappointment, a "little ugly Monster" with "nasty Claws" (374). Miss Fanny Johnson appears a votary of the goddess Wealth; her father, of the goddess Ambition. The "Butterfly," with whom Cynthia travels from Bath to London, no doubt is traveling to the court of Vanity, a "so distant a Relation" of Pride (387). Varnish, known for his unfeeling good humor, is difficult to classify. Perhaps he characterizes some aspect of the court of Pleasure or perhaps even of Pride. Spatter represents a form of Pride, known as "*Spiteful Criticism*" or "*false Ridicule*" (380). And Orgueil is clearly meant to represent Pride in its guise of false Virtue. It is important to note that in *David Simple*, David is never ensnared by Pleasure, Ambition, Avarice, or Pride; he manages to escape from each, disillusioned perhaps, but free from any lasting ill effects or long-term entanglements. Ultimately, he finds Cynthia, Valentine, and Camilla, and together they travel the path to the palace of Benevolence . . . but they get lost along the way.

In *Volume the Last*, Fielding's use of allegory intensifies. David and his three friends now have children to worry about, and David entrusts the six children to people who he believes will secure their future, ensure their financial security, and guarantee them friends in high places. David believes these individuals represent Wealth, Virtue, and Friendship. Instead, they respectively represent Avarice, Pride, and Envy. But why is David blinded to the true nature of these individuals? The answer is simple: as regards himself, David Simple has no Avarice, Pride, and Envy, but in terms of his family, particularly his children, he possesses the flaws in full. However, these particular gods demand tribute in the form of sacrifices while providing no recompense in return.

The first child sacrificed is Peter, David's elder son—and this even prior to the child being born. As noted earlier, this is David's original sin, the beginning of all his future troubles and sorrows. This is the event, the loss, the act that reverberates throughout the novel, its residual effects engendering other (poor) actions on David's part and, subsequently, other (worse) losses; this originary event fashions relicts—that is, more sufferers—from its remains.

This first-born male is offered to Mr. Ratcliff, "a Man of Fortune" (248), the textual embodiment of Avarice. David becomes ensnared by Ratcliff because he fears that recent economic losses experienced by the extended family will adversely affect the future of his son, the child's older female sibling, and those siblings and cousins who have yet to be born. At the conclusion to *David Simple*, David, Camilla, Valentine, and Cynthia possessed a combined sum of £25,000: David has inherited £15,000 from the estates of his father and uncle; Camilla and Valentine are promised £5,000 each from the "old Gentleman" (246), their father, who has chosen to live with them. However, in the opening pages of *Volume the Last*, £17,000 of that money has already been lost or is under imminent threat. Prior to transferring the money to his children, the "old Gentleman" finds himself cheated of it; he spends another £500 in trying to recover it before accepting that "the whole Money was irretrievably lost" (246). Then, the £7,000 inheritance left to David by his uncle is challenged by "a young Fellow of a very large Fortune, who had, by his Father, been put Clerk to an Attorney, and, by that means, was very learned in all the Tricks of the Law" (249). Traveling to London on this latter business and accompanied by a very pregnant Camilla, David encounters Mr. Ratcliff, a former "Acquaintance" (248), who invites them to stay with him and his wife during their time in London. Childless, Mr. Ratcliff and his wife tempt David and Camilla with an offer that seemingly will secure the future of this unborn child: "And Mr. *Ratcliff* said, that should the Child prove a Boy, he would be his God-father; and Mrs. *Ratcliff* made the same offer, should the child prove a Girl" (248). The child proves a boy, whom they name "*Peter*, after his God-father," though Camilla would have preferred that her eldest son had "borne the Name of her much-loved Husband" (248). Later, Ratcliff promises "to adopt him [Peter] as Heir to his large Fortune" (250). Misguided in their thinking, yet genuinely believing this offer to be in the child's best interests, David and Camilla agree.

As the elder male child, Peter holds an important place within the Simple household, but particularly so because he will be adopted into another household. He is the cash cow, securing the economic future of his siblings. David and Camilla "considered a large Number of Children as a larger Number of Chances for . . . worldly Prosperity; since (as they observed) it seldom happens, but out of so many, ONE will be successful; and little indeed must their Children have profited by the Precepts and Example of such Parents, if the Prosperity of ONE should not be the Prosperity of ALL" (256). Due to Ratcliff's assurances, Peter holds the most promise of being that "ONE." Adoptions of children into childless families were not uncommon in the eighteenth century—after all, Jane Austen's brother Edward was adopted by distant cousins, the Knights—but little Peter is clearly unhappy, possibly because he ends up in a liminal position, being fully part of neither one family nor the other. Even his name causes the child to sigh, demonstrating "a Regret, that he was, by a strange Adoption, in a Manner excluded from his Birthright" (255); though Peter looks an exact miniature of his father, it is his younger brother who shares the father's name. Raised with his siblings until he is seven, at which point he is sent away to school, Peter is nonetheless segregated from them by his great expectations, his superior education (which Ratcliff insists upon), and his more expensive clothing (which Ratcliff provides). Yet, time passes and still the Ratcliffs neither legally adopt little Peter nor welcome him into their home, even for a short visit.

As Ratcliff is aligned with Avarice, it behooves us to travel down that allegorical path. The guide leading the way to the den of Avarice is Labour, whose deformity is unnoticed by the pilgrims he leads, as the patched and "tattered Rags" he wears are inscribed with "*I lead to Wealth*,"[84] the only thing the pilgrims can see or, rather, wish to see. Allegorically, Labour may be interpreted as the punishing labor required of others upon which Avarice relies for its wealth. The selfish nature of Avarice is further confirmed by the actions of the pilgrims, who kick those behind them, seeking to keep anyone from gaining on them or getting ahead of them. Outside Avarice's den, several "half-starved" sycophantic retainers greet the pilgrims, "bowing and scraping."[85] Once Labour unlocks the gates of the den—a prison, in reality—the pilgrims are met by "*Horror, Affright,* and *Anxiety*," who escort the pilgrims to Avarice herself, a figure so deformed that "she did not care to appear to the Eyes, even of her Followers, but hid herself behind a large Statue made of massy Gold." Next her, upon "a little Cushion made of Nettles," sits Care, handing out bags of gold embedded with her own sharp arrows,[86] which the pilgrims gather despite the pain.

Within *Volume the Last*, numerous indications align Ratcliff with Avarice. To begin with, David never makes money by following Ratcliff's financial advice—indeed, the contrary occurs, with David's money instead lining the pockets of Ratcliff's attorney, a Mr. Parker, or Ratcliff himself. Ratcliff's numerous promises of wealth or offers of financial assistance—the guaranteed success of a Chancery lawsuit, the adoption of little Peter as his heir, and a position for David worth "Six hundred Pounds a Year" (264)—never come to fruition. Indeed, after nine years of litigation, the Chancery suit is lost—à la Jarndyce versus Jarndyce—and David finds himself "worth to the Value of One hundred Pounds, and no more" (260), a truly meager sum with which to support five adults and six children; little Peter is neither adopted nor made Ratcliff's heir, and the lucrative position is taken by Ratcliff himself, an already wealthy man. David and his family become the very image of Labour, for "if ever Poverty and Oeconomy subsisted together, it was in this Family" (276). David's constant companions become "*Horror, Affright*, and *Anxiety*," as his worries about the future transform into immediate concerns about basic necessities, such as food, shelter, and medicine; he is loaded down with the sharp arrows of Care, though *sans* the promised bags of money: "when Poverty broke in upon us, I found, that to bear the Poverty of many, was almost insupportable.—Then, indeed, my Mind began to be seized with Fear—I was no longer my former Self—Pictures of the Distress of my Family began to succeed each other in my Mind, and Terror and Timidity conquered my better Judgment" (341). By believing that Ratcliff offers the way to wealth for his eldest son and, subsequently, for that son's siblings and cousins, David finds himself metaphorically enchained in the den of Avarice: "I found my Mind in such Chains as are much worse than any Slavery of the Body" (341). David has paid court to (one man's) Avarice, and he pays for it, with Cynthia and Valentine forced to emigrate in order to find work and with the remainder of the extended family doomed to abject poverty. As the monetary and human losses increase, David is finally forced to see Ratcliff for what he is. Thus, when little Peter dies of smallpox, David feels "Joy that his Son had escaped all Possibility of having his young Mind corrupted by being formed under such a Hand" (307) as Ratcliff's.

It is worth noting that the death of little Peter is not mourned; death represents an escape from "all future Misfortunes" (307). However, during his short lifetime, the fact that he has been given to the Ratcliffs remains a constant source of sorrow, to both the child and his parents. After little Peter's death, the other children—as well as Camilla, Valentine, and their father—become "relicts" of this original loss, suffering their own indignities and disturbances from the abuses of David's so-called friends. I would also argue that the repetitive nature of events (suffering at the hands of others followed by the release of death) of *Volume the Last* is not only melancholic, as was the case with *David Simple*, but also traumatic, representing the inability (on the part of the author, on the part of the characters) to understand deliberate cruelty toward the innocent and the vulnerable and to withstand the pain of witnessing the suffering of others. But the trauma is just beginning.

Another of David's "fancied Friends" (341) is Mr. Orgueil, who functions as the allegorical equivalent of Pride or Folly, though he masquerades as Virtue, and the child sacrificed this time is Cynthia and Valentine's only child, the frail and sickly little Cynthia, who has been entrusted into the care of David and Camilla while her parents are in the West Indies. In naming the character Orgueil, Fielding's familiarity with Edmund Spenser's allegorical epic, *The Faerie Queene*, becomes evident. (In addition, a character named Una after the original in *The Faerie Queene* may be found in Fielding and Jane Collier's *The Cry*). In Book I of *The Faerie Queene*, Duessa (the Roman Catholic Church) finds the Red Crosse Knight (St. George and England), his armor abandoned, resting under the verdant growth that surrounds a bubbling fountain, whose waters are tainted by self-conceit and complaisance. He drinks; he grows "carelesse of his health, and of his fame."[87] There, the giant Orgoglio (Pride) discovers him. "Disarmd, disgrast, and inwardly dismayde, / And eke so faint in every ioynt and vaine," Red Crosse is engaged in battle, saved only by Duessa's intervention, as she offers herself as consort to the giant. Red Crosse is thrown into "a Dongeon deepe," where he lingers, pale and weak, until released by King Arthur at the intervention of Una (the "True Church").[88] Red Crosse's own pride—for such it is that enchains him—stems from a "disdainful confidence in his own virtue and a weakness for the rewards to the flesh," according to Elizabeth Heale.[89] The darkness of the dungeon in which Red Crosse is imprisoned also indicates blindness, moral and religious, on his part. As is obvious from his name, Sarah Fielding's Mr. Orgueil similarly represents Pride, and like the Red Crosse Knight, David finds himself both imprisoned and blinded by Mr. Orgueil. After many slights and insults, a single act of kindness on the part of Orgueil "renewed *David*'s former Blindness, again enslaved his mind to *Orgueil*, and fixed his Chain as strong as ever" (284).

Orgueil's connection to Pride is further confirmed by Fielding's "A Vision." The presumed path to the palace of Virtue—in reality, the palace of Pride—is led by a guide who herself purports to be Virtue. Immensely tall, her head touching the clouds, her multiple arms strong and seemingly secure, Virtue carries her devotees on what they believe to be the path of righteousness. However, the spectator, the only one who can see clearly, knows that this lofty image is an illusion. Instead, the devotees are carried by a dwarf, with an outsize head and shadowy arms, whose name is Deception. Once at the rather nondescript palace, for "*Pride* had many other Ways of gratifying her Votaries, besides that of sumptuous Palaces and magnificent Appearances" (377), the pilgrims enter and find the monarch. Seated on her throne, Pride's gigantic head lies supported by the mighty arm of her father, Folly. Like Milton's Sin, Pride has sprung forth from her father's head and mated with him, bearing hideous offspring that are bound to their mother's girdle with strong cords. The children are Insolence, Envy, Ill Nature, Cruelty, and Tyranny. Her "favorite Daughter *Envy*" has also engaged in an "incestuous Amour with her Grandfather *Folly*," and she subsequently gives birth to "*Malignity, Spiteful Criticism, false Ridicule*."[90] The pilgrims now participate in a ceremony, by which an image given by one of the inhabitants of the palace—such as Insolence or Envy—is screwed into their bosoms, wherein they believe themselves virtuous by dint of their pain.

Orgueil represents both Pride and Folly. Orgueil's lack of faith in religion, coupled with his supreme faith in himself, tallies with Spenser's giant Orgoglio, as does Orgueil's windy pronouncements about his own virtues and his essential goodness. However, the term "Folly" is often associated with Mr. Orgueil. After learning of Orgueil's true nature from Spatter, David bemoans the perfidy of Orgueil: "is it all delusion, and am I as much deceived in his *Sense* as in his *Goodness*! For surely nothing but the greatest Folly could make a Creature, who must every day, nay, every hour in the day, be conscious of a *thousand Failings*, and feel a *thousand Infirmities*, fancy himself a *Deity*, and contemplate his own Perfections" (57–58). And that "favorite Daughter Envy" is, of course, Mrs. Orgueil, whose envy of Cynthia transforms to hatred: "*Cynthia*, who, from a Spriteliness and Vivacity of Temper, generally carried the Lead in Conversation, soon became the Object of her Envy, and from thence a most inveterate Hatred of *Cynthia* took root in her mind" (258). As the daughter of Envy (Mrs. Orgueil) and Folly (Mr. Orgueil), the ill-tempered, peevish, and thoroughly spoiled Henrietta-Cassandra may be considered Ill-Nature.

Due to her "ill State of Health" (264), little Cynthia requires the healing waters of Bath, as "the only Chance she had of being cured" (265). Mrs. Orgueil invites the child to accompany her and her own daughter to Bath, as Henrietta-Cassandra requires a playmate. Urged on by Camilla, Cynthia allows her daughter to go, despite severe misgivings. Forced to ride on a hard box on the carriage floor; sent to bed in a wet, cold garret from which she acquires a "violent Cold" (271); teased and tormented by the willful Henrietta, though ill; and then beaten with "uncommon Severity" (271) by Mrs. Orgueil, little Cynthia dies within a week of her journey to Bath. Envious of Cynthia and, subsequently, envious of Cynthia's daughter, Mrs. Orgueil has vented her rage on the child. After the death of little Cynthia, Camilla is understandably reluctant to visit Mrs. Orgueil, but David insists, once Camilla's father becomes ill, as "we must not, at present, cease to grasp even the least glimmering Hope of Friendship" (278). Even after Mrs. Orgueil's egregious display of heartlessness and cruelty, David still believes that he possesses "a Friend in her Husband" (278). Through each "Act of Kindness" on the part of Mr. Orgueil, small as each is and selfishly inspired, Mr. Orgueil "again fixed *David*'s Chains" (286), from which death alone releases him.

Three of the remaining children quickly follow the fates of little Peter and little Cynthia. Little Fanny dies of "a violent Fever, occasioned by over heating herself in Play" (294); "little *David* sickened of Measles" (325), given to him by the redoubtable Henrietta-Cassandra; and little Joan, infected by the measles but then recovering, lives on in a weakened condition until dying of "a galloping Consumption" (325). The only child to survive is David and Camilla's eldest daughter, also named Camilla. Born prior to David's encounter with Avarice in the form of Ratcliff and his reacquaintance with Pride and Folly in the form of Mr. Orgueil, little Camilla alone of all the children remains untainted and thus survives. The question, then, is this: should David Simple be condemned for walking on the paths of Avarice and Pride? Yes and no.

Early in David's troubles, the usually observant narrator remarks that "David's Understanding never suffered him to go astray from the Path that led to his real Happiness" (268). However, clearly, he has strayed—not for himself, but rather for those he loves. In thinking that his children's future depends upon wealth greater than the family possesses, David is guilty of Avarice; in believing that he knows better than Providence what is best for the children, David succumbs to Pride. Paradoxically, although he lacks confidence in his ability to provide for his children, he arrogantly assumes that he knows the answer: that influential "friends" will provide. And so he has visited the den of Avarice and the palace of Pride, been stung by Care's arrows, and had his loved ones poisoned by Envy—all because he did not trust himself with the care of the children. And so he loses them, one by one. But Cynthia too must be condemned, as she permits the intimacy between the Orgueils and her own extended family to continue, despite obvious indications of the spitefulness of Mrs. Orgueil. The narrator notes that "if *Cynthia* had strenuously urged them [David, Camilla, and Valentine] to have been guided by her Judgment, an Intimacy between Persons whose Minds were so utterly incapable of having the least Sympathy with each other, would have been dropped, whatever might have been the Consequence" (252). But Cynthia doesn't object because she too is reluctant to sever any connections that might lead to a prosperous future for the children. In this, then, the parents have failed because they willfully blinded themselves into thinking of Avarice as Wealth, Pride and Folly as Virtue, and Envy as Friendship. Perhaps Camilla says it best: "And now her Folly strongly glared before her Eyes, and she condemned herself in that she had dared to imaging that she knew better than Providence, what was most for her good" (298) and, we might add, what was most for the good of the children.

Yet, Fielding would not have us condemn David or any of his friends. A fifth path exists in "A Vision" that leads to the Palace of Benevolence. Guided by Patience, a "small Party" of cheerful pilgrims walks the road to the Palace, with everyone helping "his next Neighbour as much as lay in his power."[91] Patience leads them to Truth, who conducts them onward to the palace, where the monarch

Benevolence, also known as "*real Love*," sits between "*soft Compassion*" and "*gentle Tenderness*." Those within the palace exhibit "the Height of Friendship,"[92] and though "Error and Infirmities even here crept in, . . . they served only to promote the Humility and Penitence of the Offenders, and exert the Compassion and Good-Nature of all the rest."[93] At the Palace of Benevolence, a court where Patience, Truth, Compassion, and Tenderness abide, someone like David Simple would not be condemned: "The Sentence, *They deserve no Pity because it is their own Fault*, however common it may be in the World, was never heard in this Place; on the contrary, Compassion was here heightened, in proportion, as the Grief of the Sufferer must be the greater."[94] In other words, looking out for the interest of children, David Simple lost his way, to his unending sorrow, and his attendant suffering and grief urges compassion on the part of readers.

As Ann Jessie Van Sant writes of the novel of sensibility, "ethical and literary meanings of plot become infused in an identification of plot with assaultive strategies for discovering the heart, for provoking response."[95] Within Fielding's fictive world, the trauma of earthly suffering followed by death—the loss of a loved one, the loss of many loved ones—repeats itself, over and over, with the innocent and vulnerable the only victims; each fictional death "assaults" the hearts of readers while incrementally adding to the narrative trauma and amplifying it. Unlike *David Simple*, wherein the narrative moves from melancholia to normative mourning to cure, *Volume the Last* offers only one form of solace: death itself.

The *David Simple* novels offer no hope of an afterlife, either in the form of a substantial soul, awaiting Resurrection Day, or in the shape of the Lockean conscious, free-floating and eternal. It is not that Fielding does not believe in an afterlife, but rather that the existence of an afterlife is immaterial, at least within the fictive worlds of these two novels. Indeed, the absence of an afterlife proves a source of solace to the characters in the novel; the nothingness of death offers peace and safety. As David Simple says regarding the loss of his wife, "That I have lost *Camilla* is my Pleasure" (342), or as the author writes at the conclusion to *Volume the Last*, "But I chuse to think he [David] is escaped from the Possibility of falling into any future Afflictions, and that neither the Malice of his pretended Friends, nor the Sufferings of his real ones, can ever again rend and torment his honest Heart" (342). Children and true friends function as the causes and effects of David's missteps; his original mistake, made with the best of intentions, and its subsequent consequences become like ripples on a lake, with an ever-widening sphere of damage. Relicts of this original loss take the form of suffering bodies, who can only be released from their suffering through death. Mirroring the older cultural response to death while simultaneously acknowledging the unbearable pain that the relict endures as the suffering *remnant* of earlier actions or as the sole surviving *remains* of the dead, death becomes the ultimate "friend"—in fact, the only true friend in the end.

CONCLUSION

Fielding's novelistic innovations, including her willingness to merge the realist novel with other literary genres, such as drama, allegory, history, and satire, suggest that the use of allegory in *Volume the Last* is experimental in nature, meant to highlight the nature of her protagonist's failings and, in turn, spur her readers to new levels of sympathetic response. Specifically, while the suffering and numerous deaths of innocent characters—mainly children, the elderly, or the emotionally delicate—are no doubt meant to engender extreme emotional response on the part of readers, the use of allegory suggests that Fielding thought that something more was needed: that readers needed to learn to direct their sympathy not just toward the innocent, but also toward those well-intentioned humans whose actions go horribly awry, adversely and fatally affecting others. Fielding's allegorical lesson teaches readers to blame David—and then to forgive him.

4

"IT IS ALL FOR YOU!"

Dying for Love in Samuel Richardson's
The History of Sir Charles Grandison (1753)

"AND DO *YOU* WISH IT TOO, Chevalier?—Do *you* wish to see me wounded?—To see my heart bleeding at my arm, I warrant. Say, can *you* be so hard-hearted?" So asks Clementina della Porretta of Sir Charles Grandison, the eponymous hero of Samuel Richardson's final novel. When Sir Charles doesn't answer, instead withdrawing to the window and averting his face, she adds, "Will it, will it, comfort *you* to see me bleed?—Come then, *be* comforted; I *will* bleed."[1]

The relationship between Richardson's "good man"[2] and Clementina, youngest child and only daughter of a wealthy, aristocratic Bolognese family, is a peculiar one, particularly in view of Sir Charles's characteristic attentiveness to duty and social proprieties. As the (physical and moral) savior of the youngest della Porretta son and as honorary English tutor to Clementina and two of her brothers, the punctilio-obsessed Sir Charles entangles himself in highly uncharacteristic ways with the della Porretta family, so much so that he feels obligated to marry the daughter once she becomes mad. Unlike his usual cautious self, Sir Charles has spent considerably more time with the eighteen-year-old Clementina, in his role as her tutor and "fourth brother" (III.xx; 2:122), than would seem advisable, particularly in the case of so prudent a man, particularly as he is so eminently unsuitable as a marriage prospect from the perspective of the family, being English, Protestant, a commoner (though baronet), and (relatively speaking) poor. When Sir Charles eventually departs from Bologna, Clementina's lovesick madness forces the family to recall him, offering him their daughter's hand in marriage, despite serious objections on their part. Unaware of the exact articles of settlement proposed for the marriage, though fearful of the worst— "he was afraid that the articles of Residence and Religion would not be easily compromised" (III.xx; 2:129)—Sir Charles nonetheless immediately returns to

Bologna, where his subsequent refusal to concede to the proffered terms exacerbates Clementina's madness and ultimately results in his banishment. Twenty months later, the family, desperate to restore their daughter's sanity, again urges Sir Charles's return to Bologna, willing to concede to many, if not all, of Sir Charles's wishes.

Despite all this, Sir Charles and Clementina never do marry. Instead, they become textually positioned as spouses, albeit widower and widow, respectively. Specifically, Sir Charles considers himself a "*bachelor-widower*" (V.xl; 2:650), while initially Clementina views herself as his widow and later functions in the role of (dead) first wife. Their continuing relationship is based upon the peculiar premise that the other person is metaphorically dead; each exists as the other's "relict." Nonetheless, despite Richardson's textual conceit, Sir Charles seems unwilling to play the part of grieving widower—at least not for long. The roles, then, of relict and decedent fall to Clementina alone. David L. Eng and David Kazanjian write, "loss is inseparable from what remains, for what is lost is known only by what remains of it, how these remains are produced, read, and sustained."[3] If we "read" the relict that is Clementina by what remains—that is, her damaged mind and abused body—we are confronted by the "scars, ruins, remnants, and so on" inflicted upon her lovelorn person for the sole reason that she loves Sir Charles.[4] Because of him, she suffers from madness; for him, she endures being lanced, blooded, bloodied, beaten, and straightjacketed—all for love. As Clementina informs Sir Charles, "they are very severe with me! . . . [but] *It is all for You!*" (III.xxviii; 2:222). Metaphorically, she dies for him; she dies for love.

This chapter first examines Clementina as Sir Charles's widow, a relict who bears—in the residual effects of a damaged mind and an abused body—the enduring marks of traumatic love. It then explores Clementina's role as Sir Charles's (dead) first wife, focusing on Clementina's textual haunting of Sir Charles's new love and "second" wife, Harriet Byron, and on Clementina's close association with death. In *Grandison*, Richardson abandons the substantial soul that informed Clarissa's posthumous existence. Instead, Lockean consciousness dominates, with Harriet and Clementina sharing one soul between them, with the mad Clementina conversing with a spectral Sir Charles, and with Clementina becoming something "other" than herself as well as "othered," just as death is "other" and "othered." The fact that the text metaphorically locates death in the figure of a madwoman speaks also to the epistemological dislocation that is occurring during this time within British culture as regards death and the afterlife.

"WHAT WOE WAS THERE IN IT!": THE LANGUAGE OF LOVE

After an absence of approximately twenty months,[5] Sir Charles Grandison returns to Italy at the urging of certain members of the della Porretta family—Jeronymo, the marchioness, and Father Marescotti—as Clementina remains "earnest still to see him" (IV.vii; 2:294), and they hope that by indulging her, "the noble creature's reason" (IV.vii; 2:300) may be, at least partially, restored. At her first meeting with Sir Charles, unaware as yet that he has returned, Clementina enters the room, wearing mourning attire, the very image of a grieving widow: "Her eyes were cast on the ground. Her robes were black and flowing. A veil of black gause half covered her face. What woe was there in it!" (V.i; 2:469). Although Clementina never terms herself a widow, her attire proclaims her as one, as does the lengthy duration of time that she has seemingly worn "deep mourning."[6] A 1783 engraving by Anthony Walker, taken from a drawing by Thomas Stothard, depicts Clementina attired in deepest mourning (see figure 4.1). Her "black and flowing" gown swirls about her, its long train coiling about the hem of her petticoat; on her head, she wears a muslin cap, over which a thick, heavy "veil of black gause" drapes. Clearly, Stothard interpreted Richardson's description of Clementina's clothing as indicative of widowhood and so depicted her in first or deep mourning. Her widow's weeds attest to the fact that Clementina clearly viewed herself as married to Sir Charles and that the marriage was (spiritually, psychically) consummated prior to his leaving Italy, and that she now views him as among the dead. As Sir Charles's relict—or at the very least as the relic of the ill-fated romance between Sir Charles and herself—Clementina functions textually as what "remains," and, notably, what remains is "my brain wounded, my health impaired" (V.xxiv; 2:566).

A traumatic experience is one that "is experienced too soon, too unexpectedly, to be fully known and is therefore not available to consciousness until it imposes itself, repeatedly, in the nightmares and repetitive actions of the survivor."[7] That is, the conscious mind is unable to comprehend and/or assimilate the experience—indeed, it may not remember it (the experience being too disturbing to recall) or may even not view it as traumatic while it is occurring (the individual being intent upon survival and/or unable to comprehend fully what is happening). Yet, the unconscious mind seeks to express this experience, to understand it, to move beyond it, and so it repeats the event or series of events, through dreams (nightmares), hallucinations, or metaphorically representative actions. The narrative of trauma, then, is "a kind of double telling . . . between the story of the unbearable nature of an event and the story of the unbearable nature of its survival."[8] Richardson would have us believe that Clementina's madness originates

Figure 4.1 *Sir Charles Grandison* (London: Heinemann, 1902). Engraving by Anthony Walker from a drawing by Thomas Stothard (1783). "Quitting her mother's hand, now changing pale, now reddening, she arose, and threw her arms about her Camilla." Collection of K. M. Oliver. Photograph by Charles Parkhill, 2017.

in the conflict between her religious faith and her love of Sir Charles, a heretic in her eyes, and certainly this conflict is an integral part of her years-long malady. However, if the chief identifying mark of trauma is repetition of an unprocessed event,[9] then the origins of Clementina's trauma appear to lie elsewhere—that is, in her silencing by others, beginning with Sir Charles, and by the unexplained (to her) nature of his repeated absences. In order to demonstrate this, this section examines Clementina's role as relict through the focal point of language—specifically, through her sudden inability to speak English, a language in which she was formerly proficient, and through the language of her abused body.

The love affair between Sir Charles and Clementina, if we can call it that (as it is never certain that Sir Charles returns Clementina's ardent love),[10] commences sometime during several months of English language lessons, with Sir Charles as tutor and with Clementina and her two brothers, the Bishop and Jeronymo, as his pupils. From the beginning, Clementina shows great aptitude for her studies: "*She* also called me her tutor; and, tho' she was not half so often present at the lectures as they were, made a greater proficiency than either of her brothers" (III.xx; 2:123). The Englishwoman, Mrs. Beaumont, later comments, "I was surprised at her proficiency in my native tongue," though Beaumont attributes this remarkable competence to Sir Charles's "admirable manner of teaching" (III.xxiv; 2:165), searching for a telltale blush on Clementina's pale cheek. However, all this occurs prior to Sir Charles's departure for England; twenty months later, when he returns, Clementina is unable to speak English or, at best, can speak it only haltingly: "Sometimes she aimed to speak to me in English: But her ideas were too much unfixed, and her memory too much shattered, to make herself understood for a sentence together, in the tongue she had so lately learned, and for some time disused" (V.iii; 2:481). At first glance, it appears that madness has robbed her of her newly acquired language—though she remains fluent in Italian, French, and Latin—but even when she regains some semblance of mental normality, she remains unable to speak Sir Charles's native tongue: "But, Chevalier, I have quite forgot my English. I shall never recover it" (V.iii; 2:482). Later, when she ventures to England, with only her maid and a young male attendant, she does so unable to converse in the language. Jeronymo writes to Sir Charles in alarm, lamenting how little "she knows of the English tongue!" (VII.xvii; 3:327), and when Sir Charles meets Clementina in London, he offers to speak, on her behalf, to "the gentlewoman of the house" where she is staying, "as you have almost forgotten your English" (VII.xxvi; 3:344). Clementina speaks in French to Mr. and Mrs. Selby, as they "spoke not Italian" (VII.xxxi; 3:357), and Harriet must speak in "broken Italian" (VII.xxx; 3:354) to Clementina. It is not that Clementina has forgotten English words, syntax, or grammar, for, as Harriet notes, "she reads English extremely well"

(VII.xlv; 3:416). It is that she can no longer speak it. But why this loss of verbal fluency in a language in which she had formerly "delighted to speak" (IV.vii; 2:296)?

Cathy Caruth suggests that, "there is . . . perhaps, a certain loss of self implicit in the speaking of another's language."[11] Richardson surely expected his readers to intuit that Clementina's proficiency in and love of English stems from her (initially unconscious) love for Sir Charles. Yet, in learning English and in loving Sir Charles, she loses something of herself, whether it be her prejudices or her pride (in both of which she abounds), or the boundaries between self and another/Other. In Clementina's case, however, the problem is not simply the acquisition of the beloved's language, but the beloved's sudden and unexplained unwillingness to converse with her in that language (which, for her, is the language of love). Having given up/offered something of herself, having spoken using the beloved's words, Clementina's English-language conversations with Sir Charles are abruptly halted, indefinitely postponed, always promised in the future, but never arriving. The conversation becomes determinedly one-sided, with Clementina left literally speaking to herself. As the marchioness notes, Clementina has been "taking lessons for learning a tongue, that never . . . was likely to be of use to her" (III.xx; 2:125), but not for the reasons the marchioness assumes.

Let us retrace Sir Charles's (textual) footsteps. After residing with the della Porrettas for months on end, Sir Charles leaves Bologna for Vienna, not because he believes Clementina to be in love with him and not because he believes insurmountable obstacles exist to a marriage between them (though he does believe both at different times), but rather because Clementina's spoken words in English profoundly disturb him. The occasion is the advances made in Scotland and England by the rebel forces under Catholic Charles Stuart (Bonnie Prince Charlie), in his attempt to regain the English throne for the Stuarts.[12] The della Porrettas—and indeed, all the Italians of Sir Charles's acquaintance—rejoice in the Young Pretender's progress, and they let Sir Charles know this: "Hardly any thing else was talked of, in Italy, but the progress, and supposed certainty of success, of the young invader. I was often obliged to stand the triumphs and exultations of persons of rank and figure; being known to be warm in the interest of my country. I had a great deal of this kind of spirit to contend with, even in this more moderate Italian family; and this frequently brought on debates which I would gladly have avoided holding: But it was impossible" (III.xx; 2:124). Worse, Clementina joins these debates, and damningly, she does so in English: "Every new advice from England revived the disagreeable subject; for the success of the rebels, it was not doubted, would be attended by the restoration of what they called the Catholic religion: And Clementina particularly pleased herself, that then her *heretic tutor* would take refuge in the bosom of his holy mother, the church: And she delighted to say things of this nature in the language I was teaching her, and which, by this time, she spoke very intelligibly" (III.xx; 2:124). It is not so much that Clementina has joined with her compatriots in celebrating the advances of "the young invader," though this is problem enough, but that Clementina has "particularly pleased herself" by teasing Sir Charles with the possibility of his religious conversion, in the event of Charles Stuart's victory, and "she delighted to say things of this nature" in *English*. At this point in the text, Sir Charles determines to leave Italy and "to retire to Vienna, or to some one of the German courts" (III.xx; 2:124), safe from the "triumphs and exultations of persons of rank and figure" and safe from Clementina's English-language prognostications of his future religious conversion.

Clementina's abuse of language—an abuse, at least, from Sir Charles's point of view—is immediately followed by mention of Olivia's indiscreet talk: "the displeasure of Olivia against me began to grow serious, and to be talked of, even by herself, with less discretion than was consistent with her high spirit, her noble birth, and ample fortune" (III.xx; 2:124). Presumably, Olivia threatens Sir Charles with words in Italian, not in English, but her indiscreet "talk," positioned as it is immediately after mention of Clementina's "delight" in saying "things" in English that torment Sir Charles, suggests that Clementina's proficiency in the English language profoundly disturbs Sir Charles as much if not more than Olivia's indiscreet talk. It is not that Sir Charles—or Richardson for that matter—is against women's speech, but there is an unruliness associated with the speech of the Italian women that Harriet Byron's "amiable frankness!" (III.xvii; 2:91) in letters and conversation does not possess.

Sir Charles first communicates his intention of "quitting Italy" (III.xx; 2:124) to the marchioness, who begs for him to delay for "some weeks" (III.xx; 2:125), ostensibly to probe whether Sir Charles "was in Love with her Clementina" and to ascertain if Clementina's rejection of "every [marital] proposal that had been made her" (III.xx; 2:125) proceeds from her being in love with Sir Charles. During this interval, aware of Sir Charles's impending departure, Clementina displays the first signs of madness, which are "silence" and symptoms of "deep melancholy" when with others. However, "she generally assumed a chearful air while she was with *him*, but said little; yet seemed pleased with every thing he said to her; and the little she did answer, 'tho he spoke in Italian or French, was in her newly acquired language" (III.xx; 2:125). When at last Sir Charles departs for Germany, Clementina offers him her cheek to kiss, saying, "God preserve my tutor where-ever he sets his foot (and, in English, God convert you too, Chevalier!)" (III.xx; 2:126).

Sir Charles having fled, Clementina's madness enters a new phase, one in which she converses to an invisible other. Initially, this other is herself, but later it is (the presumably dead) Sir Charles. The first instance of this one-way conversation occurs within days of Sir Charles's departure. Sitting in her chamber, "setting her chair ... over-against a closet in the room, after a profound silence, she bent forwards, and, in a low voice, seemed to be communing with a person in the closet.—'And you say he is actually gone? Gone for ever? No, not for ever!'" (III.xx; 2:127). Because her servant cannot understand English (and it is she who reports this conversation), we must assume Clementina is speaking in Italian, but to whom? Apparently to herself, which suggests an inability to obtain answers from others. Clementina's words express uncertainty over Sir Charles's absence, whether short term, long term, or "for ever!" While Clementina's love of English is symptomatic of her love for Sir Charles, Sir Charles's refusal to listen to her uncomfortable (for him) attempts to convert him, using English, suggests a desire on his part to silence her—or at the very least not to listen to her—for she uses his own language against him.

When Sir Charles subsequently returns from Vienna, unaware of the marital conditions to be imposed but suspecting their nature, he attempts to circumvent the della Porrettas by speaking directly with Clementina. However, she refuses to listen, precisely because she knows that there "are preliminaries to be settled; and, till they are, I that *know* there are, do not think myself at liberty to hear you upon *any* subject that may tend to prepossession" (III.xxv; 2:179). Of course, this is correct behavior on her part, and so Sir Charles concurs, though he later writes to Dr. Bartlett that her "modesty" was a source of discouragement to him (III.xxv; 2:180). When Sir Charles subsequently rejects the conditions imposed upon him by the della Porrettas, Clementina takes the rejection personally: "*To be despised*!—And by an English Protestant! Who can bear that!" She becomes "spiritless, her eyes fixed, and as gloomy as ever"; she responds with silence to questions asked of her, but when she does finally speak, she does so "with wildness." In her "passion and hurry," she "speaks to herself, and answers herself" (III.xxvi; 2:185). Clementina's self-conversations seek to account for Sir Charles's rejection of her, not once but twice, and they attempt to provide her with knowledge that she lacks, precisely because no one takes the time to inform her. As her mother says, "We took it for granted, that *she* knew it all, because *we* did" (III.xxviii; 2:206).

Twice more, Sir Charles attempts to speak with Clementina, but both conversations are aborted: the first because she is being blooded; the second because her mother interrupts it, fearful that Clementina will capitulate to Sir Charles's terms, and because Sir Charles censors his own comments, ostensibly out of consideration for Clementina's malady. Attempting yet again to gain Clementina's approval of his conditions, he halts in mid-speech, turning to her mother: "May I presume, madam, to put the question in my own way?—But yet I think it may distress the dear Lady, and not answer the desirable end, if I may not have hope of *your* interest in my favour; and of the acquiescence of the Marquis and your sons with my proposals" (III.xxviii; 2:210). Interestingly, Sir Charles's principle concern, in this and in the earlier conversation with Clementina, is to present *his* terms and conditions, which in turn, if agreed to, would require that Clementina deliberately rebel against her family's wishes and her own inclinations. No one asks Clementina what *she* thinks or wishes; both Sir Charles and the della Porrettas rigidly insist upon their diametrically opposed conditions of marriage. In sum, Sir Charles will not or cannot speak to Clementina directly (in her own language or in his), prohibited by social mores and concerns for her mental health, angry della Porrettas, and his own disinclination to offer compromise or conciliation. At this point, Sir Charles is banished from the della Porretta household, leaving Clementina to seek her own answers, though still "earnest for an interview" with Sir Charles (III.xxviii; 2:201). Sir Charles is not permitted to "take leave of the dear Lady" (III.xxviii; 2:214), who every moment, every day, expects to see him. However, Clementina does manage to get a letter to Sir Charles, complaining of her family's harshness toward her, warning him of the danger threatened toward him by her family, particularly her eldest brother, the General, and urging Sir Charles to "Get away to England, as soon as you can" (III.xxviii; 2:222).

After Sir Charles's subsequent departure from Bologna, Clementina's one-way conversational circle extends to the "converse of the pen"[13]—that is, to her epistolary correspondence. First, Clementina writes to Sir Charles in Latin, but Madame Sforza, observing her through the closet door, quickly steps in and, "taking up the paper, read it, and took it out of the closet with her" (III.xxxi; 2:248). Later, Mrs. Beaumont informs Sir Charles that Clementina "is often for writing Letters to you; but when what she writes is privately taken from her, she makes no enquiry about it, but takes a new sheet, and begins again" (III.xxxii; 2:254). Most of the time, however, Madame Sforza and Laurana have "confined her hands" (III.xxxii; 2:253), rendering Clementina unable to write at all.

As noted previously, repetition, "the unwitting reenactment of an event that one cannot simply leave behind,"[14] is one of defining characteristics of trauma.[15] In the fictional Clementina's case, trauma appears rooted in the forever-unfinished conversation with Sir Charles and in his abrupt, unexplained, and repeated disappearances. Sir Charles departs for Vienna without providing a reason, and he does not mention whether he will return. When later he refuses the terms of marriage that the della Porrettas offer him, they deny him the opportunity to have a parting conversation with their daughter, though "She begs but for one interview; one parting interview; and she promises to make herself easy" (III.xxxi; 2:246). The repetitive nature of this absence/disappearance continues long after Sir Charles has returned to England. On her various journeys "to Urbino, to Rome, to Naples; then back to Florence, then to Milan, to Turin," Clementina "expected to see him at the end of every journey" (III.xxxii; 2:256)—and does not. This experience repeats, even when she is sequestered within the walls of a convent: "one of the sisters, to try her, having officiously asked her to go with her into the parlour, where she said, she would be allowed to converse through the grate with a *certain* English gentleman, her impatience, on her disappointment, made her more ungovernable than they had ever known her; for she had been for two hours before meditating what she would say to him" (IV.vii; 2:295). In *Beyond the Pleasure Principle*, Freud recalls a child's game of *fort-da* (gone-there), wherein the child reacts to his mother's absences by making a wooden reel with a string disappear and return. According to Freud, the child "compensated himself" for the "renunciation" that he "had made in allowing his mother to go away without protesting," "by himself staging the disappearance and return of the objects within his reach."[16] In this way, the child attempts to gain mastery of the situation through staged repetition. In Clementina's case, however, she possesses no such control over the situation, as her innumerable expectations for the "return" of Sir Charles—falsely encouraged by others in order to test her mentally and emotionally—are forever met with his absence.

It is unclear precisely what Clementina wishes to say to Sir Charles in this long-desired interview. She has already procured a statement from him (written by her and signed by him) stating that if they married, he would allow her to retain her religion, maintain a confessor, and remain in Italy (III.xxviii; 2:207). She has already assured him that her desire for his conversion was not for her own sake but for the sake of his immortal soul (III.xxvii; 2:212). And she has requested Mrs. Beaumont to ask Sir Charles not to "think of marrying till he acquaints me with it" and not to "marry a woman unworthy of him," as that would be "a disgrace . . . to me!" (III.xxxii; 2:255). Clementina will say these things yet again in her final refusal of him. In fact, her final refusal adds nothing that she has not already expressed previously. More likely, it is Sir Charles's part of the conversation that she feels is missing, incomplete, interrupted. Specifically, he never says what she wishes him to say—that he loves her above all women. And he will never say it, though Clementina now begins to treat him as her (deceased) spouse.

On the evening of Sir Charles's dismissal from the della Porretta residence, Clementina dreams of Sir Charles's death, recalling it the next day: "In the Orangegrove, I thought I stumbled over the body of a dead man!" When questioned whose body it was, she replies, "Don't you know who was threatened? And was not Somebody here to-night? And was not Somebody to sup here? And *is* he here?" (III.xxx; 2:241). He is not. Interestingly, we are presented with death, but no dying occurs and no corpse may be found, replicating textually and figuratively the cultural disappearance of the dying/dead body. From this point on, Clementina becomes Sir Charles's relict, his widow, with Sir Charles existing as a ghost who, interestingly enough, now accommodates her need for conversation, even to the point of dominating that conversation, as Mrs. Beaumont relates: "She took it into her poor head several times this day, and perhaps it will hold, to sit in particular places, to put on attentive looks, as if she were listening to somebody. She sometimes smiled, and seemed pleased; looked up, as if to somebody, and spoke English. I have no doubt, tho' I was not present when she assumed these airs, and talked English, but her disordered imagination brought before her her tutor instructing her in that tongue" (III.xxxii; 2:255).

According to Foucault, "language and madness are linked; they are part of a tangled and inextricable fabric from which there can ultimately be no separation." He notes that "Every man who speaks enjoys, at least in secret, the absolute freedom of being mad and, conversely, every man who is mad and seems, by that very fact, to have become absolutely foreign in the language of men is also a prisoner in the closed universe of language"; to wit, "madness, even when it is silent, always passes through language."[17] Specifically, madness operates within a "verbal matrix," and "if we have difficulty communicating with the insane, it's not because they don't talk but because they talk too much, in a supercharged language, a kind of tropical abundance of signs in which all the pathways of the world are jumbled together."[18] In other words, the world of the mad is constructed by and through language, as is the world of the sane.

In Clementina's case, madness expresses itself through various language modes: silence, unintelligible raving (of which Richardson only tells, not shows), disconnected speech that nonetheless conveys potent meaning ("O what eloquence in her disorder!" [III.xxvi; 2:193]); and through conversations with invisible others (self and Sir Charles), when all attempts to converse in person or in writing are repeatedly thwarted. It would seem, however, that Clementina's madness does not simply express itself through a verbal matrix, but that language itself—the English language, specifically—has caused it, for as her speaking in English with an imaginary Sir Charles demonstrates, she has internalized him, swallowed him, incorporated him;[19] no cure for her madness can occur until she has expelled this ingested "other." If we recall the discussion of mourning and melancholia from Chapter 3, the melancholic finds herself unwilling to surrender the love object and, in consequence, sustains the love relationship by ego identification with the beloved (lost) object through incorporation, a metaphorical ingesting of the love object, so that "in spite of the conflict with the loved person the love-relation need not be given up."[20] In this way, the relationship with the lost and loved object is maintained; the love object is itself retained in surrogate form. However, because the incorporated other is an object of ambivalence, deeply loved yet somehow considered unworthy of this love, a love–hate relationship occurs. Subsequently, repetitive suffering allows the incorporated "other" representation, and it offers scenarios for re-enacting the ambivalence felt toward the incorporated "other." Such suffering, such madness, ends only when the ego determines that the incorporated "other"—and by implication the original love object—is no longer worthy and is expelled from the psyche. Clementina suffers greatly, both mentally and physically, the object of her ambivalence being Sir Charles himself (as incorporated "other" and in the flesh), because he will not concede or compromise, because he will not speak to her using the language of love.

Notably, it is only upon Sir Charles's return to Italy from England, when Clementina obtains the long wished-for opportunity to converse with him, that she finds herself unable to speak the English language, and her attempts to regain command of the language, to be taught it again, are refused by Sir Charles on the grounds of her mental fragility. Clementina asks, "Are you willing, Sir, to undertake your pupil again," but Sir Charles dissuades her: "But at present, the thought, the memory, it would require you to exert, would perplex you. I am afraid the study would rather retard, than forward your recovery." When she insists, he asks her to bring an "English book" to him, but she forgets "her purpose" (V.v; 2:488). She never does have the long-awaited English-language conversation with Sir Charles, preferring to *write* her renunciation of his marriage offer and to do so in *Italian* (V.xxiv; 2:564).[21] While, at a superficial level, Clementina achieves her heart's desire—that is, for Sir Charles to offer to marry her—at a deeper level, this victory is shallow, as Sir Charles never professes love for her, and so she finally *begins* to let go of her passion. For Clementina, the English language, despite its "hard and crabbed" (III.xxii.144) nature (for such is how she describes the poetry of *Paradise Lost*), is the language of love, and if the beloved will not speak that language back, then the conversation must always be one-sided. Better not to speak the language at all. Better to become the widow or deceased first wife than the scorned lover, and Clementina does exist as the damaged relict, the battered remains, of Sir Charles's actions and of a love affair that was determinedly one-sided. In the end, Clementina's sudden inability to speak the English language signals both acceptance of the fact that Sir Charles does not return her love and of her attempts to expel Sir Charles as internalized "other." Although her thoughts continue to dwell upon Sir Charles, Clementina begins her cure.

* * *

The body also may be read within the matrix of language, as Foucault notes: "the body, the body itself, is like a language mode. Freud, that great listener, clearly understood that our body, much more than our mind, was a wit, that it was a kind of master craftsman of metaphors and took advantage of all the resources, all the richness, all the poverty of our language."[22] Specifically, the body literalizes psychic trauma, and it does so principally through metaphor. For instance, Foucault provides the example of a woman "dropped" by her lover, who subsequently suffers from hysterical paralysis and, when placed upon her feet, falls (drops) to the ground. If the conscious mind refuses to acknowledge or cannot process a traumatic experience, then the unconscious mind stages re-enactments of it. In the case of the fictional Clementina, her bodily symptoms and the various treatments she subsequently undergoes speak of trauma at the personal level (passion for Sir Charles versus passion for the Catholic faith, and whether Sir Charles loves her—a point on which she forever remains uncertain)[23] and at the familial, wherein the della Porrettas and the doctors (the family's agents) seek to excise both Clementina's madness and her love for Sir Charles.

Before proceeding, it should be noted that for eighteenth-century English men and women, madness and melancholy were bodily disorders, not mental disorders.[24] As Lady Mary Wortley Montagu insisted, "Madness is as much a corporal Distemper as the Gout or Asthma."[25] According to Dr. George Cheyne, the nervous system—comprised of highly elastic fibers filled with a "milky and watery Fluid"—was responsible for the disorders that afflicted the mind, as "all the Nerves, or Instruments of Sensation terminate" in the brain.[26] Cheyne notes that certain of the chronical passions, such as "slow and long *Grief*, *dark Melancholy*, *hopeless natural Love*," "when very intense and long indulg'd, terminate even in *Madness*,"[27] and they do so by wearing out the nervous system: "Those *Nerves* which are necessary for *considering*, *brooding* over, and *fixing* such as Set of *Ideas* on the *Imagination*, being constantly employ'd, are worn out, broken, impaired. The *rest* by Disuse, become resty and unactive, lifeless and destitute of a sufficient *Flux* of warm Blood and due Nourishment."[28] In essence, indulgence in chronical passions destroys the nerves and keeps the bodily fluids from circulating; insufficient blood is being sent to the brain. To effect a cure requires "long Time, much Care, and great Caution, unwearied Patience and Perseverance, and so long a Course of *Self-denial*, as few People are willing to undergo."[29] Cheyne also identified religious fanaticism as a source of acute melancholy. He writes, "There is a kind of *Melancholy*, which is called *Religious*, . . . And this is merely a *Bodily Disease*, produced by an ill *Habit* or *Constitution*, wherein the *Nervous System* is broken and disordered, and the *Juices* become *viscid* and *glewy*."[30] As we know, Clementina suffers both from "hopeless, natural love" and religious melancholy—two separate and distinct maladies.

As Sir Charles writes to Dr. Bartlett, "Religion and Love . . . which heightens our relish for the things of both worlds, What pity is, that they should ever run the human heart either into enthusiasm, or superstition, and thereby debase the minds they are both so well fitted to exalt!" (III.xxviii; 2:220). Dr. Richard Mead, in *Medical Precepts and Cautions* (1751), provides the following discussion of religious madness versus love madness: "Now nothing disorders the mind as much as love and religion, I mean false and vain religion, or superstition. Love is attended with hope, fear, jealousy, and sometimes with wrath and hatred arising from the latter. Superstition fills and distracts the mind with vain terrors, and notions of divine vengeance. Hence it happens, that the madness of persons in love is more generally of the maniacal, and that of superstitious people of the melancholic kind." He adds, "But these two disorders sometimes take each other's place, and undergo various degrees of combination" in terms of symptoms.[31] Thus, the symptoms of and treatments for Clementina's madness follow the contradictory courses of mania and melancholia, overlaid with Richardson's own symbolic interpretations.

In an attempt to cure their daughter of her love for Sir Charles and her madness, the della Porrettas and their family doctors inflict every known eighteenth-century treatment upon the hapless Clementina. As Hélène Dachez comments, Clementina is often "treated as an experimental object typical of case studies."[32] First, she is "bled by leaches" (III.xxvi; 2:189) and blooded with a "lancet" (III.xxvi; 2:190), and there is talk of "blistering" (III.xxvi; 2:192), all to make the blood and bodily juices flow. The blistering is never depicted, only promised, though the marchioness worries that it will take place on Clementina's head, requiring that her hair be shaved, a denunciation of sexuality and vanity practiced by many religious groups and sects, but one which, in this instance, reflects ambiguity regarding Clementina's repeated wish to become a nun, as she takes "pride . . . in her hair" (III.xxvi; 2:192). However, the blistering never occurs (at least, it is never mentioned again). Instead, blood-letting is performed. Initially, Clementina pleads against being blooded, but when Sir Charles urges her to be blooded, Clementina capitulates: "And do *you* wish it too, Chevalier?—Do *you* wish to see me wounded?—To see my heart bleeding at my arm, I warrant." She points to her bloodied arm: "As I cannot give you tears for tears, from my eyes, Shall not my arm weep!" (III.xxvi; 2:193). While medicinal in nature, the bleeding is also clearly symbolic, with the body speaking on behalf of the emotions: her heart bleeds; she weeps blood. The bleeding also holds sexual meaning, as Judith Broome notes: "In a novel where overt displays of sexual desire are missing, Clementina's morbid fascination with the spectacle of her bleeding body, with the idea of being penetrated by the surgeon's lancet, absorbs all the sexuality that cannot be spoken. . . . Clementina succeeds in transposing erotic desire (both Sir Charles's and her own) onto a suffering and wounded body."[33] To spell it out, the bleeding metaphorically re-enacts initiation into the sexual act: Clementina's fear of being penetrated, which she overcomes because she believes Sir Charles desires it; the skin pierced by a sharp (phallic) object, whence her blood flows "freely"; and, last, the procedure over, she faints away.

Clementina is also fed a "low diet" with little or no alcohol, as Cheyne recommended to his melancholic or nervous patients, one of whom was Richardson himself. But this is unnecessary, as Clementina is "so loth to take nourishment, and when she does, is so very abstemious, that the regimen is hardly necessary" (III.xxxii: 2:255). In this, she is not unlike her fictional sister, Clarissa, after Clarissa's rape. A well-fed female body was considered a sexual body. Both Clarissa and Clementina are eager to eradicate their sexuality, the former because of sexual violation, the other because her love for Sir Charles violates her religious beliefs and because her (sexual) passion for him cannot or should not be consummated (because he is a heretic, because he may not love her). There is also something penitential in Clementina's self-starvation (as in Clarissa's): to starve the fecund body is both to punish it for its transgressive desires and to hone it into a more spiritual vessel.

Travel was also considered one of the best forms of exercise for sufferers of nervous disorders, as it gently stimulated the bodily juices and fibers while quieting the mind, and Clementina spends months traveling all over Italy: The "poor Lady [is] kept in traveling motion to quiet her mind." She journeys to "Urbino, to Rome, to Naples; then back to Florence, then to Milan, to Turin" (III.xxxii; 2:.256), and then to "Leghorn to Naples, and back again (IV.vii; 2.295). The hurried travels up and down Italy mimic her own bodily movements at times, for she "neither sits nor stands with quietness—She walks up and down her room, at other times, with passion and hurry" (III.xxvi; 2:185). But more importantly, it reflects her treatment by her family. When she first acknowledges her love of Sir Charles and her desire "to conquer my passion, or die," she complains that she was given no time for reflection—"I was hurried, as I may say: I had not time given me to weigh, ponder, recollect" (III.xxiv; 2:171)—nor is she provided with time later, always teased and tormented about her ill-conceived passion, always threatened with an impending, rushed marriage to the Count of Belvedere. In other ways, however, her family attempts to confine her, both literally and figuratively. She is placed in "in bonds" (III.xxxii; 2:253); they have "confined her hands" (III.xxxii; 2:253) and "her arms" (III.xxxii; 2:254), and on more than one occasion, she is tied into a "Strait Waistcoat" (IV.vii; 2:298). Like the hectic movement from place to place, orchestrated by her family and doctors, the severe restrictions of her movements speak to her lack of freedom in terms of personal decision making. Bonnie Latimer notes, "At no point does she win an argument definitively; others know best, although they defer to her wishes out of pity or a fear of aggravating her mental illness."[34] While Clementina's madness may force her family to make some concessions—allowing her to marry Sir Charles, for instance—it is always their decision, not hers; it is always on their terms, not hers. And Sir Charles, of course, insists upon his own terms and conditions, rendering Clementina without voice or agency.

The most disconcerting of corporeal treatments inflicted upon Clementina are the beatings imposed by her cousin, Laurana. Treating mental illness through corporeal punishment was not uncommon during the eighteenth century. In his 1795 publication, *A Guide to Health*, the Reverend Joseph Townsend notes that "Strict coercion, when the patient is inclined to violence, is required, not merely to prevent mischief, but as a remedy," adding that "The most powerful restraint is fear." However, "severities" such as whippings, dragging by chains, and starvation are, in most instances, "not only needless and cruel, but extremely detrimental."[35] However, the "cruel Laurana" delights in hitting her cousin, and justifies the beatings to Father Marescotti: "O Father, said she, we are in the right way, I assure you: When we had her first, her Chevalier, and an interview with him, were ever in her mouth; but now she is in such order, that she never speaks a word of him" (IV.vii; 2:297). The beatings correlate to the silencing that Clementina undergoes by Sir Charles and her family, and they express her family's desire to excise her love for Sir Charles—literally, to beat it out of her, for though they subsequently descry these beatings, they do not stop them when they are occurring. (When Clementina first mentions the physical abuse, she accuses her mother, not Laurana: "You beat me, remember" [III.xxx; 2:239].) Later, we learn that Laurana loves the Count of Belvedere, who loves her not, and that marriage between Clementina and Sir Charles would eliminate her rival. However, Laurana also covets the large inheritance that will fall to her if Clementina retires to a nunnery—or madhouse— and so seeks to exacerbate Clementina's malady. As Broome writes, "Clementina's physical body, like that of Clarissa Harlowe, represents much more than its own material substance: the woman's body is directly linked to a body of land."[36] Last, the physical abuse functions as penance, as punishment, and as offering. Many religious (saints and sinners alike) scourged their bodies with whips to discourage and punish the physical desires of the flesh. The beatings also exist as punishment for the incorporated other (Sir Charles), as it is his name that brings on the onslaught of abuse. And, finally, the suffering explicates the extremes to which Clementina is willing to go to demonstrate her love for Sir Charles. As Clementina tells Sir Charles, "—Ah Sir! They are very severe with me! Pity me: But I know you will; for you have a tender heart. *It is all for You!*" (III.xxviii; 2:222).

As Sir Charles's widow, as his relict, as the "remains" of the strange affair of the heart between him and the lovelorn Bolognese, Clementina "speaks" in the only ways available to her: madness and her body. And the "scars, ruins, remnants, and so on"[37] of her remains suggest that Richardson intended this: that young women of marriageable age must be guided—not forced—into making the "correct" decision regarding marriage; that they do not know what is best for them but nonetheless should not be forced. Richardson is no feminist, but as he wrote to Aaron Hill, regarding Clarissa and her fictional family: "it is one of my . . . principal Views, to admonish Parents agt. forcing their Children's Inclinations, in an Article so essential to their Happiness, as Marriage; I was very desirous, that it should appear to a Reader, that had so excellent a Creature been left to her self, well as she might have liked him had he been a moral Man, she would have overcome her Liking to him; and despised him."[38] Similarly, Clementina, if left to her own resources, would have come to conclude the inappropriateness of her attachment—and overcome it—though she would never despise Sir Charles, being as he is such "a moral Man." Finally, the fact that Clementina exists as Sir Charles's relict and he as corpse acknowledges the fact that people mourn whenever any beloved person, object, or belief is lost to them—when someone or something becomes "dead to them"—whether this occurs through death, disappearance, or disinterest on the part of the beloved, or through disillusion on the part of the bereaved.

"A WIDOWER-LOVER": CLEMENTINA'S HAUNTING OF HARRIET

In a letter to Lady Bradshaigh, dated 15 December 1748, Samuel Richardson wrote, "I told you Madam that I have been twice married. Both times happily. You will guess so as to my first when I tell you that I cherish the Memory of my lost Wife to this Hour, and as to the second, when I assure you that I can do so without derogating from the Merits of, or being disallowed by my present; who speaks of her on all Occasions as respectfully, and as affectionately, as I do myself."[39] As Sylvia Kasey Marks comments, "Harriet Byron seems to have a similar capacity to speak of Clementina in the same sympathetic manner" as Richardson's second wife.[40] Yet, Harriet is haunted by Clementina, suggesting not only an intense psychic and emotional bond between the two women, but also Harriet's unease with Clementina's status as Sir Charles's first love, as first wife, as dead wife. As is, the blame for the rushed courtship and wedding between Sir Charles and Harriet rests upon the slender shoulders of Clementina, whose impassioned insistence that "You must marry!" (V.xxxviii; 2:630) is taken by Sir Charles as a sacred oath that he must honor, conjuring the image of husband fulfilling the deathbed wishes of his wife. Sir Charles, then, is not so much a bigamist,[41] as Richardson jokingly claimed, as a widower who remarries, loving the second wife but forever fondly recalling the first one, ever revering her memory.

Within Richardson's novel, it is Lady Olivia, at last swallowing the bitter draught of Sir Charles's rejection, who first terms Sir Charles a "widower." She writes to him, "There is, among your countrywomen, one who seems born for *you*, and you for *her*. If *she* can abate of a dignity, that a first and only Love alone can gratify, and accept of a second-placed Love, a widower-bachelor, as I may call you, *she*, I know, must, will be the happy woman" (V.xlii; 2:647). In a letter penned immediately after, Sir Charles refers to Lady Olivia's term "*bachelor-widower*," questioning how he can enter into the subject of marriage with "*any*-body" (V.xl; 2:650) at this time, implying that he must grieve the loss of Clementina. Further, he worries that any woman to whom he offered marriage would be offended by the suddenness of the proposal, coming so soon after the termination of his relationship with the Bolognese noblewoman, for as he solemnly informs Harriet, "I concluded myself already the husband of Clementina" (VI.xviii; 3:56). Finally, he acknowledges that his whirlwind courtship of Harriet might have been greeted with greater enthusiasm "had I taken at least the usual time of a *Widower-Lover*" (VI.xviii; 3:57).

The specter of Clementina—originally only the faintest of ghostly outlines—first materializes when Charlotte Grandison and Lady L. force Harriet to admit of her love for Sir Charles. Within minutes, the conversation turns to the possibility of Sir Charles's entanglement with "some foreign Lady." Harriet writes, "They had raised my hopes; and now, exciting my fears by so well-grounded an apprehension, they were obliged for their pains to hold Lady L.'s salts to my nose" (II. xxxi; 1:422). Further spectral hints of Clementina appear soon after in a letter penned by Dr. Bartlett's nephew, who recounts his uncle's Continental relations with young Grandison. At one point, so the nephew writes, Sir Charles sends Beauchamp and Dr. Bartlett on a "tour into some of the Eastern regions" (II.xxxvi; 1:461) at his own expense, as Sir Charles must remain in Italy, engaged as he was "in some affairs at Bologna and Florence, which gave him great embarrassment" (II.xxxvi; 1:462). Bologna is the home of Clementina, Florence that of Olivia. As Harriet's infatuation increases, Sir Charles blushingly acknowledges that he has "seen the Lady with whom, of all the women in the world, I think I could be happy" (III.xv; 2:81). However, when Charlotte questions Sir Charles regarding the identity of this lady, Sir Charles demurs, saying, "you will excuse me, if I say, that this question gives me some pain—Because it leads to *another*, that, *if* made, *I cannot at present myself answer*" (III.xv; 2:81). Again, the talk immediately turns to foreign ladies, much to Harriet's chagrin. A few days later, after Sir Charles has finished perusing Harriet's letters, praising them for their "amiable frankness!" (III. xvii; 2:91), other letters arrive, this time from Bologna (III.xviii; 2:106), which in turn force Sir Charles's attentions away from Harriet. And when Sir Charles asks to confer privately with Harriet, ostensibly over Charlotte's marital preferences, Harriet believes, hopes, that during this meeting, Sir Charles will also reveal his feelings for her. Instead, Sir Charles reveals his intricate and intimate relationship with Clementina, advising Harriet of his impending departure for Italy. Each time Harriet believes that Sir Charles's feelings for her will be revealed, the specter of the Bolognese noblewoman appears.

Even when Sir Charles is released from his engagement to Lady Clementina, Harriet is not as happy as might be expected, particularly when one considers that the long-anticipated object of desire is within her grasp. Writing to her cousin Mrs. Reeves, Harriet explains: "But were he to declare himself my Lover, my heart would not be so joyful as you seem to expect, if Lady Clementina is to be unhappy." In addition, Harriet recognizes that she must always share Sir Charles with Clementina: "Shall your Harriet sit down and think herself happy in a second-place Love?" (VI.vii; 3:14). Harriet remains concerned that Lady Clementina will "relent" (VI.ix; 3:24), changing her mind regarding marriage to Sir Charles. When Sir Charles proves late for breakfast at the Selby's, Harriet petulantly muses, "May he not have *overslept* himself?—Some *agreeable dream* of the Bologna family" (VI.xvii; 3:46)? When Sir Charles finally makes the offer, Harriet resists at first, confessing that "I am dazled, confounded, shall I say? at the superior merits of the Lady you so nobly, so like yourself, glory in esteeming as she well deserves to be esteemed" (VI.xxii; 3:77). She continues: "The poor Harriet Byron fears, she *justly* fears, when she contemplates the magnanimity of that exalted Lady, that with all her care, with all her endeavours, she never shall be able to make the figure to HERSELF, which is necessary for her own tranquillity (however *you* might generously endeavor to *assure* her doubting mind)" (VI.xxii; 3:77). Later, accepting the marital offer, Harriet nonetheless remains haunted by Clementina. She repeatedly wonders if Clementina will regret her decision (VI.xxiv; 3:92). Watching Sir Charles dance, Harriet questions if Clementina ever danced with him (VI.xxiv; 3:93). Harriet feels "humbled in the sense . . . of his and Clementina's superior merits" (VI.xxviii; 3:119). She insists that "I shrink from his dazling eye; and, compared to Him (and *Clementina*, let me add) appear to myself such a Nothing—" (VI.xxix; 3:132). She dreams that Sir Charles "upbraided me with being the cause that he had not Lady Clementina" (VI.xxxii; 3:148). Two weeks prior to her wedding, Harriet writes to Sir Charles, insisting that "I am more and more convinced, that, however distinguished my lot *may* be, Clementina only can deserve you" (VI.xxxv;

3:165). She confesses to Charlotte, "I never can deserve him. Hapless, hapless Clementina! she *only* could!" (VI.li; 3:217).

Even after marriage, Clementina haunts Harriet's thoughts—so much so that one might say Harriet conjures up the Italian's appearance in England. At her first presentation at the church near Grandison Hall, Harriet writes, "Happy Harriet!—Yet I cannot forbear now-and-then, when my joy and gratitude are at the highest, a sigh to the merits of Lady Clementina!—What I am now, should she have been, think I often!—The general admiration paid me as the wife of Sir Charles Grandison, should have been paid to her!—Lady L. Lady G. should have been her sisters!—She should have been the mistress of this house, the co-guardian of Emily, the successor of the late Lady Grandison!—Hapless Clementina!" (VII.vii; 3:278). In addition, when Clementina suddenly manifests in England, Harriet feels that she must cede her own role as wife, giving precedence to Clementina. When Sir Charles asks Harriet to "Favour me with your hand," when welcoming Clementina to their house, Harriet refuses, insisting, "That would be to insult her." Sir Charles scolds Harriet: "My dearest Life! forget not your own dignity . . . ; nor give *me* too much consequence with a Lady, who, like yourself, is all Soul" (VII.xxx; 3:354). Nonetheless, Harriet remains in awe of Clementina, representing as she does the first love, the dead wife, and the widow of Sir Charles Grandison.

A Bertha Rochester to Harriet's Jane Eyre, Clementina exists as Sir Charles's "secret wife and in a sense her [Harriet's] secret self" or "dark double."[42] Both young women are forced to admit their preference for Sir Charles against their will or inclination: Harriet by Sir Charles's sisters, Clementina by Mrs. Beaumont. Both young women attempt to stifle their passion for Sir Charles and fail, one enduring a profound mental breakdown and physical deterioration, the other, lesser versions of both. Both become his wife, one metaphorically, the other literally. One dark and one fair, they are so alike in all other respects that Sir Charles exclaims to Clementina, "My Harriet is another Clementina! You are another Harriet! *Sister*-excellencies I have called you" (VII.xxvi; 3:343). Clementina, so Sir Charles avers, is the "Miss Byron of Italy" (VI.xviii; 3:53); Harriet, the "Clementina of England" (VII.xxx; 3:353). Admittedly, Harriet does not experience religion as the impediment to marriage as Clementina does, rather Clementina herself acts as the impediment to Harriet's marriage.

Sir Charles's conflation of Clementina and Harriet suggests their interchangeability—first wife, second wife—and perhaps the interchangeability of most (good) women, while emphasizing the uniqueness of Sir Charles, the only completely "good man" to grace the multitudinous pages of Richardson's novels.

Clementina—existing both as relict of Sir Charles's past and as deceased wife—may also represent the anxiety of many second spouses. The (dead/missing) spouse represents a chapter in the beloved's life to which the second spouse has limited or no access. This first spouse was presumably well loved (at least initially); he/she was the first, a position of pre-eminence that the second (or third or fourth) can never hold. If the first spouse is deceased, the second can never compete against the first but must accept the position of second and give due respect to the first. But the fact that Clementina exists as Harriet's dark double may also speak to the trauma of loving Sir Charles—that is, Harriet's traumatic experience of loving him, which is the traumatic experience of every young woman of marriageable age who crosses Sir Charles's path. Often, as Caruth notes, it is through another's story that our own is articulated: "the story of the way in which one's own trauma is tied up with the trauma of another, the way in which trauma may lead, therefore, to the encounter with another, through the very possibility and surprise of listening to another's wound."[43] More so than Sir Charles, Harriet exists as "witness" to Clementina's sufferings because she understands first-hand what it is to love him, and while the situations that Clementina and Harriet find themselves in are not precisely the same, Harriet can empathize with Clementina in ways that Sir Charles cannot, being female and loving a man but uncertain if that love is returned. And Harriet repeats Clementina's sufferings, though in a less exhaustive manner, and thus speaks her own trauma through replication of Clementina's.

Indeed, Clementina's haunting of Harriet—her doubling for Harriet—is repeated in the love stories of virtually every other young female character within this novel, for, in Richardson's attempt to demonstrate the physical and moral attractiveness of a good man, he makes Sir Charles into a virtual "Typhoid Charlie," a man who dangerously infects every woman of marriageable age who comes into contact with him. As Clementina's brother, the General, complains, "Had he [Sir Charles] not . . . found means to fascinate Olivia, and as many women as he come into company with?" (IV.vii; 2:.299). Indeed, Clementina, Harriet, Emily, Lady Anne S., and Olivia literally become sick with love for Sir Charles, though Olivia's passion is turned outward in acts of violence, while Clementina, Harriet, Emily, and Lady Anne S. turn their passion inward. Even Sir Charles's sister is not immune to his potent charms. On her wedding day, Charlotte Grandison admits that "My brother has long made all other men indifferent to me" (IV.xvi; 2:339), and she notes, "My brother . . . can never marry but he must break half a score hearts" (I.xxvi; 1:136). Clementina, then, as the (metaphoric) deceased first wife, as the woman who dies for love, is merely the extreme of a template upon which all other female characters are modeled.

In the end, however, Clementina differs from the other female characters in one crucial aspect: she alone is aligned with death. Dressed in black, she is the grieving widow, speaking to the ghost of her lost husband. She is the dying wife, urging her living husband to (re)marry, yet admonishing him to choose a new wife of equal worth to the first. The fact that a "living" character functions as the novel's representative of death suggests the newly animated nature of death, wherein the dead continue to live through means of their consciousness, as well as inhabiting the consciousness of others. To repeat what Richardson himself wrote regarding his two wives, the first one deceased: "You will guess so as to my first when I tell you that I cherish the Memory of my lost Wife to this Hour, and as to the second, when I assure you that I can do so without derogating from the Merits of, or being disallowed by my present; who speaks of her on all Occasions as respectfully, and as affectionately, as I do myself."[44] The ghost of Richardson's first wife lives in the author's memories—and haunts the living wife, who must speak of the dead paragon often, with respect and affection. So too does Clementina function within the text of *Grandison*. Not least, the metaphoric dead—that is, Sir Charles and Clementina—are the living dead, not the literal dead. No deathbed scenes of Sir Charles or Clementina occur and their corpses are not to be found, suggesting a movement on Richardson's part toward greater acceptance of the Lockean conscious and a dismissal of the importance of the dying/dead body.

In addition, certain scenes within the novel suggest that Clementina is dead—or that she is death itself. When the della Porrettas and Sir Charles finally agree on marital terms, Clementina's choice of clothing argues for her transformation from a maiden in love to ghostly decedent: "Once she would be in black; then in colours; then her white and silver was taken out: But that, she said, would give her a bridal appearance: She at last chose her plain white satten. She looks like an Angel" (V.xxiv; 2:561). From widow, to young maid, to bride, to angel— each change of outfit signals her fluctuating moods, her altering expectations, her shifting desires, but in the end, she is "angel," an otherworldly creature. Also, after his marriage to Harriet, the newly married Sir Charles learns of Clementina's arrival in London, and he discovers the Italian in a room dimmed and darkened by "drawn window-curtains" (VII.xxvi; 3:339). Despite the dusky gloom, Sir Charles recognizes Clementina from her outline, asking, "does she not receive her brother in darkness?" (VII.xxvi; 3:340). The darkened room with heavy curtains conjures up the image of many a darkened parlor wherein the body of the newly deceased lay for viewing. And Clementina is blamed—by herself and by others—for "Harriet's near-miscarriage,"[45] brought about by the two women wandering about the woods, "Against warnings, against threatenings" (VII.xlvii; 3:419). As (dead) first wife, her constant attendance upon the pregnant Harriet breathes death. And like death itself, Clementina is "other" (Italian, Catholic, female, mad) just as death is always "other," always happening to an(other).

CONCLUSION

Samuel Richardson's final novel is not a tragedy, but a comedy in the traditional sense of the word. Few characters actually die within the confines of *Grandison*'s voluminous pages, and those who do—Sir Thomas Grandison, Sir Hargrave Pollexfen, Mercada, and Laurana—are individuals whom readers have been taught to dislike, as they are selfish and often cruel, seeking their own gratification regardless of the cost to others. No loss there, we murmur to ourselves. It is also a novel in which myriad marriages are made—indeed, no fewer than eleven marriages are arranged by Sir Charles over the entirety of the novel. Yet, the novel refuses its status as a comedy. Instead, a perverse impulse drives the text, insisting that the desired, pleasurable end will only come after a prolonged bout of suffering, with lessons learned from that suffering. Clementina injects a tragic, melancholic minor refrain into Richardson's domestic opus, which speaks directly to Richardson's need to subject even the most innocent of pleasures to the obelisk eye of Duty, but which also infuses the novel with a counterbalance to the major comic strain of the novel, adding depth and range to the reading experience and highlighting, through contrast, the ultimate felicity of Sir Charles and Harriet. In her role as widow and deceased wife, Clementina casts a giant shadow.

Written within six years of the publication of *Clarissa*, *The History of Sir Charles Grandison* suggests Richardson's greater immersion in Lockean thought and acceptance of the free-floating Lockean soul, and it does so by focusing on the spiritual connections between like-minded individuals, their sharing of a single soul or consciousness, and the spectral encounters with the (presumed) dead, as in Clementina's conversations with an absent Sir Charles or Clementina's "haunting" of Harriet. The fact that Clementina is aligned with both death and madness may also speak to the "madness" attendant upon the cultural "other-ing" of death; her beaten, bruised, and bloody body, to nascent attitudes toward the dead body. Regardless, as both Sir Charles's metaphorical "relict" and deceased first wife, Clementina enacts the intimate relationship between love and death, between *eros* and *thanatos*, for we cannot mourn the loss of that which we do not love, and when we kiss the beloved, we do so with the (conscious or unconscious) knowledge of impending loss. Although *Grandison* demonstrates no stated belief in the substantial soul or a resurrected body, it does suggest that the soul—in the form of Lockean consciousness—can transcend place and time, can merge with the soul of the beloved in ways that the substantial soul cannot. Harriet Byron writes of her feelings toward Sir Charles: "Souls may be near, when Bodies are distant. But are we not one Soul? Could yours be unaffected, when mine was so much disturbed?" (VI.xxxii; 3:150). The spectralization of the other has begun, and it affects both the living and the dead.

Ghosts

Relics/relicts possess materiality; they are the physical remains of something or someone no longer extant. Yet, relics and relicts may be found in various states and conditions, from the pristine and intact, to the well-worn and somewhat shabby, to the decrepit and broken, to ashes and dust. Specifically, material relics may become so old, so used, so fractured, fragmented, and fragile as to be barely recognized for what they are or once were. Similarly, relicts are subject to decline and decay: the once-young widow becomes the middle-aged widow becomes the elderly widow becomes the decedent in her own right.

In this section, I examine relics/relicts in their most insubstantial and fragmented forms as mere ghosts of their former selves, which nonetheless may still be read and interpreted by those willing to do so. In terming these relics/relicts "ghosts," I refer to the eighteenth-century British conception of ghosts as spectral beings who nonetheless look exactly as they did in life, speak to the living and hear them in turn, and wear the clothes worn in life (as was the case with the apparition of Mrs. Veal, a chatty ghost dressed in her usual "Scower'd Silk" gown[1]). Wraiths of once-living personages, these relicts sigh and sorrow over the dismal state of the earthly world, and like the free-floating Lockean consciousness to which they are aligned, they roam at will, sometimes intermingling with the consciousness of other beings, privy to the host's most private thoughts and witness to her/his most private actions. As material objects, ghostly relics are tattered, torn, soiled, and scattered, yet still able to speak their relationship to the departed, if only in bits and pieces, through narrative scraps threaded together like a broken string of pearls.

The uncanny ability of relic/relicts to endure, despite fragmentation and spectralization, is nonetheless countered by a surprising lack of agency. Able to know the thoughts of others, to mingle with their consciousness, relicts as ghosts are doomed by who and what they were in life, forced to sound their mournful cries, over and over, until they such time as they disappear entirely. As well-worn and tattered objects, ghostly relics are frequently dismissed as lacking in value; the living, either unwittingly or deliberately, accelerate the relic's process of degradation. As these relics/relicts exist in their fragmented or spectral forms, the living pay little attention to them, unless it is to use them as objects or things, useful only for a moment, if even for that.

I study only one novel in this section—Henry Mackenzie's *The Man of Feeling*—a text wherein the protagonist, the internal narrator (aptly named "The Ghost"), and the "found" manuscript exist as ghostly relicts/relics. These three exist as the "remains" of a certain way of life, of a certain type of person, of an idyllic past, all of whose time has passed. The manuscript—the material relic of an exemplary life—is torn, scattered, damaged, still able to speak but no longer able to tell its full story. The protagonist, Harley, is no living man, but rather an object (relic rather than relict) that is manipulated by others, most of whom lack knowledge of what the relic that is Harley represents or how it works; Harley exists as a ghost whose presence, if seen, is largely ignored or barely acknowledged. No beneficent contagion, no emulation, no intercession will occur through the figure of the saintly Harley. And the internal narrator, "The Ghost," exists as more spirit than person, moving about largely unseen except by children (a group purportedly closer to the spirit world than adults), and he is able to shift between his own consciousness and Harley's as if a single soul animates them both. In sum, Mackenzie structures his entire novel on these wispy paeans to the past. In *The Man of Feeling*, the dead are ghosts, forgotten by the living and unable to haunt them.

5

" 'TIS AT LEAST A MEMORIAL FOR THOSE WHO SURVIVE"

The It-Narrator, Death Writing, and the Ghostwriter in Henry Mackenzie's *The Man of Feeling* (1771)

PUBLISHED WHEN ITS AUTHOR Henry Mackenzie was twenty-five, *The Man of Feeling* is a novel of sensibility—indeed, one of the more extreme examples of the genre—and thus deliberately dwells upon loss and suffering with melancholic enthusiasm. One of the stranger elements of the novel is its reliance upon relics/relicts to convey meaning and emotion. Nostalgic and elegiac, *The Man of Feeling* lays claim to a dead protagonist, a dead narrator, and the remnants of a manuscript, and it celebrates and mourns a past that never existed. In other words, it is a narrative fashioned from and by ghosts.

Mackenzie's novel pits "the man of the world" against "the man of feeling."[1] The former is an earthbound pragmatist and opportunist, delighting in the world of the flesh, exhilarated by commerce, and reveling in any chance to take advantage of the weak. Whether male or female, the character exists as all flesh, all body, weighted to the earth by its love of earthly things, from food and drink, to money, to pleasure, to sexual debauchery, and the like. In contrast, the man or woman of feeling is all spirit, emotional and empathetic, not interested in things of the earth, unless these things are fellow-minded spirits with whom one's own spirit can meet and co-mingle. In *The Man of Feeling*, the Lockean disdain for the human body and its elevation of human consciousness expresses itself through the dichotomous separation of the living into two disparate types of beings: one all body, one all soul. However, strangely enough, those who are all body thrive as *subjects*, feeding upon the living carcasses of the weak and feeble, while those who exist as all soul (very often, the weak and feeble) become *objects*, the prey of others. On the one hand, the bodiless spirits of highly sensitive beings suggests their moral superiority over earthbound sensualists—"things of the flesh are not our concern"; on the other hand, mourning clusters around women and men of feeling—to be all spirit is painful.

GHOSTS

* * *

The Man of Feeling is a framed novel, with the outermost frame authored by an unnamed "editor" engaged in a day of hunting with the local curate. The sought-after birds having flown, alerted to the presence of huntsmen and dog, the editor pauses to look around, his gaze resting upon an old residence, in front of which a young woman passes, book in her hand. The curate explains that the woman is Miss Walton, the daughter of a "neighbouring gentleman" and that the house belonged to "one HARLEY . . . a whimsical sort of man," whose history is contained within a discarded manuscript, which, coincidentally enough, is being used by the curate as wadding for gunshot.[2] Intrigued, the editor takes the proffered, incomplete manuscript, which he later reads with interest, terming it "a bundle of little episodes, put together without art, and of no importance on the whole, with something of nature, and little else in them" (3). Nonetheless, he, in turn, offers the manuscript to us, perhaps because he "is a good deal affected with some very trifling passages in it" (3–4).

Embedded within this narrative frame is the manuscript proper, written by a man named The Ghost, "a grave, oddish kind of a man" (2), who has since left the parish. The torn manuscript begins with chapter XI, with the reader abruptly transported into commentary about the recently deceased Ben Silton, an elderly gentleman whom The Ghost admires for the "rust" (5) of his character. All subsequent chapters follow Harley, a young man of uncommon sensibility, as he travels to London and meets a wide array of individuals, from pimps and prostitutes, to misanthropes, madmen, and card-sharpers. The final third of the book focuses on Harley's return home, his kindness to an old soldier and the soldier's two orphaned grandchildren, and his love for Miss Walton. Comments by the unnamed editor—the hunter—intrude three times into the narrative proper: once to remind readers that only fragments of the manuscript are available; another time to suggest that a person other than The Ghost might have added his sentiments to one small section of the manuscript; and the third to provide background to the ending of Harley's story, as more and more of the manuscript is damaged or missing. The conclusion of The Ghost's narrative is the conclusion of the entire book, as no closing frame exists.

This chapter begins with an analysis of the found manuscript as a "thing" and Harley as an it-narrator, comparing them to the protagonists—the animals and objects—of eighteenth-century novels of circulation, otherwise known as "it-narratives," and arguing that Harley becomes more object than person in his role as a relic/relict of/from the past; that as a "man of feeling," his alignment with consciousness, rather than body, paradoxically renders him and his story as objects rather than subjects. The chapter then examines death writing and its relationship to memory and memorial, exploring The Ghost's narrative as a mourning relic that simultaneously expresses The Ghost's grief over Harley's death (and the changing physical, social, and cultural landscape of England) and reconnects him with Harley and the past. The chapter concludes with a discussion of the problematic narrator, The Ghost, who often merges with Harley's own spirit, through the co-optation of the latter's consciousness, and it argues for The Ghost's status as mediating spirit for the dead and as the textual embodiment of Lockean consciousness.

"'TIS EXCELLENT WADDING": THE IT-MANUSCRIPT AND THE IT-PROTAGONIST

Mark Blackwell describes the it-narrative[3] as "a type of prose fiction in which inanimate objects (coins, waistcoats, pins, corkscrews, coaches) or animals (dogs, fleas, cats, ponies) serve as the central characters. Sometimes these characters enjoy a consciousness—and thus a perspective—of their own; sometimes they are merely narrative hubs around which other people's stories accumulate, like the stick around which cotton candy winds."[4] Enormously popular during the latter half of the eighteenth century—a time when *The Man of Feeling* was written and published—it-narratives may be identified by specific characteristics, most of which may be grouped under two major categories, as Liz Bellamy delineates: first, the it-narrator "lacks independent agency"; second, the "it-narrative" is structured around "the transference of the narrator or protagonist between otherwise unconnected characters, or, in the case of narratives of static objects like buildings, the movement of unconnected characters within the precincts of the protagonist."[5] It is worth looking into these categories more deeply.

The narrator's lack of agency is depicted in several ways beyond the obvious ones of being "sold, lost, found, given, and exchanged."[6] For instance, the it-narrator requires someone *with* agency to transmit its story, whether this be by reciting its tale to a "human amanuensis, or by inspiring the hand of the author through some mystical process."[7] In addition, the tale is usually accompanied by the use of a prefatory story explaining how the manuscript happened into the hands of the "editor," which not only creates a distancing effect, but implicitly insists that human mediation is necessary for the object's or animal's story to be told.[8]

The circulation of the protagonist, from one "owner" to another, also generates other defining aspects of the sub-genre, the most notable of which is "a looseness of structure and an avoidance of thematic coherence."[9] Each new person that the object/animal encounters requires the telling of that person's tale. The narrative becomes a series of stories,[10] loosely tied together and offering few, if any, conclusions, as the it-narrator is not privy to the final outcomes.[11] These encounters/tales usually possess some sort of "explicitly didactic or humanitarian purpose," particularly as the it-narrator routinely meets individuals from "very different social groups."[12] The it-narrative often functions as a critique of the social system, as individuals frequently lose possession of the object/animal because they "have failed to survive within the commercial state."[13] To wit, it-narratives are often "anti-luxury, anti-commercial" narratives and, within species novels (i.e., fictions in which coinage or currency is the protagonist), prostitution is "one of the most common forms of exchange portrayed,"[14] perhaps as it is one of the most degrading forms of commercial exchange. Last, because the it-narrative relies on serial encounters with random characters, rather than sustained engagement with a stable set of characters, there is an avoidance of "affective ties as plot mechanism."[15] This is not to say that emotion is not involved in the various encounters or that pathos does not exist within the individual tales, but rather that affective relations between and among a specific set group of characters are not the predominant organizing structure.

The majority—if not all—of the identifying characteristics associated with the it-narrative may be found in *The Man of Feeling*, most particularly as regards Harley's London adventures as described within The Ghost's manuscript and, to a lesser extent, as regards the manuscript itself. The story of the manuscript is itself an it-narrative, albeit in miniature.[16] The Ghost, having written fifty-one chapters and a conclusion—that is, having painstakingly recorded Harley's story from beginning to end—nonetheless abandons the manuscript for reasons unknown. Perhaps writing it has assuaged The Ghost's feelings of loss at the death of Harley, and thus the manuscript itself no longer matters. Perhaps The Ghost believes the manuscript—the tale it tells, a hagiography of a sainted life—belongs in the parish where the tale is set, so that those who knew Harley may remember him all the better, or that others may benefit from reading his story. If this is the case, then the manuscript, in its role of relic, possesses meaning only in an environment where the *remains* of the dead can be directly linked to the dead themselves (which, in and of itself, suggests that relics are meaningless without context). Or perhaps the manuscript functions as form of final payment to The Ghost's landlord, the farmer. Regardless, the manuscript has lost its original owner and must find another. The farmer, perhaps illiterate, perhaps not, finds little value in the manuscript other than in its potential to curry favor with the curate. The curate, however, similarly disvalues it, but for different reasons: "the hand is intolerably bad"; the author cannot be found "in one strain for two chapters altogether; and I don't believe there's a single syllogism from beginning to end" (3). The manuscript then becomes something else altogether—wadding for a shotgun, with its pages torn, its story mangled—and it is propelled into the fields, meadows, and woods near where Harley used to walk, exploding into the air, scattering onto the fields, and embedding itself within the dead carcasses of grouse, quail, or pheasant. And, finally, its ruined remains become the affective reading material of the editor—and us. As it travels from hand to hand, it becomes a different thing to each owner: a loving tribute to a deceased friend, a wad of papers of no interest and/or a payment with no value, excellent wadding for a shotgun, or lessons in affective response. It is a relic of little value or great value, dependent upon who views it, whether believer or non-believer. In addition, despite the brevity of its textual encounters with these individuals—The Ghost, the farmer, the curate, the hunter/editor—we learn enough about them through their encounter with the manuscript to interpret them and to understand their stories. The Ghost is eccentric, gentle, sober, yet willing to play games with the neighborhood children, and wandering through the parish lanes and meadows at night. He is something of an ironist and a bit of a sentimentalist, sensitive and melancholic. In contrast, the farmer operates from motives of necessity, renting a room in his farmhouse in order to make ends meet. Even if illiterate, he is astute enough to place the manuscript in the hands of the highly literate curate, rather than use it as kindling for the fireplace or paper for the outhouse. The curate is a "man of the world," a frequenter of the local clubs, an avid hunter, and a "strenuous logician" (3), less concerned with the state of his parishioner's souls than with the state of his own comfort. The editor enjoys hunting, something we suspect Harley or The Ghost did not, but he also possesses a sensitivity that makes him *almost* weep as he reads certain parts of Harley's tale (4), though he seems embarrassed by this weakness. Thus, the manuscript functions as an "it" or "thing," lacking agency, circulating among a variety of different people, and functioning as a touchstone for evaluating its various owners, particularly in terms of their moral worth—or, shall we say, their sensibility quotient. As the material remains of Harley, it possesses value to others only if Harley possessed value to them.

However, more so than the manuscript, Harley himself functions as object or "thing." James D. Lilley touches near to the problem, when he speaks of the roving protagonist of sentimental fiction and, more particularly, of Harley: "The sentimental flâneur does not so much see or feel ruin as cast its shadow over the world: He *is* ruined feeling. Always a traveler, and destined to pass through the world, observing the decay that has been hardwired into his vision, his melancholy account of feeling's ruined thing provides a fitting accompaniment to the 'it-narrative,' a popular eighteenth-century romance form in which inanimate objects like Harley's coin and the beggar's dog come to life and tell their adventures in circulation."[17] Curiously, near as he comes to it, Lilley does not view Harley himself as an "it-narrator." Rather, the coin and the beggar's dog are "things" that possess the *potential* to become "it-narrators"; they express "the materiality and thinghood of the sentimental commodity."[18] Further, Lilley substitutes "ruined feeling" for Harley himself. For Lilley, Harley (and any other sentimental protagonist) embodies the inherent conflict of sentimentality, which values private feeling ("use-value") yet requires its public display ("exchange-value") in order to validate itself—a process that paradoxically "ruins" genuine feeling.[19] Although I admire Lilley's Marxist critique and analysis, I believe Harley himself to be a "thing," an "it-narrator,"[20] a sort of species of coin encrusted with a great deal of "rust." Harley, as an object of exchange, articulates the premise that both money and emotion should be circulated, rather than stockpiled and hoarded, and he elucidates the notion that the *separation* between monetary exchange and affective exchange is what has become ruinous. However, before proceeding further with these ideas, it is necessary first to prove that Harley himself functions as "thing"—specifically, as a relic, but one in which the numinous powers have faded, in which few believe.

To begin with, like any object or animal that functions as the protagonist of an it-narrative, Harley lacks independent agency. Harley's trip to London to secure the interest of a baronet is against his inclination. Yet, go he does because others tell him that he must: "Harley, though he had no great relish for the attempt, yet could not resist the torrent of motives that assaulted him" (11). Spurred on by the "assault" of words, Harley starts off toward London, walking across fields, through woods, and over hills. Perhaps emotion moves him as well, as Miss Walton's father is the one who has provided Harley with "a letter of introduction to a baronet of his acquaintance" (10). Once on his journey, Harley continues to be influenced by others. As Harley stops to remove a stone from his shoe, a beggar approaches him—the first of many random encounters. In London, a dandyish former footman—now an occasional pimp and full-time gauger for the baronet—smoothly maneuvers Harley to an inn for dinner and into the company of a glazier and another man, the latter cognizant of the footman's history. Then, an acquaintance of Harley's takes him for a visit to Bedlam. The next evening, that same acquaintance takes Harley to meet the Misanthrope. A chance encounter in the park later involves Harley in a game of cards, where he is cheated of his money. Intent upon meeting some acquaintances at Fleet Street, Harley is solicited by a prostitute, Miss Atkins. Leaving London to return home by carriage, Harley finds himself in the company of Ben Silton, a friend of The Ghost. Alighting from the stagecoach to walk the remainder of the way home, Harley encounters an elderly soldier, Edwards, a former neighbor conscripted into the army in place of his son; they later meet up with Edwards's orphaned grandchildren. Each and every encounter is random, the effect of chance and circumstance and certainly not the result of any direct action on the part of Harley. This does not mean that Harley entirely lacks initiative. He is generous with his money; he reconciles Miss Atkins with her father; he provides a small farm for Edwards and his orphaned grandchildren.[21] Rather, this is to say that Harley does not actively seek out people or experiences—people come *to* him; things happen *to* him. He reacts rather than acts. As Everett Zimmerman notes, "Harley's principal function in the story is as listener rather than as actor. As protagonist he is tentative and ineffectual, as audience he is responsive and active."[22] In addition, like other it-narrators, Harley does not tell his own story but leaves this to The Ghost, who functions as his amanuensis, sometimes recording Harley's experiences as presumably related to him and, other times, seemingly inspired by "some mystical process" that allows him access to Harley's most private thoughts and emotions (more on this later). And, of course, there is the framing device of the "found manuscript," accompanied by the prefatory remarks describing how the manuscript—Harley's story—came into the hands of an editor. All of these work together to strip Harley of independent agency. As relic, Harley is passed around, from one hand to another.

Approximately three-quarters of *The Man of Feeling* focuses on Harley's accidental encounters with others and with the stories that these individuals tell of themselves or that others tell of them. Thus, like an "it-narrative," *The Man of Feeling* is loosely structured in terms of plot and dominated by a series of unrelated stories, most of which offer no conclusion, as we hear no more of the gauger, though he now possesses the leases to the land adjacent to Harley's property, nor do we learn the ultimate fate of Miss Atkins, though she is rejoined with her father. As Gerard A. Barker notes, the episodic structure "indicates a conscious effort to subordinate, at times even to disregard, causality and narrative sequence."[23] Also, like an "it-narrative," the individuals that Harley encounters come from a wide range of social groups, comprised of beggars, cardsharps, glaziers, prostitutes, soldiers, the mad, and more.[24] These individuals are unrelated to each other, either by birth or by circumstance, and thus do not make an affective circle of friends, such as those found in the novels of Samuel Richardson, and so the stories are loosely held together, with Harley the slim thread that binds them.

Clearly, Mackenzie was intent upon delivering a didactic message, but what that message was has been the subject of vigorous scholarly debate, most of it centered on Harley himself, in regards to whether Mackenzie meant the character as an exemplum to be followed or shunned.[25] However, if we view Harley in the light of an "it-narrator," not unlike the coin that is Chrysal, then Harley's own circulation through London society, accompanied as it is by the circulation of his money and emotions, offers a model (albeit a flawed one) for human relations.[26] Certainly, an anti-luxury narrative prevails, wherein modesty, kindness, compassion, and honest feeling compete against greed, self-aggrandizement, self-interest, and deception—and almost *always* lose—but the point is that money, in and of itself, is not necessarily a negative within the text, nor is emotion, in and of itself, always a positive. Instead, the text suggests that money and emotions should circulate freely, rather than be greedily accumulated or selfishly hoarded; an exchange of sorts should occur, with both parties benefiting. In addition, money and emotion may be viewed as interchangeable *if* circulated properly. For instance, the Beggar shares his story, a form of affective transaction, and receives a coin in exchange. The madwoman, blessing Harley for his tears, believing them to be for her "Billy" (27), rewards him with a ring "plaited to-day from this bit of stuff" (28); Harley greets this offering by providing "a couple of guineas" (28) for her care. Within this novel, when given where there is need, money becomes the handmaiden of sentiment. Edwards, of course, remains the principal beneficiary of Harley's willingness to engage in economic and affective transactions, as Edwards and his two orphaned grandchildren become the tenants of a small farm owned by Harley, and Harley is rewarded in turn by Edward's devoted affection for him. (Unlike many of the others encountered within this novel, Edwards truly believes in Harley and thus is rewarded.) When money is not necessary to ease distress, then emotion alone may be exchanged, as happens with Harley and Ben Silton, two men from the same social station. Failed circulation comes in myriad forms. The Misanthrope proudly hoards his emotions, occasionally spewing them forth as words of contempt for his fellow human beings. No exchange is involved, as he prohibits contradiction, shutting down attempts at conversation by himself becoming abruptly silent, refusing to speak "all the night after" (30). As Gerard A. Barker notes, sensibility can "be perverted for egotistical ends."[27] The cardsharpers cheat, taking unfairly what is not legitimately theirs and offering nothing in return. And the baronet gifts the rental of the Crown lands adjacent to Harley's property to the "pimp of a gauger" (61), his own agent who has traded his services (as the baronet's tax and rent collector) and his sister (as the baronet's new "sempstress") for this honor. In this latter instance, the baronet's gift merely secures his own position—the gauger will vote for him in the next election, collect his rent for him, and pimp for him—while the gauger lives up to his name, pressuring others for rents, ordering food and drink at others' expense, and climbing up the social ladder on the coattails of his betters.

Four consecutive chapters of the novel—placed midway at the center of the novel—focus on the plight of the prostitute, a Miss Atkins, who has been beguiled and seduced by the son of a neighboring baronet, deceived into the hands of a bawd, and left to "the common use of the town" (53). Her sensibility has become her ruin, because she has entrusted her honor and virtue to someone who has cheated her. Ultimately, she must sell herself—that very valuable self-property—in order to eat and have a roof over her head. As a lover, Miss Atkins accrues nothing in return, except an unwanted pregnancy and the scorn of her seducer. As a prostitute, Miss Atkins reaps little financial reward. She gives, both affectively and economically, receiving little or nothing in exchange. As Liz Bellamy writes, "Prostitution becomes a metaphor for the mercenary and transitory nature of relationships within a society based on circulation and rapidity of exchange."[28] Yet, Harley's compassion, expressed not only emotively but economically, restores Miss Atkins to some semblance of self-ownership, removing her from the position of object. In turn, this restoration to self and subjectivity allows her to participate once again in affective circulation, as she expresses her gratitude toward Harley by telling him her story.

Earlier, I said that Harley's "circulation" offers a flawed model of social relations, and I say flawed because as many scholars have noted, a strict limit exists to what Harley has accomplished and can accomplish, with his small coins and generous sentiments. Further, this circulation of benevolent emotional and commercial exchange is anachronistic and nostalgic, pointing to a time long since passed, if indeed it ever existed, as several scholars have duly noted.[29] Circulation is also paradoxically related to sequestration, for according to Harley, "feelings . . . that applaud benevolence, and censure inhumanity" are more easily cultivated by those "who live sequestered from the noise of the multitude" (85). Mackenzie's ideal world of benevolent circulation is more clearly articulated and realized within the fictive world of his second novel, *The Man of the World*, through the figure of Henry Bolton, a young man of high integrity, fine feelings, and active engagement, who unexpectedly inherits an estate but insists upon treating his new tenants with fond paternalism, keeping their rents low, visiting their neat, clean cottages, and restraining himself from false improvements to the estate.[30] As the narrator comments, "I never envied riches so much as since I have known Mr. Bolton."[31] But Harley *is* able to make a difference in several lives, in his modest, unassuming way. Nonetheless, if he is a saint—as the text posits him—then he is one of humble powers.

In sum, *The Man of Feeling* owes much to the subgenre known as the "it-narrative," but whether Mackenzie consciously used the it-narrative as the structural basis for the novel remains unclear. Certainly, Mackenzie was familiar with

GHOSTS

the subgenre—who wasn't?—but perhaps the structure is an (un)happy coincidence rather than a conscious choice. Regardless, the "it-narrative" structure of *The Man of Feeling* has several direct consequences. First, it forces Harley into a more passive position than would be in a more conventional (canonical) novelistic structure. This, in turn, interjects a sense of fatalism or futility into the novel, as if our personality—worldly or emotive—doomed us from the start, doomed Harley from the start, and that small acts of kindness—a coin here, a sympathetic smile there—are but tiny drops of rain in the dry, parched landscape of human interactions. Second, the lack of affective relationships as binder between and among the various individuals in the novel generates a sense of aloneness—and loneliness—on the part of Harley and others. The relationships that Harley does have with others are restricted: Edwards is his social inferior, whom he helps but with whom he cannot socialize as equal; Miss Walton is an unmarried woman, with whom propriety forbids too close contact. The Ghost is Harley's friend, but he never speaks to Harley directly within the novel, that is, not until Harley is literally on his deathbed. Good people, kind people, so it seems, have few true friends. As Harley tells The Ghost, "I have been blessed with a few friends who redeem my opinion of mankind" (104)—but they are few friends indeed.

Third and finally, the it-narrative structure of *The Man of Feeling* fashions ghosts out of "men of feeling" and women of sensibility. It-narratives routinely engage in themes of loss, as the object or animal shuffles from owner to owner, because either the object/animal itself has become lost or the owner has lost the ability to pay for it or care for it. In *The Man of Feeling*, the losses do not stem from careless ownership on the part of others but because encounters tend to be brief and because good people, sensitive people, are unable to live easily in "the world." Men and women of feeling become spectral beings, living apparitions, only dimly acknowledged by others, haunting the woods around abandoned houses or sitting quietly in graveyards. They make little mark on their world, except in small private ways; few know of them or their goodness. Although *The Man of Feeling* ends with the death of Harley—a conclusion similar to many canonical novels of the period—it seems appropriate, as those possessed of feeling either are dead by the end of the novel or seem most comfortable visiting with the spirits of the dead. The Ghost lovingly lingers on his memories of Ben Silton and Harley, and when his tale of remembrance ends, he quietly fades away, going "no one knows whither" (3). As the prefatory remarks by the editor show, Miss Walton chooses to remain single, spending her days in good deeds and wandering the paths outside Harley's house. We find her there still within Mackenzie's second novel, *The Man of the World*, where she lingers within the circle where Harley's memorial stands, waiting for the day when she too will join Harley in the grave.[32]

"'TIS AT LEAST A MEMORIAL FOR THOSE WHO SURVIVE": DEATH WRITING AS RELIC

Death writing, as Elizabeth Hallam and Jenny Hockey term it, comprises a wide range of written texts: the last will and testament of decedents; descriptions of deathbed scenes; memorial inscriptions in stone (tombstones or public memorials) or on fabric (the AIDS memorial quilt); remembrances of the decedent, including condolence letters, online memorial pages, and handwritten reminiscences; autobiographical essays, books, and blogs written by the dying person; and biographies of the dead—to name just a few.[33]

Death writing is meant as witness, tribute, memory aid, memorial, and relic. It affirms the individual's prior existence; it claims that she or he once laughed, loved, wept, slept, drank, and ate. It often serves as tribute, personal or public, venerating someone for his kindness, honoring her bravery, or acknowledging his or her contributions to the living. Written reminiscences aid recall and memory; they seek to capture the central moments in the lost beloved's life, or those things that made that person unique—his hearty laugh, a lilt in the way she talked, the odd little gesture that he made. The dead wish to be remembered, and we wish to remember them. The dying write books, essays, and blogs to stand in their stead, to express to those left behind their values, ideas, loves, and hates. If a child (even an unborn one) is left behind, then the decedent must connect across time and space through words and images. The living read about the dying to learn: to understand a particular individual (his faults, her strengths), to interrogate faith (or lack thereof), and to confront death itself. The living write about the dead in order to keep them close to them, to recall their times together, and to assert their continuing importance; to acknowledge loss; and to remember when memory has begun to fade. Death writing is a form of ghost writing, as the dying seek to leave something of their spirit behind, while the living seek to reanimate the spirits of the dead. With our fingertips, we trace the names of the dead on gravestones and memorials, as if touching the name of the dead beloved somehow allows us to touch her/his material self.[34] Death writing creates presence where absence existed, the written remembrance corporeal and material, a relic that can be touched and handled. In particular, a manuscript becomes a palpable presence, with heft and bulk, able to be cradled or hugged. Death writing functions as collaboration between mourner and decedent, particularly if the mourner is also the author of the text. Together, mourner and decedent work as one to re-create moments of the decedent's life. As Hallam and Hockey note, "writing at or after the point of death for the purposes of memory is often a matter situated at the interface between body and material object," and they remind us that death writings are highly evocative not only because of "their *content*, but by virtue of their form and execution in material terms."[35] In sum, death writing engenders "Sensations of proximity to deceased relatives and friends."[36]

Within *The Man of Feeling*, the manuscript that The Ghost pens functions as witness, tribute, memory aid, memorial, and relic; it is able to conjure and connect with the dead; and it is a lament, a *cri de coeur* for lost people and places. Hagiographically, it asserts that a man once existed whom many dismissed as inconsequential, a sentimental fool, but who was sensitive, caring, and worthy of remembrance. In *The Man of the World*, Lucy Sindall admits to Miss Walton that she has "scarcely ever heard of the name" of Harley, though she has lived in the neighborhood all her life. In reply, Miss Walton notes, "his actions were not of a kind that is loudly talked of."[37] The Ghost's manuscript bears witness to Harley's life, confirming that he existed. Further, the manuscript functions as a tribute, as, in the end, we are meant to admire Harley, not only for his gentle kindness, but also for his peaceful acceptance of his impending death, which corroborates his goodness. The manuscript also aids in recalling the small but significant moments in a quiet life, the things that The Ghost loved about Harley and the characteristics that made Harley a unique person, such as his willful naivety, his compassion toward others, his worshipful adoration of Miss Walton, and his unwillingness to "put himself forward," unless on behalf of others. We learn little about Harley's outward appearance but a great deal about his inner self. In addition, the patchy way the manuscript is put together—as the curate says, "I could never find the author in one strain for two chapters together" (3)—with its serial encounters and small heartfelt moments mimics memory itself. In fact, the subsequent disintegration of the full, intact manuscript into bits of wadding and "a bundle of little episodes" (3) recalls the degeneration and dissolution of memory. Further, the manuscript functions as memorial, much in the same manner as Harley's gravestone or as the plinth and urn erected to his memory by Miss Walton. As The Ghost remarks when looking down upon Harley's grave, "'tis at least a memorial for those who survive," acknowledging the fact that memorials are erected more for the living than the dead. The Ghost continues, commenting that "for some indeed a slender memorial will serve" (107), and so it is that the slender manuscript functions as memorial for Harley, whereas more substantial memorials exist for others (such as Richardson's Clarissa!). And, as Lucy Razzall notes, books and manuscripts were frequently viewed in a manner similar to sacred relics in Post-Reformation England,[38] and so The Ghost's manuscript exists as relic, enclosing within it the remains of Harley's life.

More than that, the manuscript allows author/mourner to connect with subject/mourned. By describing events in Harley's life, as well as his thoughts, actions, and emotions, it reanimates him, bringing him back into the land of the living, where he again sighs, weeps, and struggles against his true nature. As relic, the manuscript creates presence, but it also does so through content as well. And The Ghost becomes the saint's biographer who conjures up the dead, as his putting pen to paper, his remembering and recalling, are what make Harley whole again, if only for a short period of time, and in this way, the manuscript becomes a collaboration between author and subject, between the living and the dead, between The Ghost and Harley. However, if the manuscript possesses the power to reanimate Harley, then why does The Ghost ultimately abandon it? Perhaps because the act of writing has performed the job it needed to do effectively and well, allowing The Ghost to move on (literally)? Or perhaps it works too well, in that by reanimating Harley, it also re-creates his loss, forcing The Ghost to relive the pain of separation over again.

In the end, the manuscript documents repeated loss, and so the manuscript as death writing becomes not only a lament for the dead, but also a way of articulating The Ghost's own pain and grief, a narrative of mourning. Toward the end of the manuscript, The Ghost remarks, "HARLEY was one of those few friends whom the malevolence of fortune had yet left me!" (103), and then Harley is taken from him as well. Ben Silton too is gone—and forgotten by all, except The Ghost— "He is now forgotten and gone!" (6)—and the manuscript becomes a way to say goodbye to him as well: "Once more, my honoured friend, farewell!" (68). Perhaps too it is a lament for the ephemeral nature of human existence, with few remembering the dead except those rare individuals possessed of sensibility—and they too are disappearing, just like The Ghost does, when he "went no body knows whither" (3), leaving only Miss Walton behind to mourn and remember.

"WE SHALL MEET AGAIN, MY FRIEND": THE GHOST AND GHOSTWRITING

The Ghost, author of the found manuscript, is a somewhat problematic narrator, as his attitude toward his subject—Harley—and his distance from his subject are unstable, and because The Ghost's textual presence fades in and out, as befits his appellation. At certain rare points in the narrative, The Ghost exists as a palpable physical presence, spitefully pinching the ears of a spoiled lapdog, forgetfully purloining Harley's love poem "Lavinia," or climbing into the branches of an old tree. Other times, he exists as a palpable textual presence, injecting himself into the narrative with an "I" or a "we," philosophically commenting upon the condition of mankind, or gently mocking his friend Harley for his naivety and innocence.[39]

And, still other times, The Ghost disappears entirely from the narrative, so subsumed into Harley's consciousness that he becomes the (psychic) medium through which Harley's inner thoughts are revealed.[40] Whence this waxing and waning of The Ghost—and why? What is its significance?

The narrative contains nineteen chapters, three "fragments," and a conclusion. The manuscript begins with chapter XI, at which point The Ghost's presence is clearly evident. As narrator, he speaks from the position of "I" while recording his own long ago conversation with Ben Silton, and thus functions doubly as a speaking subject. Further, his actions intrude into the scene, as he pinches the lapdog's ears and discretely sheds a single tear in Silton's memory. In contrast, Harley's initial textual presence is negligible. He is mentioned only in the final paragraph of this beginning chapter and then minimally, with the reference to his ancestral lineage crowded out by talk of the "merchants" and the "sons of stewards" (7) who have likewise crowded out members of the lesser gentry. The past tense is used when speaking of Harley, though readers do not know that Harley is dead, assuming instead that the use of the past is merely writerly convention. The next chapter (XII) introduces Harley more thoroughly, though the tone remains impersonal, providing summary details of Harley's life leading up to his London journey. The Ghost retains a strong narrative presence, making general observations on character, speaking as "I" and making ironic remarks. However, a subtle shift occurs in the third chapter (XIII): The Ghost begins to refer to himself as "we," a sort of indirect appeal to the reader, seemingly meant to establish the narrator's veracity—"We would conceal nothing" (11)—and to urge the reader to align herself or himself subtly with the narrator. Also, The Ghost finally begins to reveal some of Harley's thoughts, though with narrative distancing still employed, as when he says, "A blush, a phrase of affability to an inferior, a tear at a moving tale, were to him [Harley], like the cestus of Cytherea, unequalled in conferring beauty" (11–12). However, despite the tentative steps into Harley's consciousness, The Ghost nonetheless remains a palpable and distinct presence, rending critical judgment on Harley: "he was a child in the drama of the world"; and "minds like Harley's are not very apt to make this distinction" (13).

Once, however, Harley sets out on the road to London (chapter XIV), the narrative voice begins to assume the perspective of Harley. At the opening of the chapter, The Ghost still refers to himself as "we" when referring to the "faithful fellow" (15) Peter, Harley's servant, whom Harley has left behind, but other than that, Harley's thoughts, feelings, actions dominate, so much so that readers become immersed in Harley's viewpoint, accessing his private thoughts at one point and witnessing his struggle between upright "Virtue" (18) and compassion, in gifting the beggar with a coin. The next chapter (XIX) follows the same format, with an

" 'TIS AT LEAST A MEMORIAL FOR THOSE WHO SURVIVE"

introductory "We" statement leading into immersion in Harley's perspective. However, abruptly, midway through the chapter, the narrator speaks directly as "I" in order to interject an opinion about the influence of ideas on objects, necessary to account to readers for Harley's vulnerability to false impressions. After this brief interlude, the narrative voice disappears entirely in chapters XX and XXI, on Harley's visit to Bedlam and his subsequent visit to the Misanthrope. A break occurs in the sequencing of the chapters—chapter XXI leads into chapter XXV—but throughout the remainder of Harley's time in London (through the first Fragment), the narrator has all but disappeared, and Harley's thoughts, words, and deeds become the lens through which readers see. Only at the end of Harley's carriage ride home, when we find out that the fellow traveler whose conversation he esteems is none other than Ben Silton, does the voice of The Ghost reappear in order to praise his long-deceased friend, Silton. In chapter XXXIV, after alighting from the carriage, Harley travels now on foot, and a slight distance between the narrative voice and Harley's perspective appears in order to explain Harley's eccentricities to the readers. But once again, the distance between narrator and Harley then all but disappears as Harley encounters Edwards and, in the next chapter, his orphaned grandchildren. (Harley's perspective dominates when he sees Edwards, as figure 5.1 suggests). As Harley approaches his home, accompanied by Edwards and the children, the narrative voice asserts itself again, with The Ghost's textual presence becoming increasingly apparent, a trend that continues throughout the remainder of the novel, particularly when Harley lays dying. At this point, The Ghost physically manifests within the narrative as he worriedly visits the infirm Harley; only then do we learn that The Ghost's name is Charles. After Harley's death, The Ghost sits in the hollow of a tree above Harley's grave, thinking about his deceased friend. His voice dominates the conclusion, and the narrative separation between narrator and subject—mimicking the physical separation of the living from the dead—is clearly defined.

Several things should be noted. First, prior to the trip to London and during it, the narrator intrudes with "I" when he and Harley's perspectives are at variance; after the trip, the "I" is used to provide eyewitness testimony as to Harley's goodness. "We" is most often used when The Ghost wishes to proffer some general philosophical comment, which reflects somehow on Harley and which sometimes works in Harley's favor and sometimes does not. It is also employed to make promises to the reader or subtle appeals for the reader's agreement. Second, physical distance impacts the narrative perspective, for when Harley and The Ghost are in close physical proximity, an obvious split occurs in perspective; when they are physically distant, the two personas merge into one. From a writing perspective, this merging of perspective—this indirect discourse—is necessary if Harley

Figure 5.1 *The Man of Feeling* (Paris: Theophilus Barrois, 1807). Engraving by C. L'Epine from a drawing by Louis Lafitte. "'Thou art old,' said Harley to himself, 'but age has not brought thee rest for its infirmities.'" Collection of K. M. Oliver. Photograph by Charles Parkhill, 2017.

himself is not allowed to narrate his own experiences. However, considering the narrator is called The Ghost and Harley himself is dead by the end of the narrative, the intermingling of narrator and subject is worth exploring more fully, particularly in view of The Ghost's spectral nature.

The Ghost has presumably been given his moniker due to his nocturnal wanderings, his avoidance of local clubs and pubs, his grave demeanor, and his and Harley's predilection for sitting in the churchyard, counting the graves. Physically, The Ghost moves about unseen by the vast majority of others. For instance, when he draws "near unperceived" to the lapdog in order to pinch its ear; the dog's mistress does "not suspect the author of its misfortune" (6), even though The Ghost himself has taken the dog's place in Ben Silton's old chair. Unseen, he also materializes in places where he can witness Harley's goodness, such as when he sees Harley hard "at work" (83) in the little garden attached to Edward's house, and he—in spirit at least—appears to have accompanied Harley to London, where he is privy to Harley's private conversations and witness to all of Harley's encounters. We know others have seen The Ghost—the curate himself attests to his own sighting—but even when The Ghost is physically present, others see right through him, as when Edwards enters Harley's room immediately after the latter's death. Although The Ghost looks Edwards "full in the face," Edward's "eye was fixed on another object" (107)—that is, the dead Harley. Although he is meant to be a real, physical character, The Ghost seems more spirit than material being. After Harley's death, he just fades away, leaving the parish to go "no body knows whither" (3), leaving behind but a single material trace that he ever existed: the manuscript. Within Mackenzie's novel, The Ghost exists as ephemeral, wispy presence—now we see him, now we don't—and his chief job, his mission on earth, so to speak, is to provide the living with a narrative of the dead—that is, with Harley's story. "The Ghost" writes Harley's consciousness; at times, he *is* Harley's consciousness.

But The Ghost is not the only ghost in the story. The dead haunt the landscape of Mackenzie's fictive world. When he learns that Miss Walton may marry Sir Harry Benson, Harley hovers around the grounds surrounding her home "like some troubled ghost" (91–92), and of course, Harley is dead by the end of the narrative, though whether he died before or during the writing of The Ghost's manuscript remains unclear, blurring the boundaries between the living and the dead. In contrast, readers are informed up front that Ben Silton has already died when the story begins; he lives on only within the manuscript, a jovial spirit, full of arcane wisdom and sage advice. Ghosts of the dead appear everywhere, even at dilapidated school houses, where Harley envisions the ghosts of children dancing upon the adjacent lawn, stringing garlands around the stump of a tree, or picnicking upon apples (78). In addition, many of the living have become ghostlike. For instance, Miss Walton haunts the grounds of Harley's old home, where she has been "seen walking there more than once" (2), and, in Mackenzie's subsequent novel, *The Man of the World*, she functions as Harley's executrix, dispensing the remainder of his wealth to the poor of the community, and, with a sigh, hinting that one day—perhaps soon—her name will join Harley's on the funerary monument.[41] The point is this: within Mackenzie's novel, those possessed of sensibility live in a world crowded with the spirits of the dead, while those who are "men of the world" see only the material world. In his dying moments, Harley tells The Ghost that "This world, my dear Charles, was a scene in which I never much delighted" (103), and he informs him that he looks eagerly forward to entering "into the society of the blessed, wise as angels, with the simplicity of children" (104). However, for those who enjoy (or bear the burden of) exquisite sensitivity, the boundary between the living and the dead is permeable—or so Mackenzie's novel would have it. People such as Harley, Miss Walton, and The Ghost live forever in the borderlands, unlike the "men of the world" whose feet remain solidly on *terra firma*.

According to the *Oxford English Dictionary*, the term "ghostwriter" first appeared in print during the late 1920s in the United States. Originally a pejorative term referring to "a hack writer who does the work for which another person takes credit," the term might be favorably applied in relation to The Ghost and Harley in *The Man of Feeling*. In this instance, The Ghost has penned a period in Harley's life—as Harley himself *felt* it and *experienced* it. The Ghost has channeled the consciousness of the dead and brought it to life, much as a psychic medium channels the spirits from beyond the grave. In doing so, The Ghost himself becomes a mediating spirit for the dead, a temporary abode for their roving consciousness. Thus, when Harley tells The Ghost that "we shall meet again, my friend" (104), there is no reason to assume not, as The Ghost has already connected with the realm of spirits—with Harley's spirit—and he is more than half spirit himself.

CONCLUSION

The Man of Feeling is a ghostly text, comprised of the wispy fragments of a more conventional novel, preoccupied with suffering, loss, and death, and insistent that those filled with feeling live in a world of ghosts, of sheer consciousness, forever envisioning what no longer exists materially but only within the realm of imagination. It suggests that the "man of the world" is just that—one who lives entirely in the material world, indulging in the sensual, consumed by objects, by prestige, by power and status, but nonetheless solid, weighty, and substantial. For the highly sensitive, whether dead or living, the corporeal body is unnecessary; it weighs the individual down, tethering him or her to the earth. The Lockean conscious has severed its connection to the material world. Those possessed of great feeling—those who are "all soul"—inhabit a world wherein the boundaries between the past and present and between the dead and the living are permeable, a world of memories inhabited by the spectral beings of the dead, by relics and relicts of the dead.

CONCLUSION

Death and the Novel

DEATH AND LOSS HAUNT the eighteenth-century British novel: living corpses walk the streets of Defoe's plague-ridden London; Clarissa Harlowe's emaciated body lies in its coffin; Orlando Faulkland commits suicide; and Harley dies, a victim of his exquisite sensibility. Madame Montoni feverishly wastes away at the Castle of Udolpho, while Antonia is raped and murdered in the sepulcher beneath the convent of St. Clare. Forlorn orphans, despairing lovers, and disillusioned dreamers wander landscapes thick with loss and longing—and littered with relics of the dead, the past, the absent, the vanished.

Both cultural influences and formalistic aspects contribute to the eighteenth-century novel's preoccupation with death and loss, with relics and relicts. Formally, its linearity, tracing the lives and histories of its fictional protagonists, mimics the lived trajectory of human life, at least as experienced in eighteenth-century Britain; its ending, the abrupt confrontation with the blank page, announces the termination of the fictional narrative and, with it, the textual death of its characters. Culturally, the realist novel's detailed presentation of material objects recreates the expansion of consumerism and consumer products, including those relative to death culture. The novel's preoccupation with the influence of past actions upon present and future circumstances mirrors the culture's newly awakened sense of its own history; its focus on interiority—revealing the most intimate thoughts of its characters—reflects the influence of Locke's theory of consciousness, of the centrality of mind to personhood and identity; and, last, its interest in death and loss acknowledges the historical reality of early and sudden deaths, from plague, fever, or smallpox, from the common cold or a sinus infection, from myriad other diseases, and also the slowly changing relationship between the living and the dead.

Two subgenres of the eighteenth-century British novel speak most clearly to the interrelated themes of consciousness, death, and loss: the novel of sensibility and the Gothic novel. The novel of sensibility, a genre that blossomed mid-century only to die an early death, relies heavily on suffering and loss for its emotive

CONCLUSION

effects. Specifically, the novel of sensibility's desire to provoke emotional responses on the part of its readers, offering scenes of suffering as witnessed by empathetic protagonists, necessarily engages with death culture, the dead being the least in need of our sympathy yet the most likely to provoke it. As Adam Smith writes, "We sympathize even with the dead. . . . It is miserable, we think, to be deprived of the light of the sun; to be shut out from life and conversation; to be laid in the cold grave, a prey to corruption and the reptiles of the earth; to be no more thought of in this world, but to be obliterated, in a little time, from the affections, and almost from the memory, of their dearest friends and relations." This excess of sentiment spent upon the dead, which "can have no influence upon their happiness" nor "afford them . . . consolation," nonetheless permits an overflow of unreciprocated emotions, presumably influencing the treatment of the living.[1] The novel of sensibility similarly invests material objects—including those associated with the dead—with sentimental and emotive value, symbols of shared sentiment between one person and another, between the living and the dead. In addition, the repetitive nature of the novel of sensibility as enacted through its myriad vignettes of distress and suffering replicates the repetitive nature of trauma and melancholia, especially as regards death and loss. Finally, sensibility's compulsion to record emotions and explore thoughts rhetorically reproduces Lockean consciousness.

Unlike the novel of sensibility, the Gothic—like the un-dead that frequently populate it—remains a living genre, perhaps because it is the only genre that consistently insists upon confronting the dead, their "missing" bodies, and their spectralization. As the dead and dying became increasingly isolated from the living, the Gothic novel replicated this cultural experience within its fictive worlds, with the dying individual imprisoned within thick walls, her emaciated or his bloodied body found by those seeking something or someone else; or, when dead, their brittle skeletons are recovered years later, pronouncing the fact of their murder. The Gothic confronts the disappearing bodies of the dying and dead, but it also distances death, making it mysterious, "other," transforming it into something horrific that only happens to someone else, not to us.

And so it is no coincidence that each of the six novels examined within this book may be categorized as either a novel of sensibility or a Gothic novel, and each, in its own way, provides textual evidence of cultural transformations regarding the treatment of the dying and/or dead body and the rejection or acceptance of consciousness as the new soul of humanity. Samuel Richardson's *Clarissa*, published in 1748, views death as the portal to otherworldly existence, with Clarissa awaiting her guaranteed entry into her heavenly home, Mrs. Sinclair her certain expulsion into a fiery hell, and Lovelace his journey to parts unknown. Clarissa's dead body, uncorrupt and lovingly arranged within its coffin, will be buried next to that of her beloved grandfather, within the local churchyard, where it will await Resurrection Day and be reunited with her soul. The relics Clarissa leaves behind—quasi-sacred ones, containing the actual remains of her deceased body—will be cherished as reminders of this saintly young woman, serve as talismans against evil, and provide assurances of future reunion with the beloved decedent. Clarissa's relics will not replace her, but they will offer remembrance of her as intimate connections to the decedent, and they pledge faith in future (heavenly) meetings.

By 1753, this confidence in the substantial soul—for that is what Clarissa appears to possess—and its reunion with the corporeal body on Resurrection Day begins to falter, even within Richardson's oeuvre. In *Grandison*, a measure of uncertainty regarding death seeps into the text: two living beings treat each other as if dead; (dead) wives haunt living ones; and like-minded individuals share the same consciousness. If Clementina metaphorically functions as death or, at the very least, the handmaiden of death, then death does not mean a dead body, but rather it is spectral (a madness of the mind) and "other"-ed (mad, Italian, female). The dead continue to exist, free-floating forms of consciousness that, across continents and seas, haunt those who would replace them.

Also published in 1753, Sarah Fielding's *Volume the Last* treats the dead body and the soul in radically different fashion from *Grandison*. Nonetheless, it is not the death of earlier ages. In *Volume the Last*, death holds no promise of a heavenly abode or afterlife. The only thing death promises is oblivion and relief from earthly pain, whether physical or mental. Death is *unconsciousness* not consciousness. No soul finds its way to a heavenly home; no consciousness remains on earth. Body and soul are dust, ashes. The body, a mere container, is a burden to be left behind, neither sacred nor esteemed. Within *David Simple* and *Volume the Last*, bodies (in the form of "friends") are discarded with unseemly abandon, never (except for Orgueil) to be seen again. No gravesides will be visited; no whispered prayers will be said for the dead. The dead just disappear.

In Mackenzie's 1771 *The Man of Feeling*, those possessed of extreme sensibility, whether dead or alive, exist as spectral beings, unmoored from the earth, their consciousness able to enter the minds of like-minded beings. Dead or alive, it hardly matters, as in corporeal or spectral form, they exist virtually unnoticed by most "worldly" creatures. Indeed, they are deemed unworthy of notice. These spectral creatures mourn, but they themselves are not mourned, except by others of their own kind, a select and endangered species. These spectral beings do not forget, though they themselves are forgotten. They disappear without trace, or in the rare event that a trace does remain, it is fractured, scattered, neglected, abused. Individuals of great sensibility are creatures without corporeal bodies, without substantial souls. They are compositions of consciousness alone, their mournful ghosts left to haunt the landscapes, solitary and alone.

And, last, by 1794, Radcliffe's *The Mysteries of Udolpho* looks for—and finds—the missing dead bodies of specific (dispensable) characters, and it also provides a waxy surrogate for Death itself. However, no indication exists that dead bodies are valuable, either as companions to the soul or as containers of consciousness. People exist within the confines of other people's minds, or within objects associated with them. Relics speak for individuals, and they often do so in ways more satisfactory than the real.

In a world of epistemological uncertainty, with the demise of the substantial soul, with the birth of consciousness that transcends time and place and body, and with a body that no longer possesses sanctity or value, whether dead or alive, relics/relicts—the material remains of the dead—become increasingly important as evidence of lives lived and of bodies buried or burned. Relic/relicts become necessary tropes within literature and other artistic genres in order to express these lives and these dead bodies, but only as long as relics/relicts (and lives and dead bodies) remain relevant within the larger culture—when the past and the dead are deemed worthy of remembrance, when lost things and places and people are mourned. And because we still mourn, the remains of the dead continue to take new forms, but ones that today express our continued cultural avoidance of death and our newfound societal attempts to deny any need to mourn. Specifically, the dead themselves—in reanimated or virtual form—function as their own relics/relicts in the twenty-first century, appearing within the arts as vampires, zombies, ghosts, and holograms and within everyday life as virtual presences, still living through social media memorial pages, holographic images, and virtual avatars. In the twenty-first century, every day is Resurrection Day.

ACKNOWLEDGMENTS

My thanks and appreciation to the amazing editors (past, acting, present) with whom I have worked at Bucknell University Press—Greg Clingham, Amy McCready, Suzanne E. Guiod, and Pamelia Dailey—as well as to the *Transit* series editors—Kate Parker and Miriam Wallace. My especial thanks to Miriam Wallace for her advocacy. In addition, the anonymous readers of the original manuscript deserve my heartfelt gratitude, as they provided detailed and thoughtful commentary that has served to unify the book and deepen the ideas within it; very special thanks to the "second reader" for reviewing the manuscript several times. Thanks are due also to Daryl Brower at Rutgers University Press and to Cheryl Hirsch at Westchester Publishing Services, for serving as production editors, and to Luane Hutchinson, for serving as copyeditor.

    I would also like to thank the Interlibrary Loan staff at the University of Central Florida for providing me with scholarly essays otherwise unobtainable. My thanks as well to those institutions and their respective representatives that allowed for the reprinting of essays or the publishing of images for this book: *Eighteenth-Century Fiction* and Jacqueline Langille; the Science and Society Picture Library and Jasmine Rodgers; and Art Resource. My appreciation too to the Yale Center for British Art for generously allowing scholars to publish beautifully photographed images at no cost.

    Marita Oliver and Andy Lehrer drove me around the cemeteries of Brooklyn and Queens on a frigid March morning so that I could take photographs of funerary statuary and mausoleums (which, unfortunately, I was unable to use due to unforeseen legalities). My thanks to both of them for their patience and their support. As well, a tip of the hat to Eileen Degenhart for her support. Thanks to Charles Parkhill for taking photographs of items in my collection and, as always, for providing me with support and encouragement in this project and in everything I do. Thanks to Sobrino and Golly for keeping me company as I read and wrote—and for keeping me warm in the hot Florida weather. And, last but not least, my thanks to Pinkie, who should have been acknowledged in my first book but was not.

NOTES

INTRODUCTION

1. John Donne, "The Relique," in *The Poems of John Donne*, ed. H.J.C. Grierson (London: Oxford University Press; Humphrey Milford, 1929): 55–56, line 10.
2. Christopher Fox, *Locke and the Scriblerians: Identity and Consciousness in Early Eighteenth-Century Britain* (Berkeley: University of California Press, 1988), 15.
3. Lucia Dacome, "Resurrecting by Numbers in Eighteenth-Century England," *Past & Present* 193 (November 2006): 73–110; 76.
4. Dacome, "Resurrecting by Numbers," 83. Dacome uses as an example Henry Felton's *Resurrection of the Same Numerical Body, and its Reunion to the Same Soul: Asserted in a Sermon Preached before the University of Oxford, at St. Mary's, on Easter-Monday, 1725* (London, 1725), 2.
5. Dacome, "Resurrecting by Numbers," 74; Fox, *Locke and the Scriblerians*, 31.
6. Fox, *Locke and the Scriblerians*, 46.
7. John Locke, *An Essay Concerning Human Understanding*, 2 vols. (New York: Dover Publications, 1959), I:463–464.
8. Dacome, "Resurrecting by Numbers," 76.
9. Locke, *An Essay*, I:448–449.
10. Locke, *An Essay*, I:448.
11. Locke, *An Essay*, I:454.
12. See Dacome, "Resurrecting by Numbers," 81. Dacome specifically mentions Thomas Beconsall's *The Doctrine of a General Resurrection: Wherein the Identity of the Rising Body Is Asserted, against Socinians and Scepticks. In a Sermon Preach'd before the University, at St. Mary's in Oxford, on Easter-Monday, Apr. 5* (Oxford, 1697).
13. See Philippe Ariès, *The Hour of Our Death: The Classic History of Western Attitudes toward Death over the Last One Thousand Years*, trans. Helen Weaver (1981; New York: Barnes & Noble, 2000), and Thomas W. Laqueur, *The Work of the Dead: A Cultural History of Mortal Remains* (Princeton: Princeton University Press, 2015). Both Ariès and Laqueur make similar arguments, though Ariès focuses principally on France and the continent, and Laqueur on England.
14. Laqueur, *The Work of the Dead*, 97.
15. Laqueur, *The Work of the Dead*, 137.
16. Laqueur, *The Work of the Dead*, 138.
17. Laqueur, *The Work of the Dead*, 113.
18. Mary Nash, *The Provoked Wife: The Life and Times of Susannah Cibber* (Boston: Little, Brown and Company, 1977), 10–11. Susannah Cibber's father, Thomas Arne, was an upholsterer and undertaker prior to managing his daughter's theatrical career. In regards to eighteenth-century development of the undertaking trade, Nash references Richard Davey, *A History of Mourning* (London: Jay's, 1889), 109, footnote a.
19. Laqueur, *The Work of the Dead*, 279.
20. See Laqueur, *The Work of the Dead*, 215–238.

21. While the nineteenth century saw the most pronounced changes in the medical profession, these changes initiated in the eighteenth century. For instance, Erasmus Darwin (1731–1802) sought the "means of preventing old age" (as quoted in Porter, 284); artificial respiration was taught; and major hospitals and infirmaries were established. As Roy Porter notes, "Increasingly, doctors hoped to cure, not just to relieve" (284). See Roy Porter, *English Society in the Eighteenth Century*, rev. ed. (London: Penguin, 1990).
22. See Ariès, *The Hour of Our Death*, and Laqueur, *The Work of the Dead*.
23. Ariès, *The Hour of Our Death*, Part IV, "The Death of the Other," 407–601. See also Terry Castle, "The Spectralization of the Other in *The Mysteries of Udolpho*," in *The New 18th Century: Theory, Politics, English Literature*, eds. Felicity Nussbaum and Laura Brown (New York: Methuen, 1987), 231–253.
24. As Lou Taylor notes, "It was Victoria, the middle-class ideal of Christian widowhood, who fanned the cult of mourning, spreading it to all classes of society during her lifetime" (122). Further, "the etiquette of mourning increased too. The mourning periods grew longer and even the remotest relatives were now mourned, though fortunately only for three to six weeks. The rules became impossibly complicated and the social pitfalls more and more numerous" (133). See Lou Taylor, *Mourning Dress: A Costume and Social History* (1983; Abingdon, UK: Routledge, 2009).
25. As Julie Rugg writes, "Relatively high levels of spending on funerals were not restricted to families of the middling classes. The poor also endeavored to give an appropriate funeral to their loved ones, and so avoid the stigma of death on the parish" (221). See Julie Rugg, "From Reason to Regulation: 1760–1850," in *Death in England: An Illustrated History*, eds. Peter C. Jupp and Clare Gittings (New Brunswick, NJ: Rutgers University Press, 2000): 202–229. See also Laqueur, *The Work of the Dead*, 312–336.
26. Maureen DeLorme, *Mourning Art & Jewelry* (Atglen, PA: Schiffer Publishing Ltd., 2004), 66.
27. See Jim Murrell, "The Craft of the Miniaturist," in *The English Miniature*, by John Murdoch, Jim Murrell, Patrick J. Noon, and Roy Strong (New Haven, CT: Yale University Press, 1981), 1–24; Patrick J. Noon, "Miniatures on the Market," in *The English Miniature*, 163–209; Daphne Foskett, *British Portrait Miniatures: A History* (1963; London: Spring Books, 1968); Katherine Coombs, *The Portrait Miniature in England* (London: Victoria and Albert Publications, 1998); and Marcia Pointon, "'Surrounded with Brilliants': Miniature Portraits in Eighteenth-Century England," *Art Bulletin* 83, no. 1 (March 2001): 48–71.
28. Taylor, *Mourning Dress*, 105.
29. Rugg, "From Reason to Regulation," 221.
30. G. W. Bernard, *The King's Reformation: Henry VIII and the Remaking of the English Church* (New Haven, CT: Yale University Press, 2005), 254–255, 276, 288–292, 326, 489–490.
31. See Alexandra Walsham, "Skeletons in the Cupboard: Relics after the English Reformation," *Past & Present* (2010), Supplement 5: 121–143; and Robyn Malo, "Intimate Devotion: Recusant Martyrs and the Making of Relics in Post-Reformation England," *Journal of Medieval and Early Modern Studies* 44, no. 3 (Fall 2014): 531–548.
32. While hair jewelry, particularly in the form of rings and bracelets, and locks of hair seem primarily to have been prized as love tokens rather than sureties of reunion on Judgment Day, they were viewed as being imbued with the spiritual nature of their original owner, and many poems that mention the lover's hair also contain religious and political imagery. See Megan Kathleen Smith, "Reading It Wrong to Get It Right: Sacramental and Excremental Encounters with Early Modern Poems about Hair Jewelry," *Philological Quarterly* 94, no. 4 (2015): 353–375.

33. Lucy Razzall, "'A good Booke is the pretious life-blood of a master-spirit': Recollecting Relics in Post-Reformation English Writing," *Journal of the Northern Renaissance* 2 (2010): par. 5. Accessed 6 November 2018, http://northernrenaissance.org.
34. Razzall, "'A good Booke,'" par. 16; par. 2.
35. See Razzall, "'A good Booke,'" par. 17. See also Alexandra Walsham, "Jewels for Gentlewomen: Religious Books as Artefacts in Late Medieval and Early Modern England," in *The Church and the Book*, ed. R. N. Swanson (Woodbridge, UK: Boydell & Brewer, 2004), 123–142; 124–125, 141.
36. Razzall, "'A good Booke,'" par. 2.
37. Razzall, "'A good Booke,'" par. 25.
38. Malo, "Intimate Devotion," 533–534.
39. Malo, "Intimate Devotion," 533.
40. William Godwin, *An Essay on Sepulchres: Or a Proposal for Erecting Some Memorial of the Illustrious Dead in All Ages, on the Spot Where Their Remains Have Been Interred* (New York: Printed for M. and W. Ward, 1809), 23.
41. Alexandra Walsham, "Introduction: Relics and Remains," *Past & Present* (2010), Supplement 5: 9–36; 11.
42. Edwidge Danticat, *The Art of Death: Writing the Final Story* (Minneapolis: Graywolf Press, 2017), 37.
43. Cathy Caruth, "Trauma and Experience: Introduction," in *Trauma: Explorations in Memory*, ed. Cathy Caruth (Baltimore: Johns Hopkins University Press, 1995), 3–12; 4–5.
44. David L. Eng and David Kazanjian, "Introduction: Mourning Remains," in *Loss: The Politics of Mourning*, eds. David L. Eng and David Kazanjian (Berkeley: University of California Press, 2003), 1–25; 2.
45. Jacques Derrida, *Specters of Marx: The State of Debt, the Work of Mourning, and the New International*, trans. Peggy Kamuf (New York: Routledge, 1994), 97.
46. It should be noted that some psychologists would disagree with Derrida's assessment. For instance, Jerrold R. Brandell writes, "mourning, the process through which psychic equilibrium is reestablished after an object loss, is incompatible with the experience of trauma; indeed, successful mourning carries with it the great likelihood that a loss will not be experienced as an enduring trauma." See Jerrold R. Brandell, "Psychoanalytic Theory (Part I)," in *Trauma: Contemporary Directions in Theory, Practice, and Research*, eds. Shoshana Ringel and Jerrold R. Brandell (Los Angeles: Sage Publications, 2012), 41–61; 46. However, as trauma always involves loss (at the very least in the sense that a lived experience has undermined the individual's former perception of and relationship to the world so much so that this new experience cannot be consciously processed), then it would seem that melancholia (which Jahan Ramazani views as another form of mourning) would reasonably follow. In "normative" mourning, the individual (after a reasonable amount of time) processes the event; in "non-normative" mourning—that is, in melancholia—the event remains in the unconscious, as consistent with trauma. For Ramazani's nuanced and persuasive redefinition of melancholia as a form of mourning, see Jahan Ramazani, *The Poetry of Mourning: The Modern Elegy from Hardy to Heaney* (Chicago: University of Chicago Press, 1994), xi.
47. Michel de Certeau, "The Unnamable," in *The Practice of Everyday Life*, trans. Steven Rendall (Berkeley: University of California Press, 1984), 190–198; 193.
48. de Certeau, "The Unnamable," 195, 194.
49. de Certeau, "The Unnamable," 195.
50. de Certeau, "The Unnamable," 198, 195.
51. de Certeau, "The Unnamable," 195.

52. Michel Foucault, "Language to Infinity," in *Language, Counter-memory, Practice: Selected Essays and Interviews*, ed. D. F. Bouchard, trans. D. F. Bouchard and Sherry Simon (Oxford: Oxford University Press, 1977), 53.
53. Maurice Blanchot, "Literature and the Right to Death," in *The Work of Fire*, reprint edition, trans. Charlotte Mandell (Stanford, CA: Stanford University Press, 1995), 300–344; 323, 322, 336.
54. Henry Staten, *Eros in Mourning: Homer to Lacan* (Baltimore: Johns Hopkins University Press, 1995), xi.
55. Nouri Gana, *Signifying Loss: Towards a Poetics of Narrative Mourning* (Lewisburg, PA: Bucknell University Press, 2011), 13.
56. Jolene Zigarovich, *Writing Death and Absence in the Victorian Novel: Engraved Narratives* (New York: Palgrave Macmillan, 2012), 6.
57. Zigarovich, *Writing Death and Absence*, 7.
58. Deborah Lutz, *Relics of Death in Victorian Literature and Culture* (Cambridge: Cambridge University Press, 2015), 8.
59. Lutz, *Relics of Death*, 4.
60. Lutz, *Relics of Death*, 3.
61. See Ariès, *The Hour of Our Death*.

1. "WITH MY HAIR IN CRYSTAL"

A version of this chapter was published under the title of "'With My Hair in Crystal': Mourning Clarissa," in *Eighteenth-Century Fiction* 23, no. 1 (2010): 35–60.

1. Samuel Richardson, *Clarissa; or, The History of a Young Lady*, 3rd ed., 8 vols. (London: S. Richardson, 1751; New York: AMS Press, 1990), 8:135. All citations are from this edition of the text, and all subsequent citations are noted parenthetically.
2. C. Jeanenne Bell, *Collector's Encyclopedia of Hairwork Jewelry* (Paducah, KY: Collector Books, 1998), 10.
3. Maureen DeLorme, *Mourning Art & Jewelry* (Atglen, PA: Schiffer Publishing Ltd., 2004), 65.
4. In his will, Pepys bequeathed a mourning ring worth ten shillings (the lowest level of mourning ring) to Jane Penny (formerly Birch), his first maid. See Appendix "A List of all Persons to Whom Rings and Mourning were Presented upon the Occasion of Mr. Pepys's Death and Burial," in John Ashton's *Social Life in the Reign of Queen Anne* (New York: Scribner and Welford, 1883), 441–444.
5. See Shirley Bury, *An Introduction to Sentimental Jewellery* (London: Her Majesty's Stationery Office, 1985), 15–32; Delorme, *Mourning Art & Jewelry*, 65–115; and Lou Taylor, *Mourning Dress: A Costume and Social History* (1983; Abingdon, UK: Routledge, 2009), 224–247.
6. See Bell, *Collector's Encyclopedia*; Bury, *Introduction to Sentimental Jewellery*, 33–45; Marcia Pointon, "Materializing Mourning: Hair, Jewellery and the Body," in *Material Memories: Design and Evocation*, eds. Marius Kwint, Christopher Breward, and Jeremy Aynsle (Oxford: Berg, 1999), 39–57; Marcia Pointon, "Wearing Memory: Mourning, Jewellery and the Body," in *Trauer Tragen—Trauer Zeigen; Inszenierungen der Geschlechter*, ed. G. Ecker (Munich: Fink, 1999), 65–81; and Helen Sheumaker, "'This Lock You See: Nineteenth-Century Hair Work as the Commodified Self," *Fashion Theory* 1, no. 4 (1997): 421–446.
7. Mary Delany, *The Autobiography and Correspondence of Mrs. Delany*, revised from Lady Llanover's edition, ed. Sarah Chauncey Woolsey, 2 vols. (Boston: Roberts Brothers, 1879), 2.381.

8. Henry Fielding, *Amelia*, ed. David Blewett (1751; London: Penguin, 1987), 101–102.
9. Charles C. F. Greville, *The Greville Memoirs: A Journal of the Reigns of King George IV and King William IV*, ed. Henry Reeve, 3 vols. (London: Longmans, Green and Co., 1874), II:190. Accessed 26 June 2019. books.google.com.
10. Frances Burney, *The Diary and Letters of Madame D'Arblay* (1778–1840), ed. Charlotte Barrett; preface and notes by Austin Dobson, 6 vols. (London: Macmillan, 1904–1905), 3: 351.
11. James Boswell to Anna Seward, 18 May 1784, Letters of James Boswell, Yale University, Beinecke Rare Book and Manuscript Library, MS L 1143, fol. 1277, cited in Teresa Barnard, *Anna Seward, A Constructed Life: A Critical Biography* (Surrey, UK: Ashgate, 2009), 137.
12. DeLorme, *Mourning Art & Jewelry*, 66.
13. Bell, *Collector's Encyclopedia*, 11.
14. See William Pietz, "The Problem of Fetish, I," *Res* 9 (1985): 5–17; "The Problem of the Fetish, II, *Res* 13 (1987): 23–45; and "The Problem of the Fetish, IIIa," *Res* 16 (1988): 105–123. The fetish is a European construct initially used to depict the peoples and cultures of West Africa as the primitive, irrational, and erratic "other." I argue that the popularity of hair jewelry during the eighteenth and nineteenth centuries existed in part as a reaction against Enlightenment privileging the rational, the technological, and the commercial over the spiritual, the psychic, and the personal.
15. Philippe Ariès, *The Hour of Our Death: The Classic History of Western Attitudes Toward Death over the Last One Thousand Years*, trans. Helen Weaver (1981; New York: Barnes and Noble, 2000), 356.
16. Ruth Richardson, *Death, Dissection and the Destitute*, 2nd ed. (Chicago: University of Chicago Press, 2000), 15. Richardson's research is specific to England from the late seventeenth century to early nineteenth century. Belief in the sentience of the corpse dates from medieval times or earlier, and appears to originate in uncertainty over the spiritual afterlife of the soul (where it resided, whether or not it "slept" until Judgment Day); over the physical moment of death, as corpses emitted noises, continued growing hair and nails, and even exhibited involuntary movement; and over the relationship between body and soul.
17. Ariès, *The Hour of Our Death*, 355.
18. Ariès, *The Hour of Our Death*, 360.
19. Ariès, *The Hour of Our Death*, 387.
20. Ariès, *The Hour of Our Death*, 461, 462.
21. Terry Castle, *Clarissa's Ciphers: Meaning and Disruption in Richardson's Clarissa* (Ithaca, NY: Cornell University Press, 1982), 138.
22. Castle, *Clarissa's Ciphers*, 138, 141.
23. Raymond F. Hilliard, "Clarissa and Ritual Cannibalism," *PMLA* 105, no. 5 (October 1990): 1083–1097; 1093.
24. Allan Wendt, "Clarissa's Coffin," *Philological Quarterly* 39, no. 4 (October 1960): 481–495; 484.
25. Ariès, *The Hour of Our Death*, 209.
26. Charles Dickens, *Great Expectations* (Garden City, NY: Nelson Doubleday, n.d.), 188–189.
27. Adam Smith, *The Theory of Moral Sentiments*, ed. Ryan Patrick Hanley (1759; New York: Penguin, 2009), 17.
28. Pointon, "Materializing Mourning," 57.
29. The third bequest is a piece of embroidery.
30. Susan Stewart, *On Longing: Narratives of the Miniature, the Gigantic, the Souvenir, the Collection* (Durham, NC: Duke University Press, 1993), 126.

31. Stewart, *On Longing*, 126.
32. Samuel Richardson to Lady Bradshaigh, 15 December 1748, in *Selected Letters of Samuel Richardson*, ed. John Carroll (Oxford: Clarendon Press, 1964), 116.

2. "YOU KNOW ME THEN"

1. Ann Radcliffe, *The Mysteries of Udolpho*, ed. Bonamy Dobrée (Oxford: Oxford University Press, 1998), 672. All citations are from this edition of the text, and all subsequent citations are noted parenthetically.
2. Marcia Pointon, *Hanging the Head: Portraiture and Social Formation in Eighteenth-Century England* (New Haven, CT: Yale University Press for The Paul Mellon Centre for Studies in British Art, 1993), 2.
3. Portraits of individuals of low birth and low social status were also painted, but almost always because "something extraordinary" had occurred that rendered them socially significant. See Pointon, *Hanging the Head*, 85.
4. In regards to the preference for sloping shoulders, see Pointon, *Hanging the Head*, 44, description of plate 64. Also, according to A. D. Harvey, the preference for sloping shoulders was related to a preference for a smooth expanse of skin from neck to bosom: "The idea was to increase the area of flat succulent flesh at the top of the chest and prevent the appearance of cleavage. A round-shouldered posture would also contribute to the desired effect and accordingly shoulders were admired in proportion to their not being square." See A. D. Harvey, *Sex in Georgian England: Attitudes and Prejudices from the 1720s to the 1820s* (New York: St. Martin's Press, 1994), 15. William Hogarth's *The Analysis of Beauty*, ed. Ronald Paulson (New Haven, CT: Yale University Press for the Paul Mellon Centre for British Art, 1997) offers an extensive examination of what constitutes beauty in eighteenth-century England, with particular attention to the curved line (see in particular chapters VII, IX, and X).
5. Shearer West, *Portraiture*, Oxford History of Art (Oxford: Oxford University Press, 2004), 11.
6. Limning on ivory was first introduced in England in 1707, and by the 1720s, almost all miniature portraits were on ivory. For information on miniatures in eighteenth-century England, see Jim Murrell, "The Craft of the Miniaturist," in *The English Miniature*, by John Murdoch, Jim Murrell, Patrick J. Noon, and Roy Strong (New Haven, CT: Yale University Press, 1981), 1–24; Patrick J. Noon, "Miniatures on the Market," in *The English Miniature*, 163–209; Daphne Foskett, *British Portrait Miniatures: A History* (1963; London: Spring Books, 1968); Katherine Coombs, *The Portrait Miniature in England* (London: Victoria and Albert Publications, 1998); and Marcia Pointon, "'Surrounded with Brilliants': Miniature Portraits in Eighteenth-Century England," *Art Bulletin* 83, no.1 (March 2001): 48–71. Most likely, Radcliffe was familiar with the work of Rosalba Carrera, as the heroine of Radcliffe's novel, *The Italian*, is named Ellena Rosalba, and other characters within that same novel, Father Schedoni and Vivaldi, employ the family names, respectively, of Bartolomeo Schedoni (1578–1615), a painter from Reggio Emilia, and Antonio Vivaldi (1678–1741), the Venetian composer.
7. Noon, "Miniatures on the Market," 169.
8. Richard Wendorf, *The Elements of Life: Biography and Portrait-Painting in Stuart and Georgian England* (Oxford: Clarendon Press, 1990), 130.
9. Wendorf, *The Elements of Life*, 130.
10. Marcia Pointon, *Portrayal and the Search for Identity* (London: Reaktion Books, 2013), 17.
11. Antonia Fraser, *Cromwell: The Lord Protector* (New York: Grove Press, 1973), 472.
12. West, *Portraiture*, 62.

13. Pointon, *Portrayal*, 32.
14. West, *Portraiture*, 62–63.
15. Kate Retford, "A Death in the Family: Posthumous Portraiture in Eighteenth-Century England," *Art History* 33, no. 1 (1 February 2010): 74–97.
16. Marianne Koos, "Wandering Things: Agency and Embodiment in Late Sixteenth-Century English Miniature Portraits," *Art History* 37, no. 5 (November 2014): 836–859; 837, 837–838.
17. Steven J. Gores, "The Miniature as Reduction and Talisman in Fielding's *Amelia*," *SEL: Studies in English Literature* 37, no. 3 (1997): 573–593; 578.
18. Alison Conway, *Private Interests: Women, Portraiture, and the Visual Culture of the English Novel, 1709–1791* (Toronto: University of Toronto Press, 2001), 117, 118.
19. Conway, *Private Interests*, 118–119; 119.
20. Conway, *Private Interests*, 119.
21. Pointon, "'Surrounded with Brilliants,'" 51.
22. Terry Castle, "The Spectralization of the Other in *The Mysteries of Udolpho*," in *The New 18th Century: Theory, Politics, English Literature*, eds. Felicity Nussbaum and Laura Brown (New York: Methuen, 1987), 231–253; 238, 239.
23. Jean Baudrillard, "The Precession of Simulacra," from *Simulations*, trans. Paul Foss, Paul Patton, and Philip Beitchman. (New York: Semiotext(e), Inc., 1983), 1–5; 1.
24. This is not to suggest that these portraits exist as simulacra in the sense that Baudrillard uses—that is, they are not "hyper-real," a simulation of something that never existed.
25. Sigmund Freud, *Beyond the Pleasure Principle*, standard edition, trans. and ed. James Strachey (1920; New York and London: W. W. Norton & Company, 1961), 16.
26. John Milton, *Paradise Lost*, in *John Milton: Complete Poems and Major Prose*, ed. Merritt Y. Hughes (Indianapolis, IN: Hackett Publishing Company, 1957), I.i.65–67.
27. Jordan Harrison's play, *Marjorie Prime* (New York: Theatre Communications Group, 2016) addresses many of these questions. The "primes" of the play are holographic images of dead beloveds. One question raised by the play is how the living—as lovers, as mourners—determine what age they wish the reincarnated beloved to be. Another question raised is how memory is often altered by longing or forgetfulness.
28. Jane Austen, *Northanger Abbey*, in *Northanger Abbey/Persuasion*, ed. R. W. Chapman, 3rd ed. (Oxford: Oxford University Press, 1923), 39–40.
29. Sir Walter Scott, "Mrs. Ann Radcliffe," in *The Miscellaneous Prose Works of Sir Walter Scott, Bart.*, 28 vols. (Edinburgh: Robert Cadell; London: Whittaker and Co., 1834): 3: 337–389; 375, 377. Accessed 26 June 2019. books.google.com.
30. Thomas W. Laqueur, *The Work of the Dead: A Cultural History of Mortal Remains* (Princeton: Princeton University Press, 2015), 184. See also Philippe Ariès, *The Hour of Our Death*, trans. Helen Weaver (New York: Barnes & Noble, 1981).
31. Laqueur, *The Work of the Dead*, 211–361.
32. Laqueur, *The Work of the Dead*, 212.
33. See Julius Von Schlosser, *History of Portraiture in Wax* (1910–1911), trans. James Michael Loughridge, in *Ephemeral Bodies: Wax Sculpture and the Human Figure*, ed. Roberta Panzanelli (Los Angeles: The Getty Research Institute, 1998), 171–314.
34. They may be seen today in the Westminster Museum.
35. *A View of the Wax Work Figures in King Henry the 7th's Chapel, Westminster Abbey: Exhibited in Several Curious Copper-Plate Prints, Drawn on the Spot by James Roberts, and Accurately Engraved by Henry Roberts. With an Historical Account of Each of the Great Personages whose Effigies are Here Represented.* (London: Printed for H. Roberts, 1769). *Eighteenth-Century Collections Online*. Gale. University of Central Florida. (Gale Reference Number: CB3326687850).

[171]

36. John Timbs, "Mrs. Salmon's Waxworks," in *Romance of London: Strange Stories, Scene and Remarkable Persons of the Great Town*, 3 vols. (London: Richard Bentley, 1865): II. 279–282. Accessed 16 June 2019. books.google.com. After Mrs. Clark's death, the collection was "sold, it is said, for less than 50l. Many of the figures were removed to a house at the west corner of Water Lane, and there exhibited for a few pence" (II.281) until 1831.
37. Uta Kornmeier argues that Salmon's Wax-work and other early waxwork exhibitions tended toward allegorical representations, as well as representations of "powerful historical figures" notable for "ethical ideals," whereas Madame Tussaud's wax figures represented only figures (historical or criminal) who had obtained some degree of "celebrity." See Uta Kornmeier, "The Famous and the Infamous: Waxworks as Retailers of Renown," *International Journal of Cultural Studies* 11, no. 3: 276–288; 282, 285.
38. *Mrs. Salmon's Royal Wax-Work (London, England). At Mrs. Salmon's Royal Wax-work* (London: 1763?). *Eighteenth-Century Collections Online*. Gale. University of Central Florida. (Gale Document Number: CW3302381051).
39. John Thomas Smith, *Nollekens and His Times*, 2 vols. (1828; Cambridge: Cambridge University Press, 2014), 1:175.
40. Lyceum Theatre (Westminster, London, England). *For the inspection of the curious. In the grand saloon, at the Lyceum, near Exeter Change, in the Strand, is an entire new exhibition, just arrived from Paris, containing a cabinet of royal figures. Most curiously moulded in wax.* (London: 1785?). *Eighteenth-Century Collections Online*. Gale. University of Central Florida. (Gale Document Number: CW3305692672).
41. Lyceum Theatre (Westminster, London, England). *For the inspection of the curious. At the Lyceum, near Exeter Change, in the Strand, is an entire new exhibition, just arrived from Constantinople, a cabinet containing an exact representation of a seraglio, most curiously moulded in wax.* (London: 1785?). *Eighteenth-Century Collections Online*. Gale. University of Central Florida. (Gale Document Number: CW3305692673).
42. Rackstrow's Museum. *A Brief Description of Those Curious and Excellent Figures of the Human Anatomy in Wax.* (London: 1790). *Eighteenth-Century Collections Online*. Gale. University of Central Florida. (Gale Document Number: CW3306584874). According to Francesco de Ceglia, "Visiting a collection of anatomical wax models was for a young woman a sort of pre-deflowering, and was sometimes even planned" by parents. See Francesco de Ceglia, "Rotten Corpses, a Disembowelled Woman, a Flayed Man. Images of the Body from the End of the 17th to the Beginning of the 19th Century. Florentine Wax Models in the First-hand Accounts of Visitors," *Perspectives on Science* 14, no. 4 (2006): 417–456; 439.
43. Knowledge of human anatomy was extremely important in the development of medicine as a profession. Dissections were performed in operating theatres, with students and spectators in attendance (with the latter often paying for the privilege). Up through the mid-eighteenth century, the Company of Barber-Surgeons (established during the medieval period) enjoyed "a monopoly of dissection rights," and they, in turn, allowed The Royal College of Physicians to give the rare dissection demonstration. In 1745, a split occurred between the barbers and surgeons, which allowed the College of Surgeons "to organize a teaching center that included dissection," to secure corpses directly, and to assume all dissecting privileges. However, although the College of Surgeons now controlled dissection rights, the availability of corpses remained limited. The Murder Act of 1752 provided more corpses for dissection, as the Act established that the bodies of murderers could not be buried. The Anatomy Act of 1832 allowed for the dissection of any "friendless" body—that is, the body of anyone who died alone and was unclaimed by relatives or friends. See "Medical Education," *Britain in the Hanoverian Age, 1714–1837: An Encyclopedia*, ed. Gerald Newman (New York: Garland Publishing, 1997), 442–444; 443.

44. See Joan B. Landes, "Wax Fibers, Wax Bodies, and Moving Figures: Artifice and Nature in Eighteenth-Century Anatomy," in *Ephemeral Bodies: Wax Sculpture and the Human Figure*, ed. Roberta Panzanelli (Los Angeles: The Getty Research Institute, 2008), 41–65; 55.
45. Landes, "Wax Fibers," 45.
46. Rackstrow's Museum, *A Brief Description*, 8, 9, 12.
47. In addition to the all-wax anatomical model, "the preparation specimen or écorché created from the remains of a deceased body" was also used, sometimes augmented with wax elements, as well as wooden anatomical models. See Landes, "Wax Fibers," 45.
48. Lyle Massey, "On Waxes and Wombs: Eighteenth-Century Representations of the Gravid Uterus." In *Ephemeral Bodies: Wax Sculpture and the Human Figure*, ed. Roberta Panzanelli (Los Angeles: The Getty Research Institute, 1998), 83–105; 83.
49. Lisa Jardine, "Inside Out," *New Statesman* 129, no. 4514 (27 November 2000): 40–41; 41.
50. de Ceglia, "Rotten Corpses," 438.
51. Almost all female anatomical models displayed a fetus in the womb, and they almost always represent the female as passive, in either a sitting or reclining position; in contrast, the male is generally staged as active, standing upright and erect. See Ludmilla J. Jordanova, *Sexual Visions: Images of Gender in Science and Medicine between the Eighteenth and Twentieth Centuries* (Madison: University of Wisconsin Press, 1989), 43–65. See also de Ceglia, "Rotten Corpses," 435–447.
52. Landes, "Wax Fibers," 55.
53. Roberta Panzanelli, "Introduction: The Body in Wax, the Body of Wax," in *Ephemeral Bodies: Wax Sculpture and the Human Figure*, ed. Roberta Panzanelli (Los Angeles: The Getty Research Institute, 2008), 1–11; 1.
54. Uta Kornmeier, "Almost Alive: The Spectacle of Verisimilitude in Madame Tussaud's Waxworks," in *Ephemeral Bodies: Wax Sculpture and the Human Figure*, ed. Roberta Panzanelli (Los Angeles: The Getty Research Institute, 2008), 67–81; 76.
55. Beth Kowaleski Wallace, "Representing Corporeal 'Truth' in the Work of Anna Morandi Manzolini and Madame Tussaud," in *Women and the Material Culture of Death*, eds. Maureen Daly Goggin and Beth Fowkes Tobin (Farnham, UK: Ashgate, 2013): 283–309; 286.
56. Landes, "Wax Fibers," 43.
57. *The Mystery at the Wax Museum*. Directed by Michael Curtiz, performances by Lionel Atwill, Fay Wray, Glenda Farrell, and Frank McHugh. Warner Brothers, 1933. Also, *House of Wax*. Directed by Andre DeToth, performances by Vincent Price, Frank Lovejoy, Charles Buchinsky, Carolyn Jones, and Phyllis Kirk. Warner Brothers, 1953. In both movies, the sculptor murders individuals in order to make them into wax museum figures.
58. Many wax sculptors were women. Beth Kowaleski Wallace ("Representing Corporeal 'Truth'") notes: "Throughout history, wax modeling was uniquely accessible to women artists who wanted to work in the plastic arts and who may have been barred from working in more durable media like wood or stone. Where working with other forms of sculpture required physical strength or training in a restricted, male environment, working with wax easily occurred in a domestic setting: wax was easy to obtain, clean and easy to prepare and preserve, and it does not need fire or cracking. A female sculptor would not need specialist tools, training, strength or extra space to work in this medium" (287). See also Marjan Sterckx, "'Une fleur que ses yeux étents ne peuvent plus contempler': Women's Sculptures for the Dead," in *Women and the Material Culture of Death*, eds. Maureen Daly Goggin and Beth Fowkes Tobin (Farnham, UK: Ashgate, 2013): 169–190.
59. Kornmeier, "Almost Alive," 67.
60. Kornmeier, "Almost Alive," 73.

61. Georges Didi-Huberman, "Viscosities and Survivals: Art History Put to the Test by Material," trans. Jane Marie Todd, in *Ephemeral Bodies: Wax Sculpture and the Human Figure*, ed. Roberta Panzanelli (Los Angeles: Getty Research Institute, 2008), 154–169; 155.
62. As quoted in Thomas N. Haviland and Lawrence Charles Parish, "A Brief Account of the Use of Wax Models in the Study of Medicine," *Journal of the History of Medicine and Allied Sciences* 25, no. 1 (1970): 52–75; 61. The quote comes from Kathleen F. Lander, "Study of Anatomy by Women before the Nineteenth Century," *Proceedings of the Third International Congress of the History of Medicine. London, July 17th to 22nd, 1922* (London: 1922; Printed in Antwerp: Imprimerie De Vlijt, 1923), 125–134.
63. de Ceglia, "Rotten Corpses," 425; 426.
64. No. 24, Thursday 11 June (1730). *Memoirs of the Society of Grub-Street*, 2 vols. (London: Printed for J. Wilford, 1737): 1:127. *Eighteenth-Century Collections Online*. Gale. University of Central Florida. (Gale Document Number: CW3300917439). Also, according to Thomas Davies, the Duchess commissioned "an automaton, or small statue of ivory, made exactly to resemble him, which every day was brought to table. A glass was put in the hand of the statue, which was supposed to bow to her Grace, and to nod in approbation of what she spoke to it." See Thomas Davies, *Dramatic Miscellanies: Consisting of Critical Observations on Several Plays of Shakespeare*, 3 vols. (London: Printed for the Author, 1784–1785), 3:407. *Eighteenth-Century Collections Online*. Gale. University of Central Florida. (Gale Document Number: CW3315910067).
65. Theophilus Cibber, *Lives of the Poets of Great Britain and Ireland*, 4 vols. (London: 1753): 4:92. *Eighteenth-Century Collections Online*. Gale. University of Central Florida. (Gale Document Number: CW3312486703).
66. Andrew Kippis, *Biographia Britannica; or the Lives of the Most Eminent Persons who have Flourished in Great-Britain and Ireland*, 2nd ed., 5 vols. (London: Rivington and Marshall, 1789): 4:79. Accessed 26 June 2019. books.google.com.
67. *Daily Post*, no. 3997 (15 July 1732). As quoted in Julie Park, *The Self and It: Novel Objects in Eighteenth-Century England* (Stanford, CA: Stanford University Press, 2009), 241, footnote 37.
68. Castle, "Spectralization of the Other," 237.
69. Castle, "Spectralization of the Other," 234.
70. Castle, "Spectralization of the Other," 244, 245.
71. Castle, "Spectralization of the Other," 243. Yael Shapira also notes Radcliffe's avoidance of bodies, particularly dead ones: "Corpses make an occasional appearance in her fiction, but their presence is limited and highly uncertain.... In most cases there is no body at all, only its alleged remnants." See Yael Shapira, "Where the Bodies Are Hidden: Ann Radcliffe's 'Delicate' Gothic," *Eighteenth-Century Fiction* 18, no. 4 (2006): 453–476; 465.
72. I am not the only scholar to notice the dead bodies. Carol Margaret Davison notes the "rich and complex thanatological semiotics of *The Mysteries of Udolpho*" as expressed through "bodies—dead, living, uncanny, spectral, and living-dead" (40). Carol Margaret Davison, "Trafficking in Death and (Un)dead Bodies: Necro-Politics and Poetics in the Works of Ann Radcliffe," *The Irish Journal of Gothic and Horror Studies* 14 (Summer 2015): 37–47. Davison's essay focuses on death and mourning practices within Radcliffe's novel in terms of a renegotiation of the social contract.
73. The terms "tame" and "untamed" death come from Ariès (*The Hour of Our Death*), who uses them in conjunction with older attitudes toward death and newer ones.
74. Ariès, *The Hour of Our Death*, 411.
75. Ya-Feng Wu, "Blazoning the Paired Tableaux: *The Mysteries of Udolpho* and *The Monk*," *Sun Yat-sen Journal of Humanities* 27 (September 2009): 1–32; 13.
76. Wu, "Blazoning the Paired Tableaux," 12.

77. Ariès, *The Hour of Our Death*, 328.
78. It is a fact that to the untrained eye (and often to the trained eye), skeletal remains are extremely difficult to identify when it comes to sex and race. Usually, sex is determined by comparing the pelvis (the pubic, ischial, and iliac bones) of the skeleton to that of other contemporaneous skeletons. Generally (not always), a female possesses a smoother, smaller pelvis; slightly longer and more rectangular pubic bones; a U-shaped subpubic angle, with a bony ridge; etc. In addition, normally, female skulls are slightly smaller and often rounder. See William A. Cox, "Identification of Skeletal Remains" (5 November 5, 2010): 31 pages; n.p. *Forensic Medicine with Dr. Cox: Learning More about Forensic Pathology & Neuropathology*. www.forensicjournals.com. Accessed 10 September 2017. https://forensicmd.files.wordpress.com/2010/11/identification-of-skeletal-remains.pdf. However, it should be noted that the size and structural differences between male and female skeletal remains are small—a few millimeters—and that identification is best made when confronting other skeletal remains from the same time, place, and group of people. Race is almost entirely determined by skull measurements, such as facial width and length, nasal and orbital openings, etc. and, in most instances, is difficult to determine with any measure of certainty.
79. In Horace Walpole's *The Castle of Otranto*, the ghost of Alfonso the Good wreaks havoc on Manfred and his descendants; another ghost, albeit with "the fleshless jaws and empty sockets of a skeleton," warns Frederic not to pursue his lust for Manfred's daughter Matilda. See Horace Walpole, *The Castle of Otranto*, in *The Castle of Otranto and Hieroglyphic Tales*, ed. Robert L. Mack (London: J. M. Dent; Rutland, Vermont: Charles E. Tuttle Co., 1993), 95. In Clara Reeve's *The Old English Baron*, the ghosts of Edmund's parents appear in a dream, informing their son of his birthright and assuring the restoration of his title; the skeleton of his murdered father is there simply to provide proof of the foul deed. See Clara Reeve, *The Old English Baron*, ed. James Trainer (Oxford: Oxford University Press, 2003). Even in Matthew Lewis's *The Monk*, the Bleeding Nun psychically sucks the life from her kinsman Raymond, her "restless soul" seeking the burial of her bones. See Matthew Lewis, *The Monk*, ed. Howard Anderson (Oxford: Oxford University Press, 1995), 175. However, it should be noted that Lewis is by no means afraid of dead or dying bodies—or of depicting murder in the act.
80. According to Ariès, the transi "constitutes only a marginal and passing episode" in the historical depiction of death, and while the focus of the macabre is the decay of all things earthly (which simultaneously argues for the eternal afterlife of the spirit), Ariès argues that the transi betrays a love of earthly things: "They are a sign of passionate love for this world and a painful awareness of the failure to which each human life is condemned"; the transi "express[es] the bitterness of having to leave the exquisite things of this life." See Ariès, *The Hour of Our Death*, 114, 130, 244. However, I believe that the transi means something quite different in Radcliffe's novel and in other novels of the time period, when it does make its rare appearance.
81. Robert Miles, "The Surprising Mrs. Radcliffe: *Udolpho*'s Artful Mysteries," *Women's Writing* 22, no. 3 (2015): 300–316; 301.
82. Landes, "Wax Fibers," 45.
83. Gary Farnell, "The Gothic and the Thing," *Gothic Studies* 11, no. 1 (May 2009): 113–123; 118. Farnell defines the "Thing" and "the Real" as follows: ". . . the Thing is a phantasmic reference to an unnameable void at the centre of the Real, that amorphous, chaotic, meaningless physical level beyond all reference that both resists and provokes symbolization. This Thing, in other words, is not of the order of signifiers within the symbolic order; hence its un-nameability except as the Thing" (113).

84. Much has been written about veils in Radcliffe's fictions. See, for instance, Elizabeth Broadwell, "The Veil Image in Ann Radcliffe's 'The Italian,'" *South Atlantic Bulletin* 40, no. 4 (November 1975): 76–87; Eve Kosofsky Sedgwick, "The Character in the Veil: Imagery of the Surface in the Gothic Novel," in *The Coherence of Gothic Conventions* (New York: Methuen, 1980), 140–175; Susan Greenfield, "Veiled Desire: Mother–Daughter Love and Sexual Imagery in Ann Radcliffe's *The Italian*," *The Eighteenth Century: Theory and Interpretation* 33, no. 1 (1992): 73–89; and Yael Shapira, "Where the Bodies Are Hidden," 468–469.
85. Sigmund Freud, "The 'Uncanny,'" in *The Standard Edition of the Complete Psychological Works of Sigmund Freud*, ed. and trans. James Strachey (based on original English translation by Alix Strachey), 24 vols. (London: Hogarth Press, 1919), 17:217–256; 17:237, 17:225.
86. Freud, "The 'Uncanny,'" 17:241.
87. Freud, "The 'Uncanny,'" 17:226.
88. Ariès, *The Hour of Our Death*, 6, 14, 15, 27, 14.
89. Terry Castle argues that the spectralization of the (dead or absent) other and the missing physical dead bodies are part of the same phenomena; that is, that if one has incorporated the other into one's psyche, then the physical body is no longer necessary. However, in my reading of Radcliffe's work, the dead body is necessary for spectralization/incorporation to occur.
90. Shapira, "Where the Bodies Are Hidden," 456.
91. See Thomas W. Laqueur, *Making Sex: Body and Gender from the Greeks to Freud* (Cambridge, MA: Harvard University Press, 1990), and Randolph Trumbach, *Sex and the Gender Revolution*, vol. I, *Heterosexuality and the Third Gender in Enlightenment London* (Chicago: University of Chicago Press, 1998).
92. Ariès, *The Hour of Our Death*, 406.
93. Wu, "Blazoning the Paired Tableaux," 12.
94. In *The Work of the Dead*, Laqueur notes that the word "obituary" as "a newspaper announcement of a death and, more generally, an appreciation of someone who had recently died" first entered the English language in 1738 (405).

PERSONS

1. Nouri Gana, *Signifying Loss: Towards a Poetics of Narrative Mourning* (Lewisburg, PA: Bucknell University Press, 2011), 13.
2. *The Annual Register; or a View of History, Politicks, and Literature for the Year 1759*, fifth edition (London, 1769), 43. *Eighteenth-Century Collections Online*. Gale. University of Central Florida. (Gale Document Number CW3325944577).
3. John Dryden, *All for Love; or The World Well Lost. A Tragedy* (London: Printed for J. Tonson and T. Bennet, 1703), Act I, page 9. Note: The play has no scenes or line numbers. *Eighteenth-Century Collections Online*. Gale. University of Central Florida. (Gale Document Number: CB3327571280).
4. Carla Mazzio and Douglas Trevor, "Dreams of History: An Introduction," in *Historicism, Psychoanalysis, and Early Modern Culture*, eds. Carla Mazzio and Douglas Trevor (New York: Routledge, 2000), 1–18; 3.
5. Cynthia Marshall, "Psychoanalyzing the Prepsychoanalytic Subject," *PMLA* 117, no. 5 (October 2002): 1207–1216; 1208; 1207.
6. See Hélène Dachez, "'I Don't Know Where to Go for a Quiet Mind': A Case Study of Samuel Richardson's Clementina," *Studies in the Literary Imagination* 48, no. 1 (Spring 2015): 1–15. Dachez persuasively argues that Richardson, using medical texts as his foundational texts, presents Clementina "in a manner redolent of a case study" (1).

3. "ALL THE HORRORS OF FRIENDSHIP"

1. Sarah Fielding, *The Adventures of David Simple and Volume the Last*, ed. Peter Sabor (Lexington: University of Kentucky Press, 1998), 195. All citations are from this edition of the text, and all subsequent citations are noted parenthetically.
2. Juliana Schiesari, *The Gendering of Melancholia: Feminism, Psychoanalysis, and the Symbolics of Loss in Renaissance Literature* (Ithaca, NY: Cornell University Press, 1992), 33.
3. Abraham and Torok's interpretation of the causes and outcomes of mourning and melancholia differs in some significant ways from Freud's, and yet, in other ways, it extends and deepens Freud's ideas. For instance, Abraham and Torok view parental dysfunction or trauma as a possible/probable cause of a child's act of incorporation, and some of Abraham and Torok's work on mourning and melancholia relates more directly to what we would term split or multiple personality disorder; they also differ from Freud in suggesting that incorporation occurs in the "preconscious-conscious" rather than in the unconscious. However, their work on mourning and melancholia also complements and supplements Freud's theory in many ways, particularly in their extended theorization and examination of incorporation. See Nicolas Abraham and Maria Torok, *The Shell and the Kernel*, trans. and ed. Nicholas T. Rand, 2 vols. (Chicago: University of Chicago Press, 1994), 1:135.
4. Abraham and Torok, *The Shell and the Kernel*, 1:135.
5. Sigmund Freud, "Mourning and Melancholia," in *The Standard Edition of the Complete Psychological Works of Sigmund Freud*, trans. and ed. James Strachey, 24 vols. (London: Hogarth, 1964), 14:243–261; 14:244.
6. James Kim, "Mourning, Melancholia, and Modernity: Sentimental Irony and Downward Mobility in David Simple," *Eighteenth-Century Fiction* 22, no. 3 (Spring 2010): 477–502; 478, 492, 498. Kim notes the underlying melancholy of David Simple, suggesting that it originates in Fielding's own ambivalent attitude toward the downward mobility of the lesser gentry, a social group to which she belonged. Through analysis of passages from *David Simple* that employ the rhetorical strategy of "sentimental irony," Kim concludes that Fielding's novel anguishes over downward social mobility while at the same time offering "an egalitarian social vision" (497). Because Kim's essay focuses principally on economics and sentimental irony, his analysis of mourning and melancholia within David Simple is understandably brief (fewer than six pages), giving short shrift (a paragraph) to the differences between mourning and melancholia.
7. Freud, "Mourning and Melancholia," 245.
8. Freud, "Mourning and Melancholia," 245.
9. Freud, "Mourning and Melancholia," 245.
10. Schiesari, *The Gendering of Melancholia*, 42.
11. Schiesari, *The Gendering of Melancholia*, 37.
12. Freud, "Mourning and Melancholia," 255.
13. Schiesari, *The Gendering of Melancholia*, 38.
14. Freud, "Mourning and Melancholia," 249.
15. Freud, "Mourning and Melancholia," 249.
16. Freud, "Mourning and Melancholia," 249.
17. Abraham and Torok, *The Shell and the Kernel*, 1.127.
18. Freud, "Mourning and Melancholia," 245.
19. Schiesari, *The Gendering of Melancholia*, 44.
20. Schiesari, *The Gendering of Melancholia*, 43.
21. Freud, "Mourning and Melancholia," 251.
22. Freud, "Mourning and Melancholia," 247.
23. Schiesari, *The Gendering of Melancholia*, 42–43.
24. Schiesari, *The Gendering of Melancholia*, 43.

25. Freud, "Mourning and Melancholia," 246.
26. Schiesari, *The Gendering of Melancholia*, 52–53.
27. Nicholas T. Rand, "Editor's Note. Part IV: New Perspectives in Metapsychology: Cryptic Mourning and Secret Love," *The Shell and the Kernel*, trans. and ed. Nicholas T. Rand, 2 vols. (Chicago: The University of Chicago Press, 1994), 1.99–106; 1.100, 1.101.
28. Rand, "Editor's Note," 1.101.
29. Freud, "Mourning and Melancholia," 252.
30. Freud, "Mourning and Melancholia," 254.
31. Freud, "Mourning and Melancholia," 253.
32. Freud, "Mourning and Melancholia," 252.
33. Freud, "Mourning and Melancholia," 258, 257.
34. See Luce Irigaray, *Speculum of the Other Woman*, trans. Gillian C. Gill (Ithaca, NY: Cornell University Press, 1985) and Julia Kristeva, *Black Sun: Depression and Melancholia*, trans. Leon S. Roudiez (New York: Columbia University Press, 1989). For a discussion of these two texts, see Schiesari, *The Gendering of Melancholia*, 63–95.
35. E. L. McCallum, *Object Lessons: How to Do Things with Fetishism* (Albany: State University of New York Press, 1999), 123.
36. Schiesari, *The Gendering of Melancholia*, 68.
37. Schiesari, *The Gendering of Melancholia*, 12, 14.
38. Schiesari, *The Gendering of Melancholia*, 12.
39. See Schiesari, *The Gendering of Melancholia*, 11–14.
40. E. L. McCallum, *Object Lessons*, 115.
41. Freud, "Mourning and Melancholia," 248, 252.
42. Sigmund Freud, "Character and Anal Eroticism," in *The Freud Reader*, ed. Peter Gay (New York: W. W. Norton, 1989), 293–297; 295.
43. Freud, "Mourning and Melancholia," 249–250.
44. Abraham and Torok, *The Shell and the Kernel*, 1.126.
45. Abraham and Torok, *The Shell and the Kernel*, 1.131.
46. Abraham and Torok, *The Shell and the Kernel*, 1.126.
47. Jahan Ramazani, *The Poetry of Mourning: The Modern Elegy from Hardy to Heaney* (Chicago: University of Chicago Press, 1994), xi.
48. The original will stipulated that David and Daniel be "Joint-Heirs" (9) of £11,000 (11). David receives £500 pounds under the forged will, leaving Daniel in possession of £10,500. By the time that David's uncle has uncovered the forgery, Daniel has squandered away a portion of the fortune on "Women and Sots" (19), leaving only £8,000, all of which Daniel is forced to hand over to David, under threat of prosecution. Thus, instead of David receiving £5,500, as his father intended, he received £8,000. David also is promised an inheritance of "seven thousand Pounds" (20) from his uncle's estate.
49. Shawn Lisa Maurer, "Happy Men? Mid-Eighteenth-Century Women Writers and Ideal Masculinity," in *Women Constructing Men: Female Novelists and Their Male Characters, 1750–2000*, eds. Sarah S. G. Frantz and Katharina Rennhak (Lanham, MD: Lexington Books, 2010), 11–30; 16.
50. Freud, "Mourning and Melancholia," 251.
51. George E. Haggerty, *Unnatural Affections: Women and Fiction in the Later 18th Century* (Bloomington: Indiana University Press, 1998), 24.
52. Abraham and Torok, *The Shell and the Kernel*, 1.131.
53. Betty A. Schellenberg, *The Conversational Circle: Re-reading the English Novel, 1740–1775* (Lexington: The University Press of Kentucky, 1996), 24.
54. Liz Bellamy, *Commerce, Morality and the Eighteenth-Century Novel* (Cambridge: Cambridge University Press, 1998), 133.

55. Adam Smith, *The Theory of Moral Sentiments*, ed. Ryan Patrick Hanley (1759; London: Penguin, 2009), 18.
56. Smith, *The Theory of Moral Sentiments*, 13.
57. Smith, *The Theory of Moral Sentiments*, 13.
58. George Cheyne, *The English Malady; or A Treatise of Nervous Diseases of All Kinds* (London: Printed for G. Strahan in Cornhill, and J. Leake in Bath, 1733), 366. *Eighteenth-Century Collections Online*. Gale. University of Central Florida. (Gale Document Number: CW3307864112).
59. G. J. Barker-Benfield, *The Culture of Sensibility: Sex and Society in Eighteenth-Century Britain* (Chicago: University of Chicago Press, 1992), 9.
60. Joseph F. Bartolomeo, "A Fragile Utopia of Sensibility," in *Gender and Utopia in the Eighteenth Century: Essays in English and French Utopian Writing*, eds. Nicole Pohl and Brenda Tooley (Aldershot, UK: Ashgate, 2007), 39–52; 40.
61. Robert Palfrey Utter and Gwendolyn Bridges Needham, *Pamela's Daughters* (1936; New York: Russell & Russell, 1972), 114.
62. Felicity Nussbaum, "Effeminacy and Femininity: Domestic Prose Satire and *David Simple*," *Eighteenth-Century Fiction* 11, no. 4 (July 1999): 421–444; 436.
63. Sara Gadeken, "Sarah Fielding and the Salic Law of Wit," *Studies in English Literature* 42, no. 3 (Summer 2002): 541–557; 542–543.
64. Mary Anne Schofield, *Masking and Unmasking the Female Mind: Disguising Romances in Feminine Fiction, 1713–1799* (Newark: University of Delaware Press; London: Associated University Presses, 1990), 109.
65. John Butt, *The Mid-Eighteenth Century*, ed. and completed by Geoffrey Carnall (Oxford: Oxford University Press, 1979), 451.
66. Norman Simms, "The Psychological Adventures of Sarah Fielding's *David Simple*," *Etudes Anglais* 49, no. 2 (April–June 1996): 158–167; 160.
67. Linda Bree speculates as to why Fielding might have chosen a male protagonist: "a male protagonist was essential to the presentation of satiric scenes of contemporary London life. David Simple, as a man, has access to public spaces: he visits hotels and coffee shops; he wanders alone round 'Change and St. James's Park, places where women would have had to be chaperoned. He changes his lodgings at will. If he hears the sound of weeping in the next room, he can walk in and ask what is wrong. If he decides to give his money away, nobody has the power to stop him. If he wishes to indulge his quixotic impulse to spend his time traveling 'through the whole world, rather than not meet with a real Friend' (27), he can." However, Bree also notes, "there are many ways in which David Simple is a very 'unmasculine' 18th-century hero." See Linda Bree, *Sarah Fielding* (New York: Twayne; London: Prentice Hall International, 1996), 32. Other scholars have also noted David's "feminine" tendencies. Janet Todd argues that "Sarah Fielding makes her protagonist a man although his predicament remains quintessentially female." See Janet Todd, *The Sign of Angellica: Women, Writing and Fiction, 1660–1800* (New York: Columbia University Press, 1989), 165. In "A Fragile Utopia," Bartolomeo notes, "David undoubtedly embodies qualities—such as passivity, emotionalism, and reserve—which were identified with and valued in women in the eighteenth century" (39). Similarly, in "Effeminacy and Femininity," Nussbaum suggests that, "David Simple, ruled by his passions, is less effeminate than feminized (439)."
68. Kim, "Mourning, Melancholia, and Modernity," 491.
69. Carolyn Woodward, "Sarah Fielding's Self-Destructing Utopia: *The Adventures of David Simple*," in *Living by the Pen: Early British Women Writers*, ed. Dale Spender (New York: Teachers College Press, Columbia University, 1992), 65–81; 73.
70. Maurer, "Happy Men?" 19.

71. Todd, *The Sign of Angellica*, 172.
72. Simon Stern, "Speech and Property in *David Simple*," *English Literary History* 79, no. 3 (Fall 2012): 623–654; 624.
73. Gadeken, "Sarah Fielding," 545.
74. Gillian Skinner, *Sensibility and Economics in the Novel, 1740–1800: The Price of a Tear* (Basingstoke, UK: Macmillan; New York: St. Martin's Press, 1999), 17.
75. Ann Jessie Van Sant, *Eighteenth-Century Sensibility and the Novel: The Senses in Social Context* (Cambridge: Cambridge University Press, 1993), 118.
76. Both Catharine Fielding and Henry Fielding (the son) died July 1750; Ursula died December 1750, and Beatrice in January 1751.
77. According to the Battestins, "Fielding helped Sarah with payments of £10 on 29 August 1950 and £9 on 19 March 1750/1—the latter corresponding to the time when she was being sued by Thomas Hayter, executor of the estate of his brother William Hayter, for recovery of an unspecified debt. Thomas Hayter . . . [had] purchased the Fielding farm at East Stour." See Martin C. Battestin and Ruthe R. Battestin, *Henry Fielding: A Life* (London: Routledge, 1989), 509.
78. Butt, *The Mid-Eighteenth Century*, 452.
79. Alexander Petit, "*David Simple* and the Attenuation of 'Phallic Power,'" *Eighteenth-Century Fiction* 11, no. 2 (January 1999): 169–184; 180.
80. Richard Stamelman, "The Shroud of Allegory: Death, Mourning, and Melancholy in Baudelaire's Work," *Texas Studies in Literature and Language* 25, no. 3 (Fall 1983): 390–409; 393.
81. By using a character named Una, Fielding also alludes to Edmund Spenser's allegorical epic, *The Faerie Queene*, in the experimental *The Cry*, co-authored with Jane Collier. Ros Ballaster specifically mentions *The Cry* as an example of how "allegorical prose romance" aided the development of "plausible embodied character" in the mid-century novel. See Ros Ballaster, "Satire and Embodiment: Allegorical Romance on Stage and Page in Mid-Eighteenth-Century Britain," *Eighteenth-Century Fiction* 27, nos. 3–4 (Spring—Summer 2015): 631–660; 631.
82. See Sarah Fielding, *Familiar Letters between the Principal Characters in David Simple, and Some Others. To which is Added, A Vision*. 2 vols. (London: Printed for the Author, 1747), II:352–92. *Eighteenth-Century Collections Online*. Gale. University of Central Florida. (Gale Document Number: CW3312269362).
83. Fielding, "A Vision," II:352.
84. Fielding, "A Vision," II:353.
85. Fielding, "A Vision," II:356.
86. Fielding, "A Vision," II: 358.
87. Edmund Spenser, *The Faerie Queene*, ed. Thomas P. Roche, Jr., with the assistance of C. Patrick O'Donnell, Jr. (London: Penguin, 1984), I.vii.7.
88. Spenser, *The Faerie Queene*, I.vii.11; I.vii.15.
89. Elizabeth Heale, *The Faerie Queene: A Reader's Guide* (Cambridge: Cambridge University Press, 1987), 37.
90. Fielding, "A Vision," II:380.
91. Fielding, "A Vision," II:388.
92. Fielding, "A Vision," II:390.
93. Fielding, "A Vision," II:390–391.
94. Fielding, "A Vision," II:391.
95. Van Sant, *Eighteenth-Century Sensibility*, 118.

4. "IT IS ALL FOR YOU!"

1. Samuel Richardson, *The History of Sir Charles Grandison*, ed. Jocelyn Harris, 3 vols. (London: Oxford University Press, 1972; Dunedin, New Zealand: University of Otago Press, 2001), III.xxvi; 2:193. All citations use Richardson's volume number and respective letter number, followed by the volume and pagination of the Harris edition. All subsequent citations are noted parenthetically.
2. Samuel Richardson to Lady Bradshaigh [1749], *Selected Letters of Samuel Richardson*, ed. John Carroll (Oxford: Clarendon Press, 1964), 133.
3. David L. Eng and David Kazanjian, "Introduction: Mourning Remains," in *Loss: The Politics of Mourning*, eds. David L. Eng and David Kazanjian (Berkeley: University of California Press, 2003), 1–25; 2.
4. Trevor Hoag, *Occupying Memory: Rhetoric, Trauma, Mourning* (Lanham, MD: Lexington Books, 2019), 27.
5. In a letter to Julia[n] Bere, dated 15 March 1754, which is included in the Appendix to the novel, Richardson writes that Sir Charles "had been about fifteen months in England when the Story begins" (VII.Appendix; 3:467). The novel begins in January; Sir Charles leaves for Italy in April, arriving in Bologna around 15 May.
6. In the Victorian era, widows were encouraged to wear mourning for two-and-a-half years, with the first year in "deepest mourning" of "dull black silk and crepe," the second year in "ordinary black mourning," and the final six months in half-mourning colors of "black, white, grey and mauve." See Lou Taylor, *Mourning Dress: A Costume and Social History* (London: George Allen and Unwin, 1983), 57. This was a change from the sixteenth and seventeenth centuries, when "widows continued wearing black for three or four years or even longer and often retained their heavy black veils for the rest of their lives." See Phillis Cunnington and Catherine Lucas, *Costumes for Births, Marriages, and Deaths* (New York: Barnes and Noble, 1972), 264. Although I can find no specific information on how long a Georgian widow would be expected to wear deep mourning, it makes sense that the duration would be somewhat less than that of earlier centuries, and it may have been that the mourning period in the Georgian era was less than in the Victorian era, when mourning practices, rites, and rituals became intensified. According to Anne Buck, eighteenth-century mourning clothes "varied in intensity and duration according to the degree of relationship; it also changed in detail during the century. For all except the shortest mourning the period was divided, half deep and half second mourning, with the second period sometimes divided again to make a more relaxed final quarter before dress in full colours and trimmings was once more worn." See Anne Buck, *Dress in Eighteenth-Century England* (London: B.T. Batsford, 1979), 60.
7. Cathy Caruth, *Unclaimed Experience: Trauma, Narrative, and History* (Baltimore: Johns Hopkins University Press, 1996), 4.
8. Caruth, *Unclaimed Experience*, 7.
9. Speaking of any patient suffering from repression—and trauma is an act of repression—Freud writes, "He is obliged to *repeat* the repressed material as a contemporary experience instead of, as the physician would prefer to see, *remembering* it as something belonging to the past." See Sigmund Freud, *Beyond the Pleasure Principle*, standard edition, trans. and ed. James Strachey (1920; New York: W. W. Norton & Company, 1961), 19.
10. Richardson famously teased his correspondents with the possibility that Sir Charles might marry Clementina rather than Harriet. Yet, as many scholars have noted, textual hints suggest that Clementina was never meant to become the true object of Sir Charles's affections. In an examination of the chronology of Grandison, Albert J. Rivero notes, "marriage to Clementina has all but been ruled out by the time Sir Charles returns to England

and saves Harriet from the clutches of the odious Sir Hargrave Pollexfen." See Albert J. Rivero, "Representing Clementina: 'Unnatural' Romance and the Ending of *Sir Charles Grandison*," in *New Essays on Samuel Richardson*, ed. Albert J. Rivero (New York: St. Martin's Press, 1996), 209–225; 210. See also Margaret Anne Doody, "Richardson's Politics," *Eighteenth-Century Fiction* 2, no. 2 (1990): 113–126; 125; Janine Barchas, "*Grandison*'s Grandeur as Printed Book: A Look at the Eighteenth-Century Novel's Quest for Status," *Eighteenth-Century Fiction* 14, nos. 3–4 (2002): 673–714; 697–698; and Teri Doerksen, "*Sir Charles Grandison*: The Anglican Family and the Admirable Roman Catholic," *Eighteenth-Century Fiction* 15, nos. 3–4 (2003): 539–558; 551–553. Of particular note is Bonnie Latimer's appraisal of Clementina in *Making Gender, Culture, and the Self in the Fiction of Samuel Richardson: The Novel Individual* (Farnham, UK, and Burlington, VT: Ashgate, 2013), 98–102.
11. Caruth, *Unclaimed Experience*, 49.
12. Notably, Charles Stuart's mistress was named Clementina Walkinshaw, "an Italian-bred Roman Catholic," as Margaret Doody has demonstrated. See Doody, "Richardson's Politics," 125.
13. Samuel Richardson to Sophia Westcomb [1746?], *Selected Letters of Samuel Richardson*, 65.
14. Caruth, *Unclaimed Experience*, 2.
15. A diagnosis of post-traumatic distress disorder (PTSD) is based on "three symptom clusters: reexperiencing, avoidance/numbing, and arousal." See Shelly A. Wiechelt and Jan Gryczynski, "Cultural and Historical Trauma Among Native Americans," in *Trauma: Contemporary Directions in Theory, Practice, and Research*, eds. Shoshana Ringel and Jerrold R. Brandell (Los Angeles: Sage Publications, 2012), 191–222; 193.
16. Freud, *Beyond the Pleasure Principle*, 14.
17. Michel Foucault, *Language, Madness, and Desire: On Literature*, eds. Philippe Artières, Jean-François Bert, Mathieu Potte-Bonneville, and Judith Revel, trans. Robert Bononno (Minneapolis: University of Minnesota Press, 2015), 25, 25–26, 26.
18. Foucault, *Language, Madness, and Desire*, 26, 26–27.
19. In *Language, Madness, and Desire*, Foucault writes, "we know that the persecuted individual who hears voices speaks those voices himself. He has the impression that they are coming from the outside, but in reality . . . he himself spoke those voices" (26).
20. Freud, "Mourning and Melancholia," 249.
21. We know that Clementina's letter to Sir Charles is in Italian (or perhaps Latin), rather than English because Richardson's footnote informs us Dr. Bartlett has translated the letter for Harriet Byron's perusal.
22. Foucault, *Language, Madness, and Desire*, 26.
23. In the letter to Sir Charles in which she rejects his offer of marriage, Clementina writes: "But dost thou indeed love me? Or is it owing to thy generosity, thy compassion, thy nobleness, for a creature, who, aiming to be great like thee, could not sustain the effort?" A few lines later she follows with "I know thou lovest Clementina: It is her pride to think that thou dost" (V.xxiv; 2:565). Ambiguity clouds the question of his love, not only for Clementina, but for Richardson's readers.
24. In eighteenth-century England, beliefs in the causes of "nervous disorders" and other forms of mental illness were various, as were recommended methods of treatment. The belief that divine retribution or diabolical possession caused madness continued to exist, though to a much lesser extent than in previous centuries. Other phenomena believed to induce madness either directly or indirectly were astrological occurrences (the moon, an unusual alignment of the stars or planets, or perhaps even a comet); weather, particularly a northern or an easterly wind; and climate, particularly a dark or damp climate, such as that found in England.

25. Lady Mary Wortley Montagu to the Countess of Bute, 20 October 1757. In *The Works of the Right Honourable Lady Mary Wortley Montagu, Including Her Correspondence, Poems and Essays. From Her Genuine Papers* (London: J. F. Dove, 1825), 437. Accessed 16 June 2019. books.google.com.
26. George Cheyne, *The English Malady; or A Treatise of Nervous Diseases of All Kinds* (London: Printed for G. Strahan in Cornhill, and J. Leake in Bath, 1733), 63, 4. *Eighteenth-Century Collections Online*. Gale. University of Central Florida. (Gale Document Number: CW3307864112).
27. George Cheyne, *An Essay of Health and Long Life* (London: Printed for George Strahan in Cornhill, and J. Leake at Bath, 1724), 156. *Eighteenth-Century Collections Online*. Gale. University of Central Florida. (Gale Document Number: CW3307899639).
28. Cheyne, *An Essay*, 155–156.
29. Cheyne, *An Essay*, 173.
30. Cheyne, *An Essay*, 157.
31. Richard Mead, *Medical Precepts and Cautions*, trans. Thomas Stack (London: Printed for J. Brindley, 1751), 76. *Eighteenth-Century Collections Online*. Gale. University of Central Florida. (Gale Document Number: CW3306584885).
32. Hélène Dachez, "'I Don't Know Where to Go for A Quiet Mind," *Studies in the Literary Imagination* 48, no. 1 (Spring 2015): 1–15; 5.
33. Judith Broome, "'Her lovely arm a little bloody': Richardson's Gothic Bodies," *Gothic Studies* 8, no. 1 (May 2006): 9–21; 16.
34. Latimer, *Making Gender*, 100.
35. Joseph Townsend, *A Guide to Health; Being cautions and directions in the treatment of diseases. Designed chiefly for the use of students*, 2nd ed. 2 vols. (London: 1795), II:175, II:176, II:179. *Eighteenth-Century Collections Online*. Gale. University of Central Florida. (Gale Document Number: CW3308188185).
36. Broome, "'Her lovely arm a little bloody,'" 16.
37. Hoag, *Occupying Memory*, 27.
38. Samuel Richardson to Aaron Hill, October 29, 1746. In *Selected Letters*, 73.
39. Samuel Richardson to Lady Bradshaigh, 15 December 1748. In *Selected Letters*, 109.
40. Sylvia Kasey Marks, *Sir Charles Grandison: The Compleat Conduct Book* (Lewisburg: Bucknell University Press; London: Associated University Presses, 1986), 46.
41. In a letter to Lady Bradshaigh, dated 8 December 1753, Richardson asks, "Are you yet come to that Place, where Charlotte says, she thinks he [Sir Charles] ought to have them [Harriet and Clementina] both"? He then teases his correspondent, saying, "as you are careful for Harriet, and think her out-soared by Clementina, think you not, that I should fetch her up with a Witness, if she, after the Ceremony, and she was secure, should propose to Sir Charles to leave her for one Half Year, or Year, and go over to his Italian Wife the other?" See *Selected Letters*, 252; 253.
42. Sandra Gilbert, "Plain Jane's Progress," *Signs* 2, no. 4 (Summer 1977): 779–804; 787, 796. Interestingly, Jocelyn Harris identifies an echo of *Grandison* in *Jane Eyre*: "Told to decide Sir Charles' destiny while knowing what her family want, Clementina admits her love, and in an episode that would be copied by Charlotte Bronte is chapter 32 of *Jane Eyre*, talks of him for one quarter of an hour by her English watch." See Jocelyn Harris, *Samuel Richardson* (Cambridge: Cambridge University Press, 1987), 157.
43. Caruth, *Unclaimed Experience*, 8.
44. Samuel Richardson to Lady Bradshaigh, 15 December 1748. In *Selected Letters*, 109.
45. Lois A. Chaber, "*Sir Charles Grandison* and the Human Prospect," in *New Essays on Samuel Richardson*, ed. Albert J. Rivero (New York: St. Martin's Press, 1996), 193–208; 204.

GHOSTS

1. Daniel Defoe, "True Relation of the Apparition of One Mrs. Veal, the next Day after her DEATH to One Mrs. Bargrave at Canterbury, the 8th of September, 1705." (London: Printed for B. Bragg in Pater-Noster-Row, 1706), 5. *Eighteenth-Century Collections Online*. Gale. University of Central Florida. (Gale Document Number: CW3321230723).

5. "'TIS AT LEAST A MEMORIAL FOR THOSE WHO SURVIVE"

1. The "man of the world" is the diametrically opposed counterpart to the "man of feeling." The former treasures the things of the world, particularly wealth, status, and sensual pleasures; the latter values sincerity, simplicity, and affective experiences. Mackenzie's second novel, published in 1773, is entitled *The Man of the World*.
2. Henry Mackenzie, *The Man of Feeling*, in *The Works of Henry Mackenzie, Esq. with A Sketch of the Author's Life* (London: Printed for T. Cadell and G. & W. B. Whittaker: and A. Constable and Co.; Manners and Miller; W. Blackwood; and J. Fairborn, Edinburgh, 1822): 1–108; 2. All citations are from this edition of the novel, and all subsequent citations are noted parenthetically.
3. "It-narratives" are also known as "novels of circulation," "spy novels," "object tales," and "speaking object narratives." See Mark Blackwell, "Introduction: The It-Narrative and Eighteenth-Century Thing Theory," in *The Secret Life of Things: Animals, Objects, and It-Narratives in Eighteenth-Century England*, ed. Mark Blackwell (Lewisburg, PA: Bucknell University Press, 2014): 9–14; 10.
4. Blackwell, "Introduction: The It-Narrative," 10.
5. Liz Bellamy, "It-Narrators and Circulation: Defining a Subgenre," in *The Secret Life of Things: Animals, Objects, and It-Narratives in Eighteenth-Century England*, ed. Mark Blackwell (Lewisburg, PA: Bucknell University Press, 2014): 117–146; 121.
6. Bellamy, "It-Narrators and Circulation," 118.
7. Bellamy, "It-Narrators and Circulation," 118.
8. Christopher Flint, "Speaking Objects: The Circulation of Stories in Eighteenth-Century Prose Fiction," in *The Secret Life of Things: Animals, Objects, and It-Narratives in Eighteenth-Century England*, ed. Mark Blackwell (Lewisburg, PA: Bucknell University Press, 2014): 162–186; 163. An earlier version of the essay appeared in *PMLA* 113.2 (1998): 212–226.
9. Bellamy, "It-Narrators and Circulation," 117.
10. Bellamy, "It-Narrators and Circulation," 121.
11. Bellamy, "It-Narrators and Circulation," 122.
12. Bellamy, "It-Narrators and Circulation," 122, 118.
13. Bellamy, "It-Narrators and Circulation," 120.
14. Bellamy, "It-Narrators and Circulation," 125, 127.
15. Bellamy, "It-Narrators and Circulation," 120.
16. David Fairer notes the intimate relationship between objects and people within the literature of sentiment. Referring to the "found" manuscript so frequently encountered in sentimental fiction, Fairer describes it as "a text that has been physically abused and is waiting to find a sympathetic reader," an object or "thing" seeking a new owner; further, Fairer writes, "The ideal sentimental text/object bears transferred meanings as a surrogate undergoing suffering or humiliation" (140). See David Fairer, "Sentimental Translation in Mackenzie and Sterne," *Essays in Criticism: A Quarterly Journal of Literary Criticism* 49, no. 2 (April 1999): 132–151.
17. James D. Lilley, "Henry Mackenzie's Ruined Feelings: Romance, Race, and the Afterlife of Sentimental Exchange," *New Literary History* 38, no. 4 (Autumn 2007): 649–666; 654.
18. Lilley, 652.

19. Lilley, 650.
20. Ildiko Csengei views Harley as "an object used for the production of someone else's subjectivity and passion" (959), "a mirror . . . [that] deflects the reader's gaze, shifting it away from Harley onto all those who narrate, see, and read him" (957). Despite viewing Harley as an "object," Csengei does not equate the character with "it-narrators." See Ildiko Csengei, "'I Will Not Weep': Reading through the Tears of Henry Mackenzie's *Man of Feeling,*" *Modern Language Review* 103, no. 4 (October 2008): 952–968.
21. Maureen Harkin argues for "Harley's powerlessness and incomprehension in the face of the various events of the novel" (327). See Maureen Harkin, "Mackenzie's *Man of Feeling*: Embalming Sensibility," *English Literary History* 61, no. 2 (Summer 1994): 317–340. However, W. B. Gerard counters this, saying that "Harley very effectively helps to reconstitute families: his rescue of Emily Atkins and his assistance to old Edwards and his grandchildren" (570–571). See W. B. Gerard, "Benevolent Vision: The Ideology of Sentimentality in Contemporary Illustrations of *A Sentimental Journey* and *The Man of Feeling,*" *Eighteenth-Century Fiction* 14, nos. 3–4 (April–July 2002): 533–574.
22. Everett Zimmerman, "Fragments of History and *The Man of Feeling*: From Richard Bentley to Walter Scott," *Eighteenth-Century Studies* 23, no. 3 (Spring 1990): 283–300; 288.
23. Gerard A. Barker, *Henry Mackenzie* (Boston: Twayne, 1975), 41. Other scholars have similarly found the narrative structure purposeful, even didactic. For instance, Mark E. Wildermuth comments, "The fragmented form seems intended to focus the attention of the readers and to stimulate their feelings, to enhance their spontaneous emotional reaction and to lend more power than conventional logic or story-telling allows" (38). See Mark E. Wildermuth, "The Rhetoric of Common Sense and Uncommon Sensibility in Henry Mackenzie's *The Man of Feeling,*" *Lamar Journal of the Humanities* 23, no. 2 (1997): 35–47; 38. Liz Bellamy writes, "The conspicuous flaunting of narrative and structural conventions may be read as an ironic satire on the commodification of narrative within the commercial system," and that "the gaps in the text of *The Man of Feeling appears* to represent a deliberate rejection of both the mimetic principles and the social visions which were increasingly coming to characterize the fictional form" (150). I think, though, that reading the structure as intentionally ironic is giving Mackenzie more than his due. See Liz Bellamy, *Commerce, Morality and the Eighteenth-Century Novel* (Cambridge: Cambridge University Press, 1998). Finally, Dale Kramer views *The Man of Feeling* as structurally unified, despite its fragmented nature; he suggests that it is a bildungsroman "thematically organized around the education of the hero" (191), who moves from a sentimental point of view, to disillusionment, to acknowledgement that goodness does not exist on earth. See Dale Kramer, "The Structural Unity of *The Man of Feeling,*" *Studies in Short Fiction* (1964): 191–199.
24. Carol McGuirk notes that Harley (and any sentimental protagonist) displays an unfortunate tendency toward objectifying others: "although the sentimental hero is outside society, subordination is still necessary to his stability; it just becomes subordination of all the objects in his world to his dominating sensibility. And the objects he admits into his world are the rejected—lunatics, beggars, convicts—of the society he rejects. Men of the world follow a survival principle; men of feeling look after the lost causes" (506). Such a stance, however, belies the fact that Harley himself does not seek out society's "losers," but instead they find him. See Carol McGuirk, "Sentimental Encounter in Sterne, Mackenzie, and Burns," *SEL: Studies in English Literature* 20, no. 3 (1980): 505–515. Timothy Dykstal also condemns the objectification of others found within the novel of sentiment: "The eighteenth-century cult of sensibility seems consistently blind to the social condescension that its benevolence implies. The paradigm of morality as attentive seeing, with its focus on the particular moral situation, does nothing to cure that blindness" (78). See Timothy

Dykstal, "The Sentimental Novel as Moral Philosophy: The Case of Henry Mackenzie," *Genre* 27, nos. 1–2 (1994): 59–81.

25. Among those viewing Harley as an example to be shunned are William Burling and Bahadir Eker. See William Burling, "A 'Sickly Sort of Refinement': The Problem of Sentimentalism in Mackenzie's *The Man of Feeling*," *Studies in Scottish Literature* 23, no. 1 (1988): 136–149, which suggests that Mackenzie was "contemptuous of the phenomenon of sentimentality" (136), but that "his failure to make the distinction clear in *The Man of Feeling* resulted from two artistic faults: the lack of a clearly defined, admirable protagonist; and the unfortunate decision to employ a fragmented, episodic plot" (136–137). Bahadir Eker argues that *The Man of Feeling* "presents . . . a thoroughgoing critique of sentimentalism both as a moral theory and as a mode of fiction" (96). See Bahadir Eker, "'So Unlucky a Perspective': The Critique of Moral Sentimentalism in *The Man of Feeling*," *Zeitschrift für Anglistik und Amerikanistik* 62, no. 2 (2014): 95–112.

More directly addressing the character of Harley (or other sentimental protagonists) are Janet Todd, Maureen Harkin, and R. Peter Burnham. Regarding the sentimental novel of the 1760s and 1770s, Janet Todd writes, "sentiments are clearly overflowings of emotion, rather than emotions combined with moral action, and characters teach response more than virtuous action. The hero is not a pattern for life" (92). See Janet Todd, *Sensibility: An Introduction* (London and New York: Methuen, 1986). In "Mackenzie's *Man of Feeling*," Maureen Harkin views *The Man of Feeling* as embodying the author's "attempts to negotiate conflicting positions about the possibility of sentimental literature as a form of social practice and critique" (336), and she views Harley as "an unreliable guide to modes of conduct" (330). And R. Peter Burnham believes that "the 'new humanitarianism' of Harley is undercut by a rather complacent old fashioned Toryism of Mackenzie" (124), and that the novel limits itself to "criticizing individuals and not the social structure" (129). See R. Peter Burnham, "The Social Ethos of Mackenzie's *The Man of Feeling*," *Studies in Scottish Literature* 18, no. 1 (1983): 123–137.

26. John Mullan views Mackenzie's novel in terms of sociability—and its failure. As Mullan writes, "If Mackenzie's novels attempt to imagine a virtue experienced in sociability, they perversely demonstrate such sociability at odds with 'the world'—and unusual, defeated solidarity" (280). See John Mullan, "The Language of Sentiment: Hume, Smith, and Henry Mackenzie," in *The History of Scottish Literature*, ed. Andrew Hook, 4 vols. (Aberdeen, UK: Aberdeen University Press, 1987): II.273–289. Sociability does fail within *The Man of Feeling*, but if we replace sociability with circulation, then failure is not guaranteed (though neither is success). I would also suggest that the metaphor of commerce—circulation is, after all, a principle economic metaphor—has tainted Mackenzie's representation of sociability. Specifically, Mackenzie's attempt to present the idyllic world that existed prior to commercialization must inevitably fail because sociability is understood and represented within the confines of Mackenzie's novel through the tropes of commerce, such as gain and loss, circulation and stagnation, exchange, etc.

27. Barker, *Henry Mackenzie*, 28.

28. Bellamy, "It-Narrators and Circulation," 127.

29. Harkin notes that "Harley represents modern commerce as a practice quite distinct from, and distinctly more powerful than, older, more limited forms of exchange in which each partner willingly participated and benefited" (326). In similar vein, Dale McDaniel notes that with Harley, "Mackenzie takes a nostalgic look into the past for a hero who represents the older medieval ideals that those in positions of authority, the aristocracy in particular, had an obligation to assist the less fortunate in their times of need," and that this "nostalgic" notion competes against "the social changes brought about by commercialization" (63). See Dale McDaniel, "Henry Mackenzie's Harley: A Reaction Against Commercial-

ism," *Studies in Scottish Literature* 33, no. 1 (2004): 62–70. John Mullan also notes that "the novel of sentiment continues to reproduce its own version of this figment" of "the singular, uncorrupted individual," but it necessarily does so in "an elegiac strain" (130). See John Mullan, *Sentiment and Sociability: The Language of Feeling in the Eighteenth Century* (Oxford: Clarendon Press, 1988).
30. Henry Mackenzie, *The Man of the World*, in *The Works of Henry Mackenzie, Esq. with A Sketch of the Author's Life* (London: Printed for T. Cadell and G. & W. B. Whittaker: and A. Constable and Co.; and Manners and Miller; W. Blackwood; and J. Fairbairn, Edinburgh, 1822): 173–395; 335–338.
31. Mackenzie, *The Man of the World*, 395.
32. Mackenzie, *The Man of the World*, 318.
33. Elizabeth Hallam and Jenny Hockey, *Death, Memory and Material Culture* (Oxford: Berg, 2001). See chapter 7, "Death Writing: Material Inscription and Memories," 179–202.
34. Thomas W. Laqueur writes, "We live in an age of necronominalism; we record and gather the names of the dead in ways, and in places, and in numbers as never before. We demand to know who the dead are. We find unnamed bodies and bodiless names—those of the disappeared—unbearable" (366). See Thomas W. Laqueur, *The Work of the Dead: A Cultural History of Mortal Remains* (Princeton: Princeton University Press, 2015).
35. Hallam and Hockey, *Death, Memory and Material Culture*, 155–156; 155.
36. Hallam and Hockey, *Death, Memory and Material Culture*, 175.
37. Mackenzie, *The Man of the World*, 318.
38. Lucy Razzall, "'A good Booke is the pretious life-blood of a master-spirit': Recollecting Relics in Post-Reformation Writing," *Journal of the Northern Renaissance* 2 (2010): 27 paragraphs. Accessed 6 November 2018. http://northernrenaissance.org.
39. Numerous scholars have commented on the ironic or satiric nature of the narrative voice in *The Man of Feeling*. For instance, in "Fragments of History," Zimmerman sees "the narrator's voice" as "predominantly satiric" (291), whereas Michael Rymer sees a "strong vein of irony in the novel" (65). See Michael Rymer, "Henry Mackenzie's *The Man of Feeling*," *Durham University Journal* 37 (1976): 62–69.
40. In *Sensibility: An Introduction*, Janet Todd notes that while "there is an effort at distancing through elaborate layering of narration . . . *The Man of Feeling* lacks much distancing, primarily because the narrator, who should provide it, clearly fails to do so" (107). Often, the distance between the narrator and Harley is negligible or non-existent.
41. Mackenzie, *The Man of the World*, 318.

CONCLUSION

1. Adam Smith, *The Theory of Moral Sentiments*, ed. Ryan Patrick Hanley (1759; New York: Penguin, 2009), 17.

BIBLIOGRAPHY

Abraham, Nicolas, and Maria Torok. *The Shell and the Kernel*. 2 vols. Edited and translated by Nicholas T. Rand. Chicago: University of Chicago Press, 1994.

The Annual Register; or A View of History, Politicks, and Literature for the Year 1759. 5th ed. London: 1769. Eighteenth-Century Collections Online. Gale. University of Central Florida. (Gale Document Number: CW3325944577).

Ariès, Philippe. *The Hour of Our Death: The Classic History of Western Attitudes toward Death over the Last One Thousand Years*. Translated by Helen Weaver. 1981; New York: Barnes and Noble, 2000.

Ashton, John. *Social Life in the Reign of Queen Anne*. New York: Scribner and Welford, 1883.

Austen, Jane. *Northanger Abbey/Persuasion*. Edited by R. W. Chapman. 3rd ed. 1923; Oxford: Oxford University Press, 1988.

Ballaster, Ros. "Satire and Embodiment: Allegorical Romance on Stage and Page in Mid-Eighteenth-Century Britain," *Eighteenth-Century Fiction* 27, nos. 3–4 (Spring–Summer 2015): 631–660.

Barchas, Janine. "*Grandison*'s Grandeur as Printed Book: A Look at the Eighteenth-Century Novel's Quest for Status," *Eighteenth-Century Fiction* 14, nos. 3–4 (2002): 673–714; 697–698.

Barker, Gerard A. *Henry Mackenzie*. Boston: Twayne Publishers, 1975.

Barker-Benfield, G. J. *The Cult of Sensibility Sex and Society in Eighteenth-Century Britain*. Chicago: University of Chicago Press, 1992.

Barnard, Teresa. *Anna Seward, A Constructed Life: A Critical Biography*. Surrey, UK: Ashgate, 2009.

Bartolomeo, Joseph F. "A Fragile Utopia of Sensibility." In *Gender and Utopia in the Eighteenth Century: Essays in English and French Utopian Writing*, edited by Nicole Pohl and Brenda Tooley, 39–52. Aldershot, UK: Ashgate, 2007.

Battestin, Martin C., with Ruthe R. Battestin. *Henry Fielding: A Life*. London: Routledge, 1989.

Baudrillard, Jean. "The Precession of Simulacra." From *Simulations*. Translated by Paul Foss, Paul Patton, and Philip Beitchman, 1–5. New York: Semiotext(e), Inc., 1983.

Bell, C. Jeanenne. *Collector's Encyclopedia of Hairwork Jewelry*. Paducah, KY: Collector Books, 1998.

Bellamy, Liz. *Commerce, Morality and the Eighteenth-Century Novel*. Cambridge: Cambridge University Press, 1998.

———. "It-Narrators and Circulation: Defining a Subgenre." In *The Secret Life of Things: Animals, Objects, and It-Narratives in Eighteenth-Century England*, edited by Mark Blackwell, 177–146. Lewisburg, PA: Bucknell University Press, 2014.

Bernard, G. W. *The King's Reformation: Henry VIII and the Remaking of the English Church*. New Haven, CT: Yale University Press, 2005.

Blackwell, Mark. "Introduction: The It-Narrative and Eighteenth-Century Thing Theory." In *The Secret Life of Things: Animals, Objects, and It-Narratives in Eighteenth-Century England*, edited by Mark Blackwell, 9–14. Lewisburg, PA: Bucknell University Press, 2014.

BIBLIOGRAPHY

Blanchot, Maurice. "Literature and the Right to Death." In *The Work of Fire*. Reprint edition. Translated by Charlotte Mandell, 300–344. Stanford, CA: Stanford University Press, 1995.

Brandell, Jerrold R. "Chapter 3: Psychoanalytic Theory (Part I)." In *Trauma: Contemporary Directions in Theory, Practice, and Research*, edited by Shoshana Ringel and Jerrold R. Brandell, 41–61. Los Angeles: Sage Publications, 2012.

Bree, Linda. *Sarah Fielding*. New York: Twayne; London: Prentice Hall International, 1996.

Broadwell, Elizabeth. "The Veil Image in Ann Radcliffe's 'The Italian,'" *South Atlantic Bulletin* 40, no. 4 (November 1975): 76–87.

Broome, Judith. "'Her lovely arm a little bloody': Richardson's Gothic Bodies," *Gothic Studies* 8, no. 1 (May 2006): 9–21.

Buck, Anne. *Dress in Eighteenth-Century England*. London: B. T. Batsford, 1979.

Burling, William. "A 'Sickly Sort of Refinement': The Problem of Sentimentalism in Mackenzie's *The Man of Feeling*," *Studies in Scottish Literature* 23, no. 1 (1988): 136–149.

Burney, Frances. *The Diary and Letters of Madame D'Arblay (1778–1840)*. 6 vols. Edited by Charlotte Barrett. Preface and notes by August Dobson. London: Macmillan, 1904–1905.

Burnham, R. Peter. "The Social Ethos of Mackenzie's *The Man of Feeling*," *Studies in Scottish Literature* 18, no. 1 (1983): 123–137.

Bury, Shirley. *An Introduction to Sentimental Jewellery*. London: Her Majesty's Stationery Office, 1985.

Butt, John. *The Mid-Eighteenth Century*. Edited and completed by Geoffrey Carnall. Oxford: Oxford University Press, 1979.

Caruth, Cathy. "Trauma and Experience: Introduction." In *Trauma: Explorations in Memory*, edited by Cathy Caruth, 3–12. Baltimore: Johns Hopkins University Press, 1995.

———. *Unclaimed Experience: Trauma, Narrative, and History*. Baltimore: Johns Hopkins University Press, 1996.

Castle, Terry. *Clarissa's Ciphers: Meaning and Disruption in Richardson's Clarissa*. Ithaca, NY: Cornell University Press, 1982.

———. "The Spectralization of the Other in *The Mysteries of Udolpho*." In *The New 18th Century: Theory, Politics, English Literature*, edited by Felicity Nussbaum and Laura Brown, 231–253. New York: Methuen, 1987.

Chaber, Lois A. "*Sir Charles Grandison* and the Human Prospect." In *New Essays on Samuel Richardson*, edited by Albert J. Rivero, 193–208. New York: St. Martin's Press, 1996.

Cheyne, George. *The English Malady; or A Treatise of Nervous Diseases of All Kinds*. London: Printed for G. Strahan in Cornhill, and J. Leake in Bath, 1733. *Eighteenth-Century Collections Online*. Gale. University of Central Florida. (Gale Document Number: CW3307864112).

———. *An Essay of Health and Long Life*. London: Printed for George Strahan in Cornhill, and J. Leake at Bath, 1724. *Eighteenth-Century Collections Online*. Gale. University of Central Florida. (Gale Document Number: CW3307899639).

Cibber, Theophilus. *Lives of the Poets of Great Britain and Ireland*. 4 vols. London: 1753. *Eighteenth-Century Collections Online*. Gale. University of Central Florida. (Gale Document Number: CW3312486703).

Conway, Alison. *Private Interests: Women, Portraiture, and the Visual Culture of the English Novel, 1709–1791*. Toronto: University of Toronto Press, 2001.

Coombs, Katherine. *The Portrait Miniature in England*. London: Victoria and Albert Publications, 1998.

Cox, William A. "Identification of Skeletal Remains" (5 November 2010): 31 pages; n.p. *Forensic Medicine with Dr. Cox: Learning More about Forensic Pathology & Neuropathology*. www.forensicjournals.com. Accessed 10 September 2017. https://forensicmd.files.wordpress.com/2010/11/identification-of-skeletal-remains.pdf.

Csengei, Ildiko. "'I Will Not Weep: Reading through the Tears of Henry Mackenzie's *Man of Feeling*," *Modern Language Review* 103, no. 4 (October 2008): 952–968.
Cunnington, Phillis, and Catherine Lucas. *Costumes for Births, Marriages, and Deaths*. New York: Barnes and Noble, 1972.
Dachez, Hélène. "'I Don't Know Where to Go for A Quiet Mind," *Studies in the Literary Imagination* 48, no. 1 (Spring 2015): 1–15.
Dacome, Lucia. "Resurrecting by Numbers in Eighteenth-Century England." *Past & Present* 193 (November 2006): 73–110.
Danticat, Edwidge. *The Art of Death: Writing the Final Story*. Minneapolis: Graywolf Press, 2017.
Davies, Thomas. *Dramatic Miscellanies: Consisting of Critical Observations on Several Plays of Shakespeare*. 3 vols. London: 1784–1785. *Eighteenth-Century Collections Online*. Gale. University of Central Florida. (Gale Document Number: CW3315910067).
Davison, Carol Margaret. "Trafficking in Death and (Un)dead Bodies: Necro-Politics and Poetics in the Works of Ann Radcliffe," *The Irish Journal of Gothic and Horror Studies* 14 (Summer 2015): 37–47.
de Ceglia, Francesco. "Rotten Corpses, a Disembowelled Woman, a Flayed Man. Images of the Body from the End of the 17th to the Beginning of the 19th Century. Florentine Wax Models in the First-hand Accounts of Visitors," *Perspectives on Science* 14, no. 4 (2006): 417–456.
de Certeau, Michel. "The Unnamable." In *The Practice of Everyday Life*, translated by Steven Rendall, 190–198. Berkeley: University of California Press, 1984.
Defoe, Daniel. "True Relation of the Apparition of One Mrs. Veal." London: Printed for B. Bragg in Pater-Noster-Row, 1706. *Eighteenth-Century Collections Online*. Gale. University of Central Florida. (Gale Document Number: CW3321230723).
Delany, Mary. *The Autobiography and Correspondence of Mrs. Delany*. Revised from Lady Llanover's edition. Edited by Sarah Chauncey Woolsey. 2 vols. Boston: Robert Brothers, 1879.
DeLorme, Maureen. *Mourning Art & Jewelry*. Atglen, PA: Schiffer Publishing Ltd., 2004.
Derrida, Jacques. *Specters of Marx: The State of Debt, the Work of Mourning, and the New International*. Translated by Peggy Kamuf. New York: Routledge, 1994.
Dickens, Charles. *Great Expectations*. Garden City, NY: Nelson Doubleday, n.d.
Didi-Huberman, Georges. "Viscosities and Survivals: Art History Put to the Test by Material." Translated by Jane Marie Todd. In *Ephemeral Bodies: Wax Sculpture and the Human Figure*, edited by Roberta Panzanelli, 154–169. Los Angeles: Getty Research Institute, 2008.
Doerksen, Teri. "Sir Charles Grandison: The Anglican Family and the Admirable Roman Catholic," *Eighteenth-Century Fiction* 15, nos. 3–4 (2003): 539–558.
Donne, John. *The Poems of John Donne*. Edited by H.J.C. Grierson. London: Oxford University Press; Humphrey Milford, 1929.
Doody, Margaret Anne. "Richardson's Politics," *Eighteenth-Century Fiction* 2, no. 2 (1990): 113–126.
Dryden, John. *All for Love; or The World Well Lost. A Tragedy*. London: Printed for J. Tonson and T. Bennet, 1703. *Eighteenth-Century Collections Online*. Gale. University of Central Florida. (Gale Document Number: CB3327571280).
Dykstal, Timothy. "The Sentimental Novel as Moral Philosophy: The Case of Henry Mackenzie," *Genre* 27, nos. 1–2 (1994): 59–81.
Eker, Bahadir. "'So Unlucky a Perspective': The Critique of Moral Sentimentalism in *The Man of Feeling*," *Zeitschrift für Anglistik und Amerikanistik* 62, no. 2 (2014): 95–112.
Eng, David L., and David Kazanjian. "Introduction: Mourning Remains." In *Loss: The Politics of Mourning*, edited by David L. Eng and David Kazanjian, 1–25. Berkeley: University of California Press, 2003.
Fairer, David. "Sentimental Translation in Mackenzie and Sterne," *Essays in Criticism: A Quarterly Journal of Literary Criticism* 49, no. 2 (April 1999): 132–151.

Farnell, Gary. "The Gothic and the Thing," *Gothic Studies* 11, no. 1 (May 2009): 113–123.
Fielding, Henry. *Amelia*. Edited by David Blewett. 1751; London: Penguin, 1987.
Fielding, Sarah. *The Adventures of David Simple* and *Volume the Last*. Edited by Peter Sabor. Lexington: University of Kentucky Press, 1998.
———. *Familiar Letters between the Principal Characters in David Simple, and Some Others. To which is Added, A Vision*. 2 vols. London: 1747. Eighteenth-Century Collections Online. Gale. University of Central Florida. (Gale Document Number: CW3312269362).
Flint, Christopher. "Speaking Objects: The Circulation of Stories in Eighteenth-Century Prose Fiction." In *The Secret Life of Things: Animals, Objects, and It-Narratives in Eighteenth-Century England*, edited by Mark Blackwell, 162–186. Lewisburg, PA: Bucknell University Press, 2014.
Foskett, Daphne. *British Portrait Miniatures: A History*. 1963; London: Spring Books, 1968.
Foucault, Michel. *Language, Counter-memory, Practice: Selected Essays and Interviews*. Edited by D. F. Bouchard. Translated by D. F. Bouchard and Sherry Simon. Oxford: Oxford University Press, 1977.
———. *Language, Madness, and Desire: On Literature*. Edited by Philippe Artières, Jean-François Bert, Mathieu Potte-Bonneville, and Judith Revel. Translated by Robert Bononno. Minneapolis: University of Minnesota Press, 2015.
Fox, Christopher. *Locke and the Scriblerians: Identity and Consciousness in Early Eighteenth-Century Britain*. Berkeley: University of California Press, 1988.
Fraser, Antonia. *Cromwell: The Lord Protector*. New York: Grove Press, 1973.
Freud, Sigmund. *Beyond the Pleasure Principle*. 1920. Standard edition. Translated and edited by James Strachey. New York: W. W. Norton & Company, 1961.
———. "Character and Anal Eroticism." 1908. In *The Freud Reader*, edited by Peter Gay, 293–297. New York: W. W. Norton, 1989.
———."Mourning and Melancholia." 1917. In *The Standard Edition of the Complete Psychological Works of Sigmund Freud*. 24 vols. Translated and edited by James Strachey, 14: 243–261. London: Hogarth, 1964.
———. "The 'Uncanny.'" 1919. In *The Standard Edition of the Complete Psychological Works of Sigmund Freud*. 24 vols. Translated and edited by James Strachey, 17: 217–256. London: Hogarth, 1964.
Gadeken, Sara. "Sarah Fielding and the Salic Law of Wit," *Studies in English Literature* 42, no. 3 (Summer 2002): 541–557.
Gana, Nouri. *Signifying Loss: Toward a Poetics of Narrative Mourning*. Lewisburg, PA: Bucknell University Press, 2011.
Gerard, W. B. "Benevolent Vision: The Ideology of Sentimentality in Contemporary Illustrations of *A Sentimental Journey* and *The Man of Feeling*," *Eighteenth-Century Fiction* 14, nos. 3–4 (April–July 2002): 533–574.
Gilbert, Sandra. "Plain Jane's Progress." *Signs* 2, no. 4 (Summer 1977): 779–804.
Godwin, William. *An Essay on Sepulchres: Or a Proposal for Erecting Some Memorial of the Illustrious Dead in All Ages, on the Spot where their Remains Have Been Interred*. New York: Printed for M. and W. Ward, 1809.
Gores, Steven J. "The Miniature as Reduction and Talisman in Fielding's *Amelia*," *SEL: Studies in English Literature* 37, no. 3 (1997): 573–593.
Greenfield, Susan. "Veiled Desire: Mother–Daughter Love and Sexual Imagery in Ann Radcliffe's *The Italian*," *The Eighteenth Century: Theory and Interpretation* 33, no. 1 (1992): 73–89.
Greville, Charles C. F. *The Greville Memoirs: A Journal of the Reigns of King George IV and King William IV*. 3 vols. Edited by Henry Reeve. London: Longmans, Green and Co., 1874. Accessed 26 June 2019. books.google.com.
Haggerty, George E. *Unnatural Affections: Women and Fiction in the Later 18th Century*. Bloomington: Indiana University Press, 1998.

Hallam, Elizabeth, and Jenny Hockey. *Death, Memory and Material Culture*. Oxford: Berg, 2001.
Harkin, Maureen. "Mackenzie's Man of Feeling: Embalming Sensibility," *English Literary History* 61, no. 2 (Summer 1994): 317–340.
Harris, Jocelyn Harris. *Samuel Richardson*. Cambridge: Cambridge University Press, 1987.
Harrison, Jordan. *Marjorie Prime*. New York: Theatre Communications Group, 2016.
Harvey, A. D. *Sex in Georgian England: Attitudes and Prejudices from the 1720s to the 1820s*. New York: St. Martin's Press, 1994.
Haviland, Thomas N., and Lawrence Charles Parish. "A Brief Account of the Use of Wax Models in the Study of Medicine," *Journal of the History of Medicine and Allied Sciences* 25, no. 1 (1970): 52–75.
Heale, Elizabeth. *The Faerie Queene: A Reader's Guide*. Cambridge: Cambridge University Press, 1987.
Hilliard, Raymond F. "Clarissa and Ritual Cannibalism," *PMLA* 105, no. 5 (October 1990): 1083–1097.
Hoag, Trevor. *Occupying Memory: Rhetoric, Trauma, Mourning*. Lanham, MD: Lexington Books, 2019.
Hogarth, William. *The Analysis of Beauty*. Edited by Ronald Paulson. New Haven, CT: Yale University Press for the Paul Mellon Centre for British Art, 1997.
Irigaray, Luce. *Speculum of the Other Woman*. Translated by Gillian C. Gill. Ithaca, NY: Cornell University Press, 1985.
Jardine, Lisa. "Inside Out," *New Statesman* 129, no. 4514 (27 November 2000): 40–41.
Jordanova, Ludmilla J. *Sexual Visions: Images of Gender in Science and Medicine between the Eighteenth and Twentieth Centuries*. Madison: University of Wisconsin Press, 1989.
Kim, James. "Mourning, Melancholia, and Modernity: Sentimental Irony and Downward Mobility in *David Simple*," *Eighteenth-Century Fiction* 22, no. 3 (Spring 2010): 477–502.
Kippis, Andrew. *Biographia Britannica; or the Lives of the Most Eminent Persons who have Flourished in Great-Britain and Ireland*. 2nd ed. 5 vols. London: Rivington and Marshall, 1789. Accessed 26 June 2019. books.google.com.
Koos, Marianne. "Wandering Things: Agency and Embodiment in Late Sixteenth-Century English Miniature Portraits," *Art History* 37, no. 5 (November 2014): 836–859.
Kornmeier, Uta. "Almost Alive: The Spectacle of Verisimilitude in Madame Tussaud's Waxworks." In *Ephemeral Bodies: Wax Sculpture and the Human Figure*, edited by Roberta Panzanelli, 67–81. Los Angeles: Getty Research Institute, 2008.
———. "The Famous and the Infamous: Waxworks as Retailers of Renown," *International Journal of Cultural Studies* 11, no. 3: 276–288.
Kramer, Dale. "The Structural Unity of *The Man of Feeling*," *Studies in Short Fiction* (1964): 191–199.
Kristeva, Julia. *Black Sun: Depression and Melancholia*. Translated by Leon S. Roudiez. New York: Columbia University Press, 1989.
Landes, Joan B. "Wax Fibers, Wax Bodies, and Moving Figures: Artifice and Nature in Eighteenth-Century Anatomy." In *Ephemeral Bodies: Wax Sculpture and the Human Figure*, edited by Roberta Panzanelli, 41–65. Los Angeles: Getty Research Institute, 2008.
Laqueur, Thomas W. *Making Sex: Body and Gender from the Greeks to Freud*. Cambridge, MA: Harvard University Press, 1990.
———. *The Work of the Dead: A Cultural History of Mortal Remains*. Princeton, NJ: Princeton University Press, 2015.
Latimer, Bonnie: *Making Gender, Culture, and the Self in the Fiction of Samuel Richardson: The Novel Individual*. Farnham, UK: Ashgate, 2013.
Lewis, Matthew. *The Monk*. Edited by Howard Anderson. Oxford: Oxford University Press, 1995.

Lilley, James D. "Henry Mackenzie's Ruined Feelings: Romance, Race, and the Afterlife of Sentimental Exchange," *New Literary History* 38, no. 4 (Autumn 2007): 649–666.

Locke, John. *An Essay Concerning Human Understanding.* 2 vols. Edited by Alexander Campbell Fraser. New York: Dover Publications, 1959.

Lutz, Deborah. *Relics of Death in Victorian Literature and Culture.* Cambridge: Cambridge University Press, 2015.

Lyceum Theatre (Westminster, London, England). *For the inspection of the curious. At the Lyceum, near Exeter Change, in the Strand, is an entire new exhibition, just arrived from Constantinople, a cabinet containing an exact representation of a seraglio, most curiously moulded in wax.* (London: 1785?). *Eighteenth-Century Collections Online.* Gale. University of Central Florida. (Gale Document Number: CW3305692673).

———. *For the inspection of the curious. In the grand saloon, at the Lyceum, near Exeter Change, in the Strand, is an entire new exhibition, just arrived from Paris, containing a cabinet of royal figures. Most curiously moulded in wax.* (London: 1785?). *Eighteenth-Century Collections Online.* Gale. University of Central Florida. (Gale Document Number: CW3305692672).

Mackenzie, Henry. *The Man of Feeling.* In *The Works of Henry Mackenzie, Esq. with A Sketch of the Author's Life,* 1–108. London: Printed for T. Cadell and G. & W. B. Whittaker: and A. Constable and Co.; Manners and Miller; W. Blackwood; and J. Fairbairn, Edinburgh, 1822.

———. *The Man of the World.* In *The Works of Henry Mackenzie, Esq. with A Sketch of the Author's Life,* 173–395. London: Printed for T. Cadell and G. & W. B. Whittaker: and A. Constable and Co.; and Manners and Miller; W. Blackwood; and J. Fairbairn, Edinburgh, 1822.

Malo, Robyn. "Intimate Devotion: Recusant Martyrs and the Making of Relics in Post-Reformation England." *Journal of Medieval and Early Modern Studies* 44, no. 3 (Fall 2014): 531–548.

Marks, Sylvia Kasey. *Sir Charles Grandison: The Compleat Conduct Book.* Lewisburg, PA: Bucknell University Press; London: Associated University Presses, 1986.

Marshall, Cynthia. "Psychoanalyzing the Prepsychoanalytic Subject," *PMLA* 117, no. 5 (October 2002): 1207–1216.

Massey, Lyle. "On Waxes and Wombs: Eighteenth-Century Representations of the Gravid Uterus." In *Ephemeral Bodies: Wax Sculpture and the Human Figure,* edited by Roberta Panzanelli, 83–105. Los Angeles: Getty Research Institute, 1998.

Maurer, Shawn Lisa. "Happy Men?: Mid-Eighteenth-Century Women Writers and Ideal Masculinity." In *Women Constructing Men: Female Novelists and Their Male Characters, 1750–2000,* edited by Sarah S. G. Frantz and Katharina Remmhak, 11–30. Lanham, MD: Lexington Books, 2010.

Mazzio, Carla, and Douglas Trevor. "Dreams of History: An Introduction." In *Historicism, Psychoanalysis, and Early Modern Culture,* edited by Carla Mazzion and Douglas Trevor, 1–18. New York: Routledge, 2000.

McCallum, E. L. *Object Lessons: How to Do Things with Fetishism.* Albany: State University of New York Press, 1999.

McDaniel, Dale. "Henry Mackenzie's Harley: A Reaction against Commercialism," *Studies in Scottish Literature* 33, no. 1 (2004): 62–70.

McGuirk, Carol. "Sentimental Encounter in Sterne, Mackenzie, and Burns," *SEL: Studies in English Literature* 20, no. 3 (1980): 505–515.

Mead, Richard. *Medical Precepts and Cautions.* Translated by Thomas Stack. London: Printed for J. Brindley, 1751. *Eighteenth-Century Collections Online.* Gale. University of Central Florida. (Gale Document Number: CW3306584885).

"Medical Education." *Britain in the Hanoverian Age, 1714–1837: An Encyclopedia.* Edited by Gerald Newman, 442–444. New York: Garland Publishing, 1997.

Memoirs of the Society of Grub-Street. 2 vols. London: Printed for J. Wilford, 1737. *Eighteenth-Century Collections Online*. Gale. University of Central Florida. (Gale Document Number: CW3300917439).

Miles, Robert. "The Surprising Mrs. Radcliffe: Udolpho's Artful Mysteries," *Women's Writing* 22, no. 3 (2015): 300–316.

Milton, John. *Paradise Lost*. In *John Milton: Complete Poems and Major Prose*, edited by Merritt Y. Hughes, 173–469. Indianapolis, IN: Hackett Publishing Company, 1957.

Montagu, Lady Mary Wortley. *The Works of the Right Honourable Lady Mary Wortley Montagu, Including Her Correspondence, Poems and Essays. From Her Genuine Papers*. London: J. F. Dove, 1825. Accessed 26 June 2019. books.google.com.

Mrs. Salmon's Royal Wax-Work (London, England). At Mrs. Salmon's Royal Wax-work (London: 1763?). *Eighteenth-Century Collections Online*. Gale. University of Central Florida. (Gale Document Number: CW3302381051).

Mullan, John. "The Language of Sentiment: Hume, Smith, and Henry Mackenzie." In *The History of Scottish Literature*, 4 vols. Edited by Andrew Hook, II.273–289. Aberdeen, UK: Aberdeen University Press, 1987.

———. *Sentiment and Sociability: The Language of Feeling in the Eighteenth Century*. Oxford: Clarendon Press, 1988.

Murrell, Jim. "The Craft of the Miniaturist." In *The English Miniature*, by John Murdoch, Jim Murrell, Patrick J. Noon, and Roy Strong, 1–24. New Haven, CT: Yale University Press, 1981.

Nash, Mary. *The Provoked Wife: The Life and Times of Susannah Cibber*. Boston: Little, Brown and Company, 1977.

Noon, Patrick J. "Miniatures on the Market." In *The English Miniature*, by John Murdoch, Jim Murrell, Patrick J. Noon, and Roy Strong, 163–209. New Haven, CT: Yale University Press, 1981.

Nussbaum, Felicity. "Effeminacy and Femininity: Domestic Prose Satire and *David Simple*," *Eighteenth-Century Fiction* 11, no. 4 (July 1999): 421–444.

Panzanelli, Roberta. "Introduction: The Body in Wax, the Body of Wax." In *Ephemeral Bodies: Wax Sculpture and the Human Figure*, edited by Roberta Panzanelli, 1–11. Los Angeles: Getty Research Institute, 2008.

Park, Julie. *The Self and It: Novel Objects in Eighteenth-Century England*. Stanford, CA: Stanford University Press, 2010.

Petit, Alexander. "*David Simple* and the Attenuation of 'Phallic Power,'" *Eighteenth-Century Fiction* 11, no. 2 (January 1999): 169–184.

Pietz, William. "The Problem of the Fetish, I," *Res* 9 (1985): 5–17.

———. "The Problem of the Fetish, II," *Res* 13 (1987): 23–45.

———. "The Problem of the Fetish, IIIa," *Res* 16 (1988): 105–123.

Pointon, Marcia. *Hanging the Head: Portraiture and Social Formation in Eighteenth-Century England*. New Haven, CT: Yale University Press for the Paul Mellon Centre for Studies in British Art, 1993.

———. "Materializing Mourning: Hair, Jewellery and the Body." In *Material Memories: Design and Evocation*, edited by Marius Kwint, Christopher Breward, and Jeremy Aynsle, 39–57. Oxford: Berg, 1999.

———. *Portrayal and the Search for Identity*. London: Reaktion Books, 2013.

———. "'Surrounded with Brilliants': Miniature Portraits in Eighteenth-Century England." *Art Bulletin* 83, no. 1 (March 2001): 48–71.

———. "Wearing Memory: Mourning, Jewellery and the Body." In *Trauer Tragen—Trauer Zeigen; Inszenierungen der Geschlechter*, edited by G. Ecker, 65–81. Munich: Fink, 1999.

Porter, Roy. *English Society in the Eighteenth Century*. Revised edition. London: Penguin, 1990.

Rackstrow's Museum. *A Brief Description of Those Curious and Excellent Figures of the Human Anatomy in Wax*. London: 1790. *Eighteenth-Century Collections Online*. Gale. University of Central Florida. (Gale Document Number: CW3306584874).

Radcliffe, Ann. *The Mysteries of Udolpho*. Edited by Bonamy Dobrée. 1966; Oxford: Oxford Press, 1998.

Ramazani, Jahan. *The Poetry of Mourning: The Modern Elegy from Hardy to Heaney*. Chicago: University of Chicago Press, 1994.

Rand, Nicholas T. "Editor's Note. Part IV: New Perspectives in Metapsychology, Cryptic Mourning and Secret Love." In Nicolas Abraham and Maria Torok, *The Shell and the Kernel*, 2 vols. Edited and translated by Nicholas T. Rand, 1: 99–106. Chicago: University of Chicago Press, 1994.

Razzall, Lucy. "'A good Booke is the pretious life-blood of a master-spirit': Recollecting Relics in Post-Reformation English Writing." *Journal of the Northern Renaissance* 2 (2010). Accessed 6 November 2018. http://northernrenaissance.org.

Reeve, Clara. *The Old English Baron*. Edited by James Trainer. Oxford: Oxford University Press, 2003.

Retford, Kate. "A Death in the Family: Posthumous Portraiture in Eighteenth-Century England," *Art History* 33, no. 1 (1 February 2010): 74–97.

Richardson, Ruth. *Death, Dissection and the Destitute*. 2nd ed. Chicago: University of Chicago Press, 2000.

Richardson, Samuel. *Clarissa; or, The History of a Young Lady*. 3rd ed. 8 vols. 1751; New York: AMS Press, 1990.

———. *The History of Sir Charles Grandison*. Edited by Jocelyn Harris. 3 vols. London: Oxford University Press, 1972; Dunedin, New Zealand: University of Otago Print, 2001.

———. *Selected Letters of Samuel Richardson*. Edited by John Carroll. Oxford: Clarendon Press, 1964.

Rivero, Albert J. "Representing Clementina: 'Unnatural' Romance and the Ending of *Sir Charles Grandison*." In *New Essays on Samuel Richardson*, edited by Albert J. Rivero, 209–225. New York: St. Martin's Press, 1996.

Rugg, Julie. "From Reason to Regulation: 1760–1850." In *Death in England: An Illustrated History*, edited by Peter C. Jupp and Clare Gittings, 202–229. New Brunswick, NJ: Rutgers University Press, 2000.

Rymer, Michael. "Henry Mackenzie's *The Man of Feeling*," *Durham University Journal* 37 (1976): 62–69.

Schellenberg, Betty A. *The Conversational Circle: Re-reading the English Novel, 1740–1775*. Lexington: University Press of Kentucky, 1996.

Schiesari, Juliana. *The Gendering of Melancholia: Feminism, Psychoanalysis, and the Symbolics of Loss in Renaissance Literature*. Ithaca, NY: Cornell University Press, 1992.

Schofield, Mary Anne. *Masking and Unmasking the Female Mind: Disguising Romances in Feminine Fiction, 1713–1799*. Newark: University of Delaware Press; London: Associated University Presses, 1990.

Scott, Sir Walter. "Mrs. Ann Radcliffe." In vol. 3 of *The Miscellaneous Prose Works of Sir Walter Scott, Bart.* 28 vols. Edinburgh: Robert Cadell; London: Whittaker and Co., 1834. Accessed 16 June 2019. books.google.com.

Sedgwick, Eve Kosofsky. *The Coherence of Gothic Conventions*. New York: Methuen, 1980.

Shapira, Yael. "Where the Bodies Are Hidden: Ann Radcliffe's 'Delicate' Gothic," *Eighteenth-Century Fiction* 18, no. 4 (2006): 453–476.

Sheumaker, Helen. "This Lock You See: Nineteenth-Century Hair Work as the Commodified Self," *Fashion Theory* 1, no. 4 (1997): 421–446.

Simms, Norman. "The Psychological Adventures of Sarah Fielding's *David Simple*," *Etudes Anglais* 49, no. 2 (April–June 1996): 158–167.
Skinner, Gillian. *Sensibility and Economics in the Novel, 1740–1800: The Price of a Tear*. Basingstoke, UK: Macmillan; New York: St. Martin's Press, 1999.
Smith, Adam. *The Theory of Moral Sentiments*. Edited by Ryan Patrick Hanley. 1759; New York: Penguin, 2009.
Smith, John Thomas. *Nollekens and His Times*. 2 vols. 1828; Cambridge: Cambridge University Press, 2014.
Smith, Megan Kathleen. "Reading It Wrong to Get It Right: Sacramental and Excremental Encounters in Early Modern Poems about Hair Jewelry." *Philological Quarterly* 94, no. 4 (2015): 353–375.
Spenser, Edmund. *The Faerie Queene*. Edited by Thomas P. Roche, Jr., with the assistance of C. Patrick O'Donnell, Jr. London: Penguin, 1978.
Stamelman, Richard. "The Shroud of Allegory: Death, Mourning, and Melancholy in Baudelaire's Work," *Texas Studies in Language and Literature* 25, no. 3 (Fall 1983): 390–409.
Staten, Henry. *Eros in Mourning: Homer to Lacan*. Baltimore: Johns Hopkins University Press, 1995.
Sterckx, Marjan. "'Une fleur que ses yeux étents ne peuvent plus contempler': Women's Sculptures for the Dead." In *Women and the Material Culture of Death*, edited by Maureen Daly Goggin and Beth Fowkes Tobin, 169–190. Farnham, UK: Ashgate, 2013.
Stern, Simon. "Speech and Property in *David Simple*," *English Literary History* 79, no. 3 (Fall 2012): 623–654.
Stewart, Susan. *On Longing: Narratives of the Miniature, the Gigantic, the Souvenir, the Collection*. Durham, NC: Duke University Press, 1993.
Taylor, Lou. *Mourning Dress: A Costume and Social History*. 1983; Abingdon, UK: Routledge, 2009.
Timbs, John. "Mrs. Salmon's Waxworks." In *Romance of London: Strange Stories, Scene and Remarkable Persons of the Great Town*. 3 vols. London: Richard Bentley, 1865. Accessed 26 June 2019. books.google.com.
Todd, Janet. *Sensibility: An Introduction*. London: Methuen, 1986.
———. *The Sign of Angellica: Women, Writing and Fiction, 1660–1800*. New York: Columbia University Press, 1989.
Townsend, Joseph. *A Guide to Health; Being cautions and directions in the treatment of diseases. Designed chiefly for the use of students*. 2nd ed. 2 vols. London: 1795. *Eighteenth-Century Collections Online*. Gale. University of Central Florida. (Gale Document Number: CW3308188185).
Trumbach, Randolph. *Sex and the Gender Revolution*. 2 vols. Chicago: University of Chicago Press, 1998.
Utter, Robert Palfrey, and Gwendolyn Bridges Needham. *Pamela's Daughters*. 1936; New York: Russell & Russell, 1972.
Van Sant, Ann Jessie. *Eighteenth-Century Sensibility and the Novel: The Senses in Social Context*. Cambridge: Cambridge University Press, 1993.
A View of the Wax Work Figures in King Henry the 7th's Chapel, Westminster Abbey: Exhibited in Several Curious Copper-Plate Prints, Drawn on the Spot by James Roberts, and Accurately Engraved by Henry Roberts. With an Historical Account of Each of the Great Personages whose Effigies are Here Represented. London: Printed for H. Roberts, 1769. *Eighteenth-Century Collections Online*. Gale. University of Central Florida. (Gale Document Number: CB3326687850).
Von Schlosser, Julius. *History of Portraiture in Wax* (1910–1911). Translated by James Michael Loughridge. In *Ephemeral Bodies: Wax Sculpture and the Human Figure*, edited by Roberta Panzanelli, 171–314. Los Angeles: Getty Research Institute, 1998.

Wallace, Beth Kowaleski. "Representing Corporeal 'Truth' in the Work of Anna Morandi Manzolini and Madame Tussaud." In *Women and the Material Culture of Death*, edited by Maureen Daly Goggin and Beth Fowkes Tobin, 283–309. Farnham, UK: Ashgate, 2013.

Walpole, Horace. *The Castle of Otranto*. In *The Castle of Otranto and Hieroglyphic Tales*, edited by Robert L. Mack. London: J. M. Dent; Rutland, Vermont: Charles E. Tuttle Co., 1993.

Walsham, Alexandra. "Introduction: Relics and Remains." *Past & Present* (2010), Supplement 5: 11–35.

———. "'Jewels for Gentlewomen: Religious Books as Artefacts in Late Medieval and Early Modern England." In *The Church and the Book*, edited by R. N. Swanson, 123–142. Woodbridge, UK: Boydell & Brewer, 2004.

———. "Skeletons in the Cupboard: Relics after the English Reformation," *Past & Present* (2010), Supplement 5: 121–43.

Wendorf, Richard. *The Elements of Life: Biography and Portrait-Painting in Stuart and Georgian England*. Oxford: Clarendon Press, 1990.

Wendt, Allan. "Clarissa's Coffin," *Philological Quarterly* 39, no. 4 (October 1960): 481–495.

West, Shearer. *Portraiture*. Oxford: Oxford University Press, 2004.

Wiechelt, Shelly A. and Jan Gryczynski. "Cultural and Historical Trauma Among Native Americans." In *Trauma: Contemporary Directions in Theory, Practice, and Research*, edited by Shoshana Ringel and Jerrold R. Brandell, 191–222. Los Angeles: Sage Publications, 2012.

Wildermuth, Mark E. "The Rhetoric of Common Sense and Uncommon Sensibility in Henry Mackenzie's *The Man of Feeling*," *Lamar Journal of the Humanities* 23, no. 2 (1997): 35–47.

Woodward, Carolyn. "Sarah Fielding's Self-Destructing Utopia: *The Adventures of David Simple*." In *Living by the Pen: Early British Women Writers*, edited by Dale Spender, 65–81. New York: Teachers College Press, Columbia University, 1992.

Wu, Ya-Feng. "Blazoning the Paired Tableaux: *The Mysteries of Udolpho* and *The Monk*," *Sun Yat-sen Journal of Humanities* 27 (September 2009): 1–32.

Zigarovich, Jolene. *Writing Death and Absence in the Victorian Novel: Engraved Narratives*. New York: Palgrave Macmillan, 2012.

Zimmerman, Everett. "Fragments of History and *The Man of Feeling*: From Richard Bentley to Walter Scott," *Eighteenth-Century Studies* 23, no. 3 (Spring 1990): 283–300.

INDEX

Abraham, Nicolas, and Maria Torok, 83, 85, 86, 89, 92, 177n3
Adventures of David Simple, The (Fielding), 14, 17–18; 78–79; 81–102; allegory, 14, 104; betrayal, 81, 82, 89–95; consciousness (Lockean), 18, 111; death, 18, 78, 79, 82, 89, 90–91, 102; economics, 82, 83, 88–89, 99–101, 178n48; female suffering, 96–99; friends, 17, 82, 89–102; incorporation, 85–87, 89, 92; male protagonist, 179n67; melancholia, 17, 78, 82–89, 89–102; moral superiority, 86, 95; mourning, 82–89; (fear of) poverty, 88–89, 99–101; relicts, 17, 78, 79, 82, 83, 101; (lack of) remembrance, 82; repetition, 14, 17, 78, 83, 92–93, 101–102; sensibility, 78, 88, 95, 101, 102; suffering, 78, 79, 81, 82, 86, 88, 89–102; trauma, 101
allegory, 14, 76, 78, 79, 102–112, 180n81.
  See also figures of speech
Anatomy Act of 1832, 172n43
Annual Register, The, 77
Ariès, Philippe, 17, 31, 58, 66, 71, 165n13, 174n73, 175n80
Austen, Jane, 27, 44, 57–58, 73, 106

Ballaster, Ros, 103, 180n81
Barker, Gerard A., 145, 146
Barker-Benfield, G. J., 95
Bartolomeo, Joseph F., 95, 179n67
Battestin, Martin C., and Ruthe R. Battestin, 180n77
Battie, William, 78
Baudrillard, Jean, 171n24
Beconsall, Thomas, 165n12
Bellamy, Liz, 93, 141, 147, 185n23
beneficent contagion, 8, 10, 21, 22, 25, 34, 138. *See also* relic (the): sacred
Bentham, Jeremy, 29
Biheron, Marie Marguerite, 62

Blackwell, Mark, 141
Blanchot, Maurice, 13
body (the): abused, 114, 117, 126–129, 136; as anathema, 2, 4, 6, 67, 71, 74, 161; death and, 10, 11, 65; decomposed/decomposing, 58, 68; disappearance of, 2, 6, 7, 12, 14, 15, 70, 71, 122; dying, 2, 4, 12, 64, 68–69, 134, 159; and language, 124, 126–129; Lockean disdain for, 4, 139; madness and, 12, 76, 125, 126–129; "man of the world" and, 19, 139; missing, 15, 72; and personal identity, 3, 4; and personhood, 4; reclamation of, 30; as refuse, 4; relics of, 8, 16, 29; relics worn on, 43; remains of, 7–8, 9, 10–11, 16, 161; replacement by relic, 7, 66; resurrection of, 1–2, 3, 5, 136, 160; and salvation, 2, 3; sensitive, 95; skeleton of, 66–67; and soul, 1, 2, 3–4, 7, 23, 28, 29; spectral, 71; suffering of, 78; *transi* as representation of, 66–67; trauma and, 12, 79; as unnecessary, 157; wax models of (*see* wax-work figures). *See also* corpse; dead (the); dying (the); ghosts; skeleton; *transi*
Boswell, James, 27
Bradshaigh, Lady (Dorothy), 129, 183n41
Brandell, Jerrold R., 167n46
Bree, Linda, 179n67
Broadwell, Elizabeth, 176n84
Brontë, Charlotte, 14, 132, 183n42
Broome, Judith, 126, 128
Buck, Anne, 181n6
burial sites: churchyard versus cemetery, 4, 5–6; in Mackenzie's *The Man of Feeling,* 148, 155; in Radcliffe's *The Mysteries of Udolpho,* 71; in Richardson's *Clarissa,* 160
Burling, William, 186n25
Burney, Frances, 27
Burnham, R. Peter, 186n25
Burton, Robert, 77
Butt, John, 96, 103

[199]

INDEX

Carrera, Rosalba, 41, 170n6
Caruth, Cathy, 11, 118, 133
Castle, Terry, 30, 50, 64–65, 71, 176n89
Castle of Otranto, The. *See* Walpole, Horace
cemetery. *See* burial sites
Certeau, Michel de. *See* de Certeau, Michel
Charlotte of Mecklenberg-Strelitz (queen of England), 26
Cheyne, George, 77, 95, 125, 127
chiasmus. *See* figures of speech; repetition
churchyard. *See* burial sites
Cibber, Susannah, 165n18
Clarissa; or, The History of a Young Lady (Richardson), 16–17, 22, 25–38, 159–160; beneficent contagion, 22, 25, 34; coffin, 17, 30; commemorative jewelry, 16, 22, 25, 26–38; consciousness (Lockean), 29; corpse, 29, 159–160; death, 17, 25, 159–160; hair, 16, 22, 25, 26–29, 30–38; mourning rings, 16, 22, 26–38; portraits, 34, 35, 36–37, 44; relics, 22, 25, 29, 30, 34, 37, 38, 160; remembrance, 22, 25, 29, 160; resurrection, 17, 22, 159–160; sainthood, 22, 29, 30–31. *See also* jewelry
clothing. *See* dress
College of Surgeons, 5–6, 172n43
Collier, Jane, 103, 108, 180n81
commemorative jewelry. *See* jewelry
Company of Barber-Surgeons, 5, 172n43
Congreve, William, 59, 62–63, 174n64
consciousness (Lockean): co-mingling with others, 114, 137, 138, 141, 152, 155, 156, 160; cultural acceptance of, 4, 16, 17; elevation of, 139; of the fictional dead, 16, 19, 134, 135, 155, 160; free-floating nature of, 6, 18, 44, 51, 136, 137, 160; and ghosts, 137–138; instability of, 3, 22–23; and "the man of feeling," 140–141, 156, 160–161; as new soul of humanity, 2, 3, 4, 15, 29, 159; omnipotence of, 4; and personal identity, 2, 3, 4, 158; and the relic, 15, 17, 22, 44, 51; rhetorical reproduction of, 159; severance from body, 2, 29; and trauma, 12, 115. *See also* Locke, John
Conway, Allison, 46–47
corpse: as abject, 67; as anathema, 2, 6; changing attitudes toward, 6, 28–29, 65; disappearance of, 6, 14–15, 122; and disease, 6; dissection of, 60, 172n43; moment of death, 169n16; preservation of, 29; replaced by relic, 7; sentience of, 28–29, 169n16; and *transi*, 66–68; use of in wax-work figure making, 60–61, 61–62. *See also* body (the); dead (the); ghosts; skeleton; *transi*; wax-work figures
Cox, William A., 175n78
Cromwell, Oliver, 43
Csengei, Ildiko, 185n20
Cunnington, Phillis, and Catherine Lucas, 181n6

Dachez, Hélène, 126, 176n6
Dacome, Lucia, 3, 4
Danticat, Edwidge, 10
Darwin, Erasmus, 166n21
Davey, Richard, 165n18
David Simple (*oeuvre*) (Fielding), 14, 17, 103
Davies, Thomas, 174n64
Davison, Carol Margaret, 174n72
dead (the): and afterlife (the), 1–2; changing attitudes toward, 1–2, 4–6, 16, 17, 28–29, 58, 64–65, 71, 72–73; disappearance of, 2, 6, 12, 14, 15, 65, 159, 160; as harmful to living, 4, 6; relics of/from, 2, 7, 8–9, 10, 12; remains of, 7–8, 10, 12, 29, 60, 68; remembrance of, 5, 6, 9, 10, 29, 58, 73, 149–150; sequestration of, 6; as skeletons, 66–67, 175n78; spectralization of, 6, 22, 67, 160; sympathy for, 36, 159; as *transi*, 66–67, 175n80; treatment of, 4, 7, 16–17; and treatment of living, 7, 161. *See also* body (the); corpse; death; dying (the)
death: changing attitudes toward, 1–2, 3, 4–6, 7, 58, 64–65, 70, 73–74; as companion, 7, 74; as failure, 5; and language, 12–13; and literature, 13, 158–159; as lost beloved, 64–73; moment of, 169n16; and mourning, 7; as "other," 114, 160; and sex, 65, 71; tame, 17, 65, 67, 70, 74, 174n73; trauma of, 10–11; untamed, 17, 65, 67, 68, 70–73, 174n73; as void, 73–74. *See also* corpse; dead (the); dying (the)
death writing, 141, 149–151
de Ceglia, Francesco, 172n42
de Certeau, Michel, 12–13
Defoe, Daniel, 137, 158, 184n1 (Ghosts)
Delany, Mary, 26
DeLorme, Maureen, 26
Derrida, Jacques, 12, 167n46

INDEX

Dickens, Charles, 32, 106
Didi-Huberman, Georges, 62
Donne, John, 1, 1–2, 8, 10, 16, 27
Doody, Margaret Anne, 182n12
dress: as bequest, 26; in Fielding's *The Adventures of David Simple*, 106; of ghosts, 18, 67, 137; mourning, 5, 6, 7, 88, 115, 181n6; in portraiture, 41; in Radcliffe's *The Mysteries of Udolpho*, 54, 56, 57; in Richardson's *Clarissa*, 33–34; in Richardson's *The History of Sir Charles Grandison*, 79, 115, 134; as secondary relic, 8; veils, 54, 56, 57–58, 65, 66, 69–70, 73, 115, 176n84, 181n6; on wax-work figures, 41, 59, 62, 66; widow's weeds, 88, 115
Dryden, John, 77
Duchess of Marlborough (2nd). *See* Godolphin, Henrietta
dying (the): changing attitudes toward, 2, 5–6, 7, 16–17, 64–65, 65, 134, 159–160; disappearance of, 6, 7, 14, 15, 70, 122, 159; inability to speak of death, 12–13; and language, 12–13, 149; and relics, 2, 10; trauma of, 10–11; treatment of, 4, 5–6, 7, 17, 64
Dykstal, Timothy, 185–186n24

Eker, Bahadir, 186n25
Eng, David L. and David Kazanjian, 12, 114
Essay Concerning Human Understanding. *See* consciousness (Lockean); Locke, John

Fairer, David, 184n16
Familiar Letters between the Principal Characters in David Simple (Fielding), 102, 103
Farnell, Gary, 68, 175n83
Felton, Henry, 165n4
feme covert. *See* relict
Ferrini, Giuseppe, 61
fetish, 9, 22, 28, 36, 43, 66, 77, 169n14
Fielding, Henry, 26, 44, 46–47, 103
Fielding, Sarah: deaths of family members, 102–103, 180n76; experimentation as writer, 112; fear of poverty, 99, 103; lawsuit against, 103, 180n77. See also *Adventures of David Simple, The; David Simple* (oeuvre); *Familiar Letters between the Principal Characters in David Simple*; "Vision, A"; *Volume the Last*

figures of speech: allegory, 14, 76, 78, 79, 102–112, 180n81; aporia, 14, 76; apostrophe, 14, 76; catachresis, 14, 76; chiasmus, 14, 76; metaphor, 2, 7, 9, 12, 14, 15, 22, 29, 38, 47, 51, 76, 79, 82, 89, 92, 107, 114, 115, 123, 125, 126–127, 132, 133, 134, 136, 147, 160, 186n26; metonymy, 14, 76; personification, 14, 76; prolepsis, 14, 76; prosopopoeia, 14, 76; repetition, 12, 17, 76, 78, 92, 93, 101, 103, 117, 121, 122; reversibility, 14, 76; symbolism, 2, 30, 36, 38, 41, 73, 76, 79, 126, 159, 175n83; trope, 2, 14, 76, 103, 161, 186n26. *See also* allegory; metaphor; repetition; symbolism
Foucault, Michel, 13, 123, 124–125, 182n19
Fox, Christopher, 3
Freud, Sigmund, 53, 70, 83–89, 91, 92, 122, 124–125, 177n3, 181n9
friends. *See Adventures of David Simple, The* (Fielding)
funerary professions, 5, 7

Gadeken, Sara 95, 99
Gana, Nouri, 14, 76
George IV (king of England), 26–27
Gerard, W. B., 185n21
ghosts: agency of, 138; eighteenth-century conceptions of, 67, 137; in eighteenth-century literature, 18–19, 66–67, 123, 130, 134, 137–138, 139–161, 175n79; in relation to skeletons and *transi*, 66–67; as relics/relicts, 18–19, 137–138
ghost writing, 149, 151–156. *See also* ghosts
Godolphin, Henrietta, 2nd Duchess of Marlborough, 62–63, 174n64
Godwin, William, 1, 10
Gores, Steven J., 46, 47
graveyards. *See* burial sites
Greenfield, Susan, 176n84
Gryczynski, Jan. *See* Wiechelt, Shelly A., and Jan Gryczynski

Haggerty, George, 91–92
hair: and intimacy, 25, 26–27, 31–34; jewelry, 1, 6–7, 8, 9, 10, 16, 22, 25, 26–29, 30, 31–37, 166n32, 169n14; lock of, 9, 16, 25, 27, 29, 30, 35, 36, 37–38, 166n32; as relic, 8, 9, 10, 21, 22, 28, 29, 30, 35, 166n32; and remembrance, 9, 22, 25, 27, 29, 35; and sexuality, 126; on wax-work figures, 61, 62

[201]

INDEX

hair jewelry. *See* hair; jewelry: hair
Hallam, Elizabeth, and Jenny Hockey, 149, 149–150
Harkin, Maureen, 185n21, 186n25, 186n29
Harris, Jocelyn, 183n42
Harrison, Jordan, 171n27
Harvey, A. D., 170n4
Haywood, Eliza, 44, 47
Heale, Elizabeth, 108
Henry VII's Lady Chapel, Westminster Abbey, 59
Henry VIII (king of England), 8
Hilliard, Raymond F., 30
historicism (theoretical practice), 76–77
History of Sir Charles Grandison, The (Richardson), 18, 78, 79, 113–136, 160; absence, 115, 117, 120, 121, 122, 135; bigamy, 183n41; (the) body, 79, 113, 114, 119, 122, 124–129, 160; chronology, 181n5, 181–182n10; Clementina, 18, 70, 78, 113–136, 160; Clementina as death figure, 18, 114, 134–135, 160; consciousness (Lockean), 18, 114, 115, 134, 135–136, 160; death, 18, 79, 115, 119, 122, 129, 160; dress, 79, 115, 134; Harriet Byron, 18, 79, 114, 117, 119, 129–135, 183n41; incorporation, 123–124, 128; language and silencing, 117–124, 182n21; love, 114, 117, 183n41; madness, 18, 79, 113, 114, 115–116, 117, 119, 123–129; melancholia, 119, 123, 125–126, 127, 135; "other," 114, 118, 123–124, 128, 135, 136; relict, 18, 79, 114, 115, 117, 123, 124, 135; religion, 113, 117, 118, 119, 122, 125–126, 132; repetition, 14, 79, 115, 117, 121–122, 133; sexuality, 126–127, 128–129, 133; spectralization, 79, 114, 130, 135, 136; symbolism, 79, 126–128; trauma, 79, 114, 115, 117, 121, 125, 133; widow/widower, 18, 79, 114, 115, 123, 124, 128, 129–130, 132, 133, 134, 135; wife, 79, 114, 115, 124, 129, 135, 181–182n10. *See also* madness; melancholia; trauma
Hockey, Jenny. *See* Hallam, Elizabeth, and Jenny Hockey
Hogarth, William, 170n4
House of Wax, 62, 173n57

identity. *See* personal identity
incorporation (psychoanalytical), 85, 86–87, 89, 92, 123, 176n89, 177n3
intercession, 8, 138. *See also* relic: sacred
introjection (psychoanalytical), 86–87
Irigaray, Luce, 87–88
Italian, The (Radcliffe), 44, 170n6
it-narratives, 140, 141–145, 147–148, 184n3
it-narrators, 140–141, 141–142, 144–146, 185n20

Jane Eyre. See Brontë, Charlotte
jewelry: bracelets, 1, 8, 10, 16, 26, 44, 45, 166n32; with hair, 1, 6–7, 8, 9, 10, 16, 22, 25, 26–29, 30, 37, 166n32, 169n14; lockets, 25, 26, 27, 30, 35, 37; mourning, 6–7, 16, 25, 26–29, 29–37; necklaces, 26, 61; with portraits, 35, 44, 45, 47–48; rings, 1, 6, 9, 10, 16, 22, 25, 26–36, 37
Jordanova, Ludmilla, 173n51
Judgment Day. *See* resurrection

Kazanjian, David. *See* Eng, David L. and David Kazanjian
Kim, James, 97, 177n6
King George IV. *See* George IV (king of England)
King Henry VIII. *See* Henry VIII (king of England)
Koos, Marianne, 43
Kornmeier, Uta, 62, 172n37
Kramer, Dale, 185n23
Kristeva, Julia, 87

Lander, Kathleen F., 174n62
Landes, Joan B., 60, 62, 68, 173n47
Laqueur, Thomas, 5, 6, 58, 165n13, 176n94, 187n34
La Roche, Sophia von, 27
Lewis, Matthew, 175n79
Lilley, James D., 143–144
Locke, John: afterlife, 79, 82, 134; body as irrelevant to personhood, 3–4, 139; consciousness as new soul of humanity, 3–4, 114, 159; cultural acceptance of theory of consciousness, 16–17, 158, 159; *An Essay Concerning Human Understanding,* 1–3; free-floating nature of consciousness, 18, 22–23, 44, 79, 111, 114, 134, 135, 136, 137, 141; separation of body and soul, 4, 19, 29, 139, 157. *See also* consciousness (Lockean)
Lucas, Catherine. *See* Cunnington, Phillis, and Catherine Lucas
Lutz, Deborah, 14, 15–16

INDEX

Mackenzie, Henry, 139. See also *Man of Feeling, The*; *Man of the World, The*

Madame Tussaud. *See* Tussaud, Anna Maria "Marie,"

madness: and the body, 12, 76, 124–128, 129; and death, 79, 135, 160; in eighteenth century, 12, 76, 78, 182n24; and language, 117–129; and love-sickness, 113, 114, 116; and religious enthusiasm, 115–117; and trauma, 114, 115. *See also* Freud, Sigmund; melancholia; trauma

Malo, Robin, 9

"man of feeling," 95, 139, 140–141, 148, 184n1 (chap. 5)

Man of Feeling, The (Mackenzie), 18–19, 138, 139–157, 160–161; body, (the) 139, 140, 149, 157; children and ghosts, 138; circulation, 141–142, 144, 146–147, 184n3, 186n26; consciousness (Lockean), 19, 137–138, 139, 140, 141, 152, 155, 156, 157; dead, (the), 138, 139, 141, 142, 148, 149–151, 154, 155–156, 157; death writing, 141, 149–151; "editor," 140, 141, 143, 145, 148; framed narrative, 140; The Ghost, 18, 138, 140, 141, 142, 143, 144, 145, 148, 150–151, 151–156; Harley, 18, 138, 140, 141, 142, 143–148, 150–151, 151–156; it-narratives/it-narrators, 140, 141–148, 184n3; "man of feeling," 139, 140, 184n1 (chapter 5); "man of the world," 19, 139, 143, 156, 184n1 (chapter 5), 185n24; manuscript, 18, 138, 139, 140, 141–143, 145, 149, 150–151, 151–152, 155; memory and memorial, 141, 148, 149–151; money, 139, 142, 144–146; narrator, 18, 138, 139, 140, 141–148, 151–156; novels of circulation (*see* it-narratives/it-narrators); objects, 138, 139, 140–141; past, the, 19, 139, 140, 141–142, 143–144, 147, 148, 149, 153, 156; prostitution, 142, 147; relics/relicts, 18–19, 137–138, 139, 140–141, 142, 143, 144, 145, 149–151, 157; sensibility, 19, 139, 140, 143, 146, 147, 148, 151, 156, 158; sociability, 186n26; subjectivity, 139, 140–141, 147, 185n20. *See also* ghosts; it-narratives; it-narrators

"man of the world," 139, 143, 156, 184n1 (chap. 5)

Man of the World, The (Mackenzie), 147, 150

Marks, Sylvia Kasey, 129

Marshall, Cynthia, 77

Mary I (Queen of England), 8

Maurer, Shawn Lisa, 91, 99

Mazzio, Carla, and Douglas Trevor, 77

McCallum, E. L., 83, 88, 97

McDaniel, Dale, 186–187n29

McGuirk, Carol, 185n24

Mead, Richard, 126

melancholia: and allegory, 76, 78, 78–79; ambivalence exhibited in, 83–85, 91; definition of, 83–89; in eighteenth century, 76–77, 125–126, 128; and figures of speech, 14, 76, 92; gendering of, 83, 87–88, 96–99; incorporation in, 85–86, 89, 92, 123–124, 177n3; and (unconscious nature of) loss, 83–84, 87; and moral superiority, 83, 86–87, 92, 95; versus (normative) mourning, 83–89, 167n46; as non-normative mourning, 75, 89, 167n46; and originary loss, 82; outcomes of, 87; and (fear of) poverty, 82, 83, 87, 88–89, 99–101; and the relict, 75, 82; and repetition, 17, 76, 78, 82, 83, 87, 101–102, 159; and suffering, 92–93, 95; and trauma, 12, 14, 17, 75, 76, 82, 87, 159; (eighteenth-century) treatment of, 126–128. *See also* Freud, Sigmund; madness; trauma

memento illius, 26

memento mori, 26, 66, 73

mental illness. *See* Freud, Sigmund; madness; melancholia

metaphor, 2, 7, 9, 12, 14, 15, 22, 29, 38, 47, 51, 76, 79, 82, 89, 92, 107, 114, 115, 123, 125, 126–127, 132, 133, 134, 136, 147, 160, 186n26. *See also* figures of speech

Miles, Robert, 68

Milton, John, 13, 77, 108, 124

Monk, The. See Lewis, Matthew

Montagu, Lady Mary Wortley, 125

morte secca. See skeleton

mortuary professions. *See* funerary professions

mourning: and consumerism, 7; for death itself, 7, 73–74; in eighteenth-century England, 6–7; and materiality, 2, 10, 15, 16, 21–22, 22, 149–150, 161; versus melancholia, 83–89. *See also* death writing; dress: mourning; figures of speech; jewelry: mourning; narrative mourning

mourning jewelry. *See* jewelry: mourning; mourning
Mrs. Salmon's Royal Wax-work, 59–60, 61, 172n37
Mrs. Veal. *See* Defoe, Daniel
Mullan, John, 186n26, 186–187n29
Murder Act of 1752, 172n43
Mysteries of Udolpho, The (Radcliffe), 16–17, 22–23, 39–74, 161; Beauveau, Blanche, 44, 47–49; (missing) bodies, 65–66, 67–68, 72–73; Carrera, Rosalba 170n6; consciousness (Lockean), 22, 44, 51, 74; (wax) corpse, 39, 55, 58, 64–73; the dead and dying, 51–57; death, 16, 22, 57–74; Du Pont, 44, 45–47, 57; Montoni, 46, 54–55, 56; Montoni, Madame (neé Cheron), 58, 65, 68, 69, 70, 71, 71–72; portraits, 16, 22, 40–57, 170n6; relics, 16, 22–23, 39, 40, 44, 46, 49, 50, 51, 52, 53, 55, 56, 57, 59, 62–64, 65–66, 68 73; repetition, 53, 70; Schedoni, Bartolomeo, 170n6; sex and sexuality, 50, 65, 67, 71–73; spectralization, 22, 64–65, 67, 71; St. Aubert, Emily, 39, 40, 44, 45–47, 51, 52, 53, 55, 56, 56–57, 64, 65, 66, 69–71, 71–72, 73; St. Aubert, Madame, 70; St. Aubert, Monsieur, 51–53, 68–69, 70–71; St. Foix, 40, 47–49; tame death, 17, 65, 67, 68, 70–71; *transi*, 66–68, 72; trauma, 53; di Udolpho, Laurentini, 40, 44, 49–50, 51, 54–57, 58, 65, 66, 68, 68–69, 71, 72–73; untamed death, 17, 65, 67, 68, 70, 71–73; Valancourt, 39, 45, 46, 53; veils, 54, 56, 57, 58, 65–66, 69–70, 73, 176n84; de Villeroi, Marchioness, 40, 51–54, 55–57; de Villeroi, Marquis, 44, 49–50; Vivaldi, Antonio, 170n6; wax-work figures, 16, 22, 59–63, 64–73
Mystery at the Wax Museum, The, 62, 173n57

narrative: exhaustion, 75; framing, 140; melancholia complicating, 75–76; movement, 17, 78; resolution, 75
narrative mourning, 2, 14, 15, 17, 53, 75–76, 82, 103. *See also* allegory; figures of speech; melancholia; metaphor; narrative; repetition; symbolism; trauma
nervous disorders. *See* Freud, Sigmund; madness; melancholia

novel (genre): assuagement of mourning, 39; of circulation (*see* it-narrative); and death, 158–159; the Gothic, 58, 66–67, 71, 158, 159; and relics/relicts, 158; of sensibility, 78, 95, 102, 111, 158–159; of sentiment, 184n16, 185n24, 186–187n29
novel of circulation. *See* it-narrative
novel of sensibility. *See* novel (genre)
novel of sentiment. *See* novel (genre)
Nussbaum, Felicity, 179n67

Old English Baron, The. *See* Reeve, Clara
"other": characters as, 114, 124, 135, 160; death as, 114, 135, 160; incorporated, 86, 92, 124

Panzanelli, Roberta, 61
Paradise Lost. *See* Milton, John
Pepys, Samuel, 32, 168n4
personal identity, 2, 3–4, 7, 8
Petit, Alexander, 103
Pietz, William, 169n14
Pointon, Marcia, 43, 47, 170n4
Pope, Alexander, 27
Porter, Roy, 166n21
portraits: active agency of, 44, 49, 50–51; competing with their subjects, 45, 48–49, 50–51; connecting the living with the dead or absent, 40; of the dead or dying, 16, 22, 39, 43, 51–57; as fetishes, 43; on ivory, 41, 51–52, 170n6; as jewelry, 26, 35; life-size, 35, 37, 39, 40, 40–41, 43, 51, 53–54; of the living, 22, 40, 44–51; miniature, 7, 36–37, 39, 40, 41–43, 44, 170n6; as mnemonic devices, 43; as objects of mourning, 7; possession of, 46, 48–49; and the real, 40, 45, 46, 51–55, 57; as relics, 16, 17, 22, 39, 40, 46, 50; as simulacra, 44–45, 51, 53; as surrogates, 40, 43–46, 50, 51; 54
portraiture (in England), 40
post-traumatic stress disorder (PTSD), 182n15
Pringle, Sir John, 62
psychoanalytic theory, 12, 14, 43, 76–78, 83–89, 96, 167n46

Queen Charlotte. *See* Charlotte of Mecklenberg-Strelitz

[204]

INDEX

Rackstrow's Museum, 60–61
Radcliffe, Ann. See *Italian, The*; *Mysteries of Udolpho, The*
Ramazani, Jahan, 89, 167n46
Rand, Nicholas T., 86
Rape of the Lock, The. See Pope, Alexander
Razzall, Lucy, 150
Reeve, Clara, 67, 175n79
relic (the): and beneficent contagion, 8, 10, 21; Bible as, 8–9; changing nature of, 2, 16; and consciousness (Lockean), 2, 22; continuing importance of, 2; and cult of saints, 15–16; cultural attitudes toward, 2, 8–9; and the dead, 2, 7–8, 21–22; definition of, 2, 7–8, 10, 12; and fetishism, 9, 22; and figures of speech, 2, 9; and intercession, 8; and loss, 10; materiality of, 10, 21; memory and remembrance, 9, 10, 21, 22; and narrative mourning, 2; and narrative strategy, 2, 17; as object, 9, 16–17, 21–22; as person (*see* relict); pre-versus post-Reformation, 8–9; primary, secondary, and tertiary, 8, 21; recusants and, 8, 9; and its reliquary, 9; and reunion in afterlife, 1–2, 8, 10; and Roman Catholicism, 8, 15–16; sacred, 8, 11, 16, 20; secular, 8, 9, 11, 16, 21–22; sentience of, 21, 22; as surrogate, 2; and trauma, 10, 12. *See also individual authors and their respective works*
relict: definition of, 2, 10, 12, 75; as double, 18, 75; as *feme covert*, 75; as fictional character; and loss, 10; and melancholia, 75; and repetition, 17, 75, 76; as replacement, 75; as surrogate, 75; and symbolism, 76; and trauma, 10, 75. *See also individual authors and their respective works*
relinquere, 8
reliquary, 2, 8, 9, 15, 16, 29, 30, 31
reliquiae, 7–8
repetition: as chiasmus, 14, 76; in Fielding's *David Simple* novels, 14, 78, 92, 93, 101, 103; and melancholia, 17, 76, 78; and metaphor, 12; and narrative mourning, 103; as narrative strategy, 17; in Richardson's *The History of Sir Charles Grandison*, 14, 78, 117, 121, 122; and trauma, 12, 17, 76, 78, 117, 121, 122. *See also* figures of speech

resurrection: beliefs concerning, 1–2, 3, 4, 169n16; relics assuring reunion after, 1, 8, 10, 18; in twenty-first century, 161.
Resurrection Day. *See* resurrection
Richardson, Ruth, 28, 169n16
Richardson, Samuel: nervous disorder, 127; teasing of correspondents, 181–182n10, 183n41. *See also Clarissa; or, The History of a Young Lady*; *History of Sir Charles Grandison, The* (Richardson)
Rivero, Albert J., 181–182n10
Royal College of Physicians, 172n43
Rugg, Julie, 166n25
Rymer, Michael, 187n39

Salmon's Wax-work. *See* Mrs. Salmon's Royal Wax-work
Schedoni, Bartolomeo, 170n6
Schellenberg, Betty, 93
Schiesari, Juliana, 83, 84, 84–85, 86, 87, 178n34
Scott, Sir Walter, 58, 73
Sedgwick, Eve Kosofsky, 176n84
sentimental fiction. *See* novel (genre): of sentiment
Seward, Anna, 27
Shakespeare, William, 77
Shapira, Yael, 71, 174n71, 176n84
Sir Charles Grandison. See History of Sir Charles Grandison, The (Richardson)
skeleton, 58, 66–67, 175n78
Skinner, Gillian, 101
Smith, Adam, 35, 94, 159
Smith, Megan Kathleen, 166n32
soul: beliefs regarding, 1–2, 3, 5, 8, 10, 169n16; and the body, 1–2, 3, 7, 8, 10, 15, 25, 28, 29, 58, 67, 74, 139, 160, 161; co-mingling of, 35, 114, 136, 138; and consciousness (Lockean), 2, 3–4, 15, 18, 114, 135, 138, 157, 159; substantial, 3, 4, 18, 79, 82, 111, 114, 136, 160, 160–161, 161; transmigration of, 4
spectralization: of the dead, 6, 15, 22, 64–65, 67, 71, 135, 136; and ghosts, 67; of the living, 22, 64–65, 79, 114, 130, 136; of the "other," 136. *See also* dead (the); ghosts
Spenser, Edmund, 107–108, 109, 180n81
Stamelman, Richard, 103
Staten, Henry, 13–14

[205]

INDEX

Stern, Simon, 99
Stewart, Susan, 36, 37
Stothard, Thomas, 115
Stuart, Charles ("Bonnie Prince Charlie"), 118, 119, 182n12
Susini, Clemente, 61
symbolism, 2, 30, 36, 38, 41, 73, 76, 79, 126, 159, 175n83. *See also* figures of speech

tame death. *See* death
Taylor, Lou, 166n24, 181n6
Timbs, John, 172n36
Todd, Janet, 99, 179n67, 186n25, 187n40
Torok, Maria. *See* Abraham, Nicolas, and Maria Torok
Townsend, Joseph, 128
transi, 66–68, 72, 175n80
trauma: allegory as rhetorical marker of, 76, 82, 103; of death and dying, 10–11; definition of, 11–12, 115; in eighteenth-century England, 12, 76–77; in Fielding's *David Simple* oeuvre, 18, 78, 82, 101, 107, 111; and figures of speech, 12, 76, 125; in literature, 12, 75; and melancholia, 14, 17, 75–76, 85, 87, 159, 167n46, 177n3; and mourning, 7, 12, 14, 82, 167n46, 177n3; and narrative, 14, 17, 53, 75, 101–102, 111; and post-traumatic stress disorder (PTSD), 182n15; and the relic/relict, 10–11, 12, 75–76, 82; and repetition, 11–12, 17, 53, 75, 76, 101, 111, 115, 117, 159, 181n9; in Richardson's *The History of Sir Charles Grandison*, 78, 79, 114, 117, 121, 125, 133; as "wound of the mind," 12, 77. *See also* figures of speech: allegory; figures of speech: metaphor; figures of speech: repetition; relic: trauma; relict: trauma
Trevor, Douglas. *See* Mazzio, Carla, and Douglas Trevor
"True Relation of the Apparition of One Mrs. Veal, The." *See* Defoe, Daniel
Tuke, William, 78
Tussaud, Anna Maria "Marie," 59, 61, 61–62, 172n37

undertakers. *See* funerary professions
untamed death. *See* death

Van Sant, Ann Jessie, 111
veils. *See* dress; *Mysteries of Udolpho, The* (Radcliffe)
Venus de' Medici waxwork figure, 61
"Vision, A" (Fielding), 103–104, 106, 107, 108–109, 110–111
Vivaldi, Antonio, 170n6
Volume the Last (Fielding), 17–18, 78–79, 81–82, 102–112, 160; allegory, 14, 82, 102–112; consciousness (Lockean), 18, 79, 82, 111; death, 18, 79, 82, 103, 107, 109, 111–112; didactic message, 82, 112; melancholia, 17, 111; mourning, 103, 107; relicts, 17, 105, 107, 111–112; repetition, 14, 17, 78, 103, 107; substantial soul, 79, 111; trauma, 17, 82, 103, 107, 111

Walker, Anthony, 115
Walkinshaw, Clementina, 182n12
Wallace, Beth Kowaleski, 62, 173n58
Walpole, Horace, 67, 175n79
wax-work figures: anatomical, 60–61; *cire perdue* (lost-wax process), 61; of Congreve, William, 62–63; and death, 16, 17, 22, 39, 55, 56, 58, 64, 65–68; in eighteenth-century England, 59–63; as fetishes, 66; and misrecognition, 62, 63, 64; and the real, 16, 17, 61–62, 63, 66, 67, 73, 172n36; as (problematic) relics, 39, 59, 62, 64, 65, 67; as simulacra, 63; *transi*, 66–68. *See also* Mrs. Salmon's Royal Wax-work; *transi*); Tussaud, Anna Maria "Marie,"
Wendorf, Richard, 41–42
West, Shearer, 41, 43
widow's weeds. *See* dress
widows. *See* relict
Wiechelt, Shelly A., and Jan Gryczynski, 182n15
Wildermuth, Mark E., 185n23
Willis, Francis, 78
Wolfe, James, 77
Wollstonecraft, Mary, 10, 16
Woodward, Carolyn, 99
Wu, Ya-Feng, 66, 73

Zigarovich, Jolene, 14–15
Zimmerman, Everett, 145, 187n39

ABOUT THE AUTHOR

KATHLEEN M. OLIVER is author of *Samuel Richardson, Dress, and Discourse* (2008). Her essays on Daniel Defoe, Sarah Fielding, Samuel Richardson, Frances Sheridan, Charlotte Smith, and William Wycherley have appeared in peer-reviewed journals and scholarly collections. In 2002, she received the Émilie du Châtelet Award for Independent Studies, bestowed by the Women's Caucus of the American Society for Eighteenth-Century Studies.